The
Moral
Imagination

— ✦ —

How Literature and Films
Can Stimulate Ethical Reflection
in the Business World

edited by

OLIVER F. WILLIAMS, C.S.C.

The University of Notre Dame Press
Notre Dame, Indiana

© 1997
Published by
The University of Notre Dame Press
Notre Dame, Indiana 46556
All Rights Reserved

Designed by Wendy McMillen
Set in 10/12.5 Sabon by The Book Page, Inc.
Printed in the U. S. A. by Braun-Brumfield, Inc.

Library of Congress Cataloging-in-Publication Data

The moral imagination : how literature and films can stimulate ethical reflection in the business world / edited by Oliver F. Williams.
    p. cm. — (The John W. Houck Notre Dame series in business ethics)
    Includes bibliographical references and index.
    ISBN 0-268-01432-9 (cloth : alk. paper). — ISBN 0-268-01434-5 (pbk. : alk. paper).
    1. Business ethics. 2. Business ethics in literature.
3. Business ethics in motion pictures. I. Williams, Oliver F.
II. Series.
HF5387.M648 1998
174'.4—dc21
                                          97-46844
                                          CIP

To

JOHN W. HOUCK

— ☉ —

Born
April 16, 1931

Died
December 11, 1996

A Teacher,
A Scholar,
A Lover of Life,
A Friend

"The light he lit in the hearts
of those who knew him
will never be extinguished."

Madeline Day

Contents

— ⊙ —

THE CHALLENGE

Envisioning the Good Life

— ☉ —

OLIVER F. WILLIAMS, C.S.C.

It is only fitting that a book on envisioning the good life should be dedicated to John W. Houck, for his whole life in teaching and research revolved around that theme. Born on April 16, 1931, John died unexpectedly on the morning of December 11, 1996, while preparing to leave home for his daily walk to his office. One of his projects for the fall of 1996 was organizing a conference and preparing the papers for publication. As codirector of the Center for Ethics and Religious Values in Business, a center he founded some twenty years ago, John had helped organize twelve major conferences and had coauthored or coedited eleven books. This present volume contains the papers presented at the 1996 conference, "How Literature and Films Can Stimulate Ethical Reflection in the Business World," held at the University of Notre Dame from September 30 through October 2, 1996.

The topic of John Houck's final conference is, in many ways, an appropriate capstone to his forty years in the academy. Dearly loved by his many students over the years, John was always leading those students to see that the more interesting and prior question is, Who are we? rather than, What shall we do? He believed that by cultivating the imagination through art, literature, and film, one would come to see what it might mean to be human and thus be able to answer the fundamental question, Who am I? A genuine sense of self expands an impoverished moral vision and opens the way for the largeness of heart that was so well embodied in John Houck's work with students, staff, and faculty alike.

The University of Notre Dame's Frank O'Malley Award, given annually by the student government and the Notre Dame Alumni Association, was awarded posthumously to John Houck in the spring of 1997. "Professor Houck could put morality in the coldest of souls simply through his teachings," wrote one student in nominating John for the award. "When he died, the biggest heart on campus left with him."

THE PAST AS PROLOGUE

To make moral imagination the focus of work in business ethics was not a new idea for John Houck or me. In 1978 we coauthored *Full Value: Cases in Christian Business Ethics,* which highlights the role of images and narrative theology in business practice. While the essays presented in this present volume do not draw on religious images, it may be helpful to repeat several pages of an earlier article in *Full Value* to place this new book in context.[1]

Full Value is designed to clarify how moral personality is formed in a Christian community, and how a Christian community is defined by its story.[2] The point of the work is to show how the Christian community provides a truthful narrative that so shapes its adherents that they come to see situations in a new light. For example, a manager formed in such a community has an idea of the sort of person she wants to be and the sort of company she wants to manage, and it is this vision which forms the context for all that she sees as a manager. She sees and feels differently from many others in business. She has the skills to describe afresh the situations she encounters, for she has been trained in a community which schooled her in the virtues required to be a certain sort of person. Christians, through their language, habits, and feeling, construe the world in such a way that it seems critically important to avoid laying off loyal employees, or allowing the families of chronically ill workers to suffer financial collapse.

In some religions there is no necessary connection between religion and morality, while in others the two are inextricably bound.[3] The Christian and Jewish religions are in the latter category, for at the core of their beliefs is the doctrine that God is holy, that God possesses absolute moral perfection (for example, in justice and mercy), and that his followers ought to try to imitate that perfection in their own human and fallible ways. Fidelity to the moral life, then, is essential for those who want to be pleasing to God. My theological position understands the life of Jesus to be God among us, offering a way of life that enables our full humanity to unfold. Paul echoes this theme throughout his writings: "In your minds you must be the same as Christ Jesus . . ." (Phil. 2:5). Jesus is often seen as understanding himself as *the* paradigm for his followers. For example, in teaching his disciples to use their power to serve the community, Jesus is portrayed in the gospel of John: "If I, then, the Lord and Master, have washed your feet, you should wash each other's feet. I have given you an example so that you may copy what I have done to you" (John 13:15).

In this framework, if one follows the thought of Thomas Aquinas, the moral concern is not so much to judge human performance in terms of how it measures up to some principle or set of laws, as in the Ten Commandments; rather, the emphasis is on judging how well human life approaches the ideal as embodied by Christ. God is thought of more as a literary critic than as a judge in a court of law. It is as if all of us are fashioning a piece of work, such as sculpting a statue, with our lives, and we are to be judged by how well our creation embodies the ideal. By reading the Bible and participating in the liturgy and life of the church, one slowly becomes the sort of person exemplified by Jesus. Character traits such as compassion, generosity, and forgiveness are highlighted.

For Aquinas, ethics or moral theology has to do with transforming persons so that they realize their potential and become their true selves. Knowing the *end* of human life—"Man's ultimate happiness consists solely in the contemplation of God"[4]—the ethical task is to provide the *means* to enable and realize this *end*. While becoming the sort of person who might enjoy the presence of God is thought to be possible only through a free gift (a "supernatural gift of grace"), this process entails appropriating the biblical virtues of faith, hope, and charity. For Aquinas, however, being properly oriented to God also entails development of the natural virtues of wisdom, justice, temperance, and fortitude. God, as creator of the world, has made it good, to be enjoyed. Insofar as creatures are in a proper relationship to him and to each other, they are in harmony with God's plan or God's *wisdom*. Aquinas envisions God's wisdom as the basis for moral goodness.[5]

In this synthesis, the created order embodies God's intentions, and thus all truth discovered by human intellect and will is taken to be God's intention, a "natural law" implanted in creation. Thus, reasoning takes on a crucial role, for the person becomes a cocreator through the use of intellect and will, discovering and fashioning a more humane world. However, the key here is that reason is perfected by the moral virtues.

For Aquinas virtue is not its own reward in the sense that swimming as exercise can be enjoyable; rather, it is analogous to the student of music who diligently studies for years and finally can thoroughly enjoy a symphony; so too the virtuous life transforms a person so that he or she finally "sees" the world as it is. This person is then the sort who can "enjoy God's presence" and his creation, for he or she is in a "right" relation to it. The moral virtues school us to desire rightly. In philosophical terms, practical reason perfected is both an attitude of intellect seeking the truth and an attitude of will seeking the good.[6] In this sense, a good person knows the good; there is a co-naturalizing effect, an attunement to the good as a result of living a life of generosity, forgiveness, compassion, and so on. The intellect is effectively qualified in that it is attentive to certain features of experience that it might otherwise miss or undervalue.

Full Value is an attempt to give an account of how reason is affectively qualified by participation in a Christian community. Its premise is that people are shaped by their environment and that if one is to grow in the virtues cherished by Christians it is essential to be actively involved in a church community that supports these values. The business environment tends to accent efficiency and productivity since these are clearly essential to the enterprise. *Full Value* tries to show how a Christian community, emulating the character traits exhibited by Jesus, tries to inculcate other values.[7] Although there is no definitive Christian character, seven major values from the Christian tradition need to be stressed in the face of the particular cultural distortions of our time: power as service; the understanding of stewardship over nature; the value of wealth and property; happiness; justice; deferred gratification of wants; and time. These seem to have been essential to the life of Christ and hence to the Christian community, and they also seem to be some of the values most neglected in the contemporary business world.

Unlike much of contemporary business ethics, principles and rules for those focusing on the moral imagination take on a secondary status.

> If you ask a Christian, "What are the principles of the Christian life?" he or she may have a little difficulty in providing a summary list. "Love your neighbor, forgive your enemies, be faithful to your vocation as a child of God, and always be trusting of the mercy and love of God," might be a good response. Yet when we teach children how to be Christian, usually without thinking much about it, it seems very important to read the Bible stories. It is not enough just to pass on the principles or values. We do not just tell children to love one another or respect the value of community. These principles are themselves an abstraction from the Bible stories, a kind of "skeleton" of the stories. Just as a human skeleton could never convey the beauty of a complete person, so a principle could never capture the complexity of human action.
>
> The actions of a Christian do not really flow from *principles;* rather they flow from *stories,* and in particular the story of Jesus as portrayed in the New Testament. The "story" concept helps us see that our principles ("Love your neighbor") and values (community, honesty) acquire a definite sense from their context. For this reason the Christian values revealed in the Bible

are usually set in the context of a story or event that Jesus used to teach his disciples.[8]

Christians are people who consciously strive to be other Christs—they have a model to follow. The model provides a story or pattern of meaning which serves as a context to interpret principles. Of course, this is true for any person, religious or not. The principle "Be honest" would be understood and embodied one way by an executive who is single-mindedly focused on getting promoted and rich, and quite another way by a colleague who sees his role as serving the common good of the firm as well as the wider society. The same principle, "Be honest," would have quite divergent implications for two persons with differing horizons of interpretation.

Full Value argues that business organizations can so shape persons that they do not "see" the ethical dimensions of business life. When efficiency and productivity are the only values reinforced in the organization, people are molded slowly to do whatever will "get the job done." Treating people functionally dulls their sensitivity and constricts their perspective so that their "world" is basically functional. This can affect how they describe situations. A long-time employee who is not performing adequately in his present position may be seen as "an incompetent who must be fired" or as "a man in the wrong position who must be reassigned." To a large extent, it depends on whether the cultural distortions of functionality and rationality dominate, or whether sensitivity to human dignity is shaping one's vision.

I take it that while moral images and the stories they compose shape reason "to see rightly," they do not replace reason. There is an important distinction here between *recognizing* obligations or wrongdoing and *justifying* these obligations or instances of wrongdoing.[9] The distinct contribution of theologians in business ethics is to provide an account of how appropriation of the way of life and values of Jesus so shapes the character that one is particularly attuned to recognizing obligations or wrongdoing. The Catholic tradition speaks of theologians employing "reason *informed* by faith," not *replaced* by faith. There is the conviction that the biblical message, which indeed has rules and principles, is not discontinuous with reason but rather adds depth and breath to it. Rules and principles must be justified with reason, but one must always recall that reason is in the context of an explicit Christian vision.[10] The stories and images of the Christian community help one to discover God's will but, in principle, human insight and reasoning can discover this same will in the form of moral obligations. To be sure, there are certain unique obligations Christians incur by virtue of belonging to a Christian community, such as attending church on Sunday, but these are not of special concern to moral discourse on the ethical aspects of the business world.

In the account presented here, faith and reason are not mutually exclusive domains of moral knowledge; rather, revelation completes and complements reason. This is the traditional Catholic approach whose assumptions were clearly articulated by Thomas Aquinas and have been retrieved by contemporary Catholic theologians.[11] From the fourth Gospel, Jesus Christ is taken to be the Word of God, the Logos. All creation is patterned on the Logos (in scholastic terminology, Christ is "the exemplary cause" of creation), and the incarnation completes creation in the sense that it fulfills its deepest aspirations. It might be said that the incarnation is the eighth day of creation. In this understanding of the relationship of Christ and creation, all the world is a revelation of God and Father, but it is in the words and deeds of Christ, indeed in the *person* of Christ, that revelation is brought to full clarity. Moral law is thus grounded in creation, for all truth that is discerned by use of the intellect and will is discovering God's intentions implanted in creation; creation is taken to be a participation in the eternal law of God. While it is true that because Christ came into the world evil has been overcome, he was able to come into the world and be heard only because all creation is basically good and attuned to his word. Christ offers the explicit pattern for all that is hinted at in creation. Christ is the "transformer of culture" and the exemplar in this account.[12] The significant point is that, in principle, the domains of reason and revelation should not be at odds with each other.

Thus, the philosopher and the theologian can fruitfully engage in moral argument. Although the theologian will want to maintain that his community has been transformed by Christian faith so that he might more astutely *recognize* obligation and wrongdoing, the process of *justifying* a situation as indeed a violation or an obligation will be carried on by human reason with all the tools of the philosopher. Whether it be the moral status of the corporation, the ethics of insider trading, and so on, philosopher and theologian will reason alike. It may be, however, that evidence compelling to the theologian may not be so compelling to others. It may be also that the theologian, impelled by the image of Jesus as paradigmatic, may want to invite listeners to do much more than is obligatory in the situation.[13]

HOW LITERATURE AND FILMS CAN STIMULATE ETHICAL REFLECTION IN THE BUSINESS WORLD

Since the essays that follow seldom discuss religious images and biblical narratives, it may now be obvious to the reader that this volume draws on the contemporary retrieval of narrative theology to make the wider point that all experience has a narrative quality. The assumption of this work is that some stories and their images have the capacity to widen our vision and open our eyes to what is really important. These stories that "ring true" bring us in touch with the fullness of our humanity.

Actually, the use of moral images in business ethics, as I have discussed it here, owes much to Aristotle. Many have argued that Thomas Aquinas never took his eye off Aristotle's text as he was writing his own. Much that I have said, then, can be seen as arguing for a retrieval of the Aristotelian insight on ethics for the business ethics of our time. Ethics in this perspective is not primarily concerned with analyzing situations so that one can make the right decisions, but with reflecting on what is constitutive of the good life. There is a similar concern in the work of Aristotle, particularly in the *Nicomachean Ethics* and the *Politics*. This philosophic tradition could bring a crucial corrective to the way business ethics is practiced today.

Just as theological ethics has its saints, holy persons, and paradigmatic individuals, Aristotle's moral philosophy also centered on discussing obviously good Athenians.[14] One learned the right thing to do by observing good people and by doing what they did. This insight is at the core of Aristotle's thinking:

> . . . but the virtues we get by first exercising them, as also happens in the case of the arts as well. For the things we have to learn before we can do them, we learn by doing them, e.g., men become builders by building and lyre-players by playing the lyre: so too we become just by doing just acts, temperate by doing temperate acts, brave by doing brave acts.[15]

Theological ethics reflects on the Christian community and provides an account of how the moral virtues so shape a person that the world is seen truthfully. Its claim is that without compassion, justice, loyalty, and so on, the right moral dilemmas will not even arise in one's life. Only the "good" person can make correct judgments. This is, of course, a central point for Aristotle: "the same things do not seem sweet to a man in a fever and a healthy man— nor hot to a weak man and one in good condition. The same happens in other cases. But in all such matters that which appears to the good man is thought to be really so."[16] It is the virtues which make a man good (Bk. II, Chap. 5, 1106a). Similarly in theological ethics, Aristotle stresses the key role of affectivity in moral knowledge, "for to feel delight and pain rightly or wrongly has no small effect on our actions."[17] He also stresses the need for a community of moral formation: "Hence we ought to have been brought up in a particular way from our youth, as Plato says, so as both to delight in and to be pained by the things that we ought; for this is the right education."[18]

For Aristotle, moral philosophy was a practical science, one that is learned by practicing what model individuals in the community do. Practical reason, its tool, is effectively attuned to what is good by cultivation of the moral virtues. If contemporary business ethics were to be influenced by this emphasis on virtue, business people would come to see that the field as it is now constituted is too narrow. The theories of obligation need a context, a vision of what constitutes the good life. The images of the story of this vision would then attune one to recognize obligations. Theologians have relatively little difficulty offering this vision, for they have Jesus as a paradigmatic figure; they have the broad outlines of a way of life and some sense of the origin and final destiny of all creation. For philosophers and other scholars in business ethics, it is quite another matter. While theologians have a narrative which they take to be normative in shaping the community and the individual journey through life, there is no common agreement on a *telos* among philosophers. The force of this essay is to suggest that any account of morality is incomplete without a vision of what constitutes a good life—of the kind of persons we want to be and the kind of communities we want to form.[19]

I take it that moral obligations preserve a way of life. The business ethics of philosophers needs to spell out this way of life. For a start, one might investigate and write an account of the life stories of some of the leading persons in business who are known for their moral sensitivity. The stories of businesses that are recognized for ethical awareness need to be written and read by students and managers; their "company philosophies" (*not* codes of conduct) need to be spelled out and become common knowledge.

AN EXAMPLE: THE BILL HEWLETT STORY

Several years ago I had the good fortune to have a research year at the Stanford Business School in Palo Alto, California. As a Catholic priest, I was often asked to lead the Sunday worship service in a nearby church. One Sunday morning, after leading the service, I was greeting the people leaving the church when a woman stopped to comment on my homily. She had obviously thought about my remarks and was interested in further discussions. After a brief exchange, she thanked me and suggested that I meet her husband and continue our conversations on the world of business: "My husband is in the computer business. I am Mrs. William Hewlett." "Mrs. William who?" I responded. From that precarious beginning, I came to know a rather remarkable man who cofounded what is generally regarded as one of the premier business firms, the Hewlett-Packard Company. Recognized not only as a healthy company financially, the firm is also considered to be one of the most progressive in implementing social and ethical values.[20]

Today Hewlett-Packard has over 65,000 employees in locations around the world. Sales are over $4 billion with annual earnings in the range of $400 million. Recognized by the experts "as one of the best-managed companies in the electronics industry," H-P is also invariably cited as a model firm by business ethicists. Generous profit-sharing plans, stock-purchase programs, flexible working hours, and unusually low turnover for skilled workers are just a few of H-P's notable features. Founded in 1939 by two young electrical engineering graduates, Dave Packard and Bill Hewlett, both of whom had to work their way through Stanford, H-P has always been a pioneer in recognizing the dignity of the person in the workplace. Many employee benefits, now taken to be "moral obligations" of an employer, were instituted at H-P years before it occurred to most businessmen to consider them as "obligations." It might very well be that some of the employee benefits taken for granted at H-P today, but not yet present in most firms, may be tomorrow's "moral obligations." What accounts for this sort of moral leadership evident at H-P and a small number of other major firms?

For the first twenty years H-P was a relatively small business where all the employees personally knew the bosses as Bill and Dave, and where there was always free communication. Reflecting on the early days, Bill Hewlett noted that the company came to embody his and Dave Packard's personal beliefs and values. He offers examples of how innovative policies happened. In the early days, both Bill and Dave assumed a variety of roles, from bookkeeper to janitor, and they came to know their employees well. Bill tells of one employee who, because of tuberculosis, had to take a leave of absence for two years. Although the company provided some financial assistance to the family, Bill was touched by the "devastating impact" that the illness had on the man's family. Both he and Dave resolved then that they must work toward a more permanent solution to this type of health crisis. From this experience, they were moved to develop a plan for catastrophic medical insurance, an idea that was totally new for business in the late 1940s.

Several years after founding the company, the young entrepreneurs decided that they had to fire a good friend who was their production manager. Hewlett describes the occasion as "one of the most difficult steps that I can remember," but the manager was not able to do the job and the employees under him were suffering the consequences. This painful experience was the impetus for a company policy that provides a new opportunity in the firm for a loyal employee who is not measuring up in his or her present position. Relocating such employees within the company has been a successful strategy in most cases for the last forty years.

Hewlett and Packard were not from wealthy families, and they were both deeply touched by the poverty of the Great Depression in their early years at home. They were determined that their firm would not be a "hire-and-fire operation," and that they would always strive to avoid laying off employees. This has meant that they have never sought many of the lucrative government contracts that would require a temporary large increase in employees and a subsequent layoff. In the recession of early 1970, this philosophy was tested when H-P found that they had 10 percent more employees than they needed. Determined not to lay off these employees, they managed to obtain a consensus among all the employees to take every other Friday off without pay. As soon as the recession was over, all were returned to a normal work schedule and full pay.

In 1957 Hewlett and Packard decided they should try to articulate the corporate objectives that had been implicitly guiding them for twenty years. They set out to formulate the values that "reflect the organization's basic character and personality," and developed a seven-point "Statement of Corporate Objectives." Mirroring the concern in the situations cited above, a section of the statement reads:

> The company has been built around the individual, the personal dignity of each, and the recognition of personal achievements.
>
> Job security is an important HP objective. Over the years, the company has achieved a steady growth in employment by consistently developing good new products, and by avoiding the type of contract business that requires hiring many people, then terminating them when the contract expires. The company wants HP people to have stable, long-term careers.

To pass this corporate culture along to new employees, there are training seminars in the "HP Way" and a whole series of accountability procedures. As a former MBA student of mine remarked: "You have to see this company to believe it. It is almost too good to be true. They really do believe in human dignity and they practice what they preach."

The emphasis on moral imagination helps in understanding how it is that Bill Hewlett was able to "recognize" obligations, how he was able to "see" his little world "rightly" before most other business leaders. The strength of the traditional "business ethics" is that subsequently it can provide a justification, by appealing to rules and principles, of the rightfulness of the actions of Hewlett with his employees. The process of justifying the obligations then provides warrants to insist that other, less enlightened firms follow suit and offer their employees similar benefits. While this latter task is no small contribution, it is only a part of the field of business ethics.

How is it that some people are more attuned to recognizing wrong-doing and moral obligations than others? This focus on how our reasoning is shaped by our convictions is at the core of this inquiry into the moral imagination. Discussing stories and images of a life can offer an account of Bill Hewlett's behavior that is much more satisfactory than the traditional business ethics.

In the three simple examples—initiation of catastrophic medical insurance, founding a plan to avoid firing incompetent employees, and formulating schedules to avoid layoffs in an economic slump—the common element present is that Hewlett did not feel constrained by the "givens" of the situation. No one in his league of entrepreneurs would have blamed him if the firm simply said that it must always fire those who are not performing in their assigned role, or if management laid off 10 percent of the workers when there was a decline in orders. In fact, almost everyone would have said it was the best one could do in a capitalist economy. "There are limits to what one can do for employees in an efficient business enterprise." Perhaps one could have even found a "business ethicist" who would have *justified* his decision to fire the employee or lay off the workers, or to limit company payments to victims of chronic illnesses. While Hewlett may not have been under a moral obligation to do what he did, he felt he had to act in these ways to be true to himself. The chapters that follow examine how we might educate more men and women to see the world as Hewlett and other heroes of the business world have seen it.

Chapter 1 by Michael Goldberg, makes a strong case that business people today are illiterate in the classics, resulting in an impoverished strategic and moral vision. Paraphrasing Kant, he reminds us that rational argument without imagination is blind and that imagination without rational argument is empty. Goldberg argues for major changes in the undergraduate curriculum, specifically the addition of an interdisciplinary, professional ethics program. This program would help the student discover what it means to be human and how it feels to be in various roles in society. Goldberg is concerned that our students are not learning "the skill of sustained silent contemplation and critical reflection."

John Houck is the author of chapter 2 and he offers us, in capsule summary, his philosophy of education. Discussing three films—*The Dead Poets' Society*, *Billy Budd*, and *To Kill a Mockingbird*—Houck gives us a glimpse of a great teacher at work. After reading the Houck essay, we can see that it is no wonder he is revered by countless generations of students.

Chapter 3, authored by Timothy Fort, offers the reader a blueprint for the use of the film *The Brothers Karamazov* in a class on business ethics. Fort sees two foci for learning: "The need of a good that restrains human actions and the responsibility of individuals in exercising their freedom."

In chapter 4, Eileen Bender offers the reader an account of "the woman's story" in the "American myth of success." Using a variety of literary works and films, particularly those dealing with working women, Bender provides a compelling analysis of the ambivalence about the ethic of success.

Chapter 5, by Oliver Williams, c.s.c., is an analysis of how self-deception can mar the ethical performance of business managers. Using the film *Other People's Money*, Williams argues that self-deception is the best explanatory hypothesis for the attitudes and behavior of the central character of the film, takeover artist Larry Garfield. Assuming that self-deception is a common human failing, the essay offers a way to help our students come to grips with this dimension of themselves.

Teresa Phelps, author of chapter 6, uses Shakespeare's play *Measure for Measure* and four films—*Working Girl, Wall Street, Disclosure*, and *Mr. Holland's Opus*—as a penetrating analysis of power and what it does to us. Her task is a constructive one, to "rehabilitate our notions of power so that we may use authority more profitably."

Chapter 7 is by Thomas Shaffer, who has long been an advocate of narrative theology and its use of story. He presents three possible scenarios about business people and their lawyers, and asks the reader to ponder what those stories might mean for the conduct of business.

Bernard Murchland offers an intriguing proposal in chapter 8. Drawing on the work of Marshall McLuhan, Murchland suggests that we think of business as the great story of our time, "the closest we have to a metanarrative." In this account, ethics is "primarily a matter of understanding what kind of world we live in."

Chapter 9 by Dennis McCann, focuses on three films that starred Jack Lemmon—*The Apartment, Save the Tiger*, and *Glengarry Glen Ross*. McCann points us to the deeper dimension of all ethical reflection, the struggle to become fully human. "Business ethics can pursue no higher goal than the one Harry sets out for himself, enabling ourselves and others to become fully human, not in spite of, but precisely in and through our routine business practice."

Michael Medved, author of chapter 10, treats the reader to a brilliant summary and analysis of a number of films. The entertainment industry is shown to be discouraging ethical reflection and ethical behavior in the business world. Medved's prescription: we "need more people of conscience, of religious faith to get involved in the entertainment industry."

In chapter 11 David Collins gives an insider's account on how a company might form "a business climate that stimulated not only ethical reflection but ethical actions as well."

Charles Van Doren offers a remarkable compliment to business in chapter 12. After outlining the overwhelming problems in our environment today, Van Doren issues his call: "Businessmen and business women of the world, unite to save us. . . . Can we turn back to find a better road? . . . For you too are people in need of the good, the true, and the beautiful."

Chapter 13 is by Ellen O'Connor. Drawing on organizational theory about identity production as well as literary theory and the role of narrative in organizations, she sheds much light on how some of the best organizations are shaping corporate cultures today. These cultures call for a self-transformation, to be sure, and this is cause for some concern. "My biggest concern is the extent to which organizations and organization theorists have developed and refined their theories with such little attention to the ethical dimensions of their projects."

We are most grateful for the financial assistance provided by John Caron and William Lehr, Jr., businessmen of remarkable generosity and ethical concerns. The associate director of the University Press at Notre Dame, Jeffrey L. Gainey, deserves special thanks for his guidance and support. Finally, as in most projects, there is one who has guided this project from its inception, from planning the brochure to copyediting the manuscript. That person, the center's executive coordinator, Madeline Day, deserves our praise and gratitude for her untiring efforts.

NOTES

1. The pages that follow have been previously published in somewhat different form. See Oliver F. Williams, c.s.c., "Can Business Ethics Be Theological? What Athens Can Learn from Jerusalem," *Journal of Business Ethics* 5 (1986): 471–84.

2. Oliver F. Williams and John W. Houck, *Full Value: Cases in Christian Business Ethics* (San Francisco: Harper & Row, 1978). Works by former teachers and colleagues have been helpful in my development of narrative theology. See John S. Dunne, *Time and Myth* (New York: Doubleday, 1973); Sallie Teselle, *Speaking in Parables: A Study in Metaphor and Theology* (Philadelphia: Fortress Press, 1975); James Wm. McClendon, Jr., *Biography as Theology* (Nashville: Abingdon Press, 1974); Edna Mc-Donagh, *Doing the Truth* (Notre Dame: University of Notre Dame Press, 1979); and Stanley Hauerwas, *Vision and Virtue* (Notre Dame: University of Notre Dame Press, 1974). Other works that explore the theme include Alasdair MacIntyre, *After Virtue*

(Notre Dame: University of Notre Dame Press, 1981), and Robert C. Solomon, *Ethics and Excellence* (New York: Oxford University Press, 1992).

3. For an excellent discussion of the various ways religion and morality are related, see *Religion and Morality*, Gene Outka and John P. Reeder, Jr., eds. (Garden City: Anchor Press/Doubleday, 1973).

4. Aquinas, *Summa Contra Gentiles*, III, 37.

5. Aquinas, *De Veritate*, 23, 6.

6. For a good discussion of the Catholic understanding of practical moral reason, see Daniel C. Maguire, "*Ratio practica* and the Intellectualistic Fallacy," *Journal of Religious Ethics* 10 (1982): 22–39.

7. For a succinct summary, see O. Williams, "Christian Formation for Corporate Life," *Theology Today* 36 (1979): 347–52.

8. Williams and Houck, *Full Value*, 12.

9. For an excellent analysis and survey of the literature on the interplay between character analysis and decision-making in moral theology, see Richard A. McCormick, S.J., "Notes on Moral Theology," *Theological Studies* 42 (1981): 90–100; McCormick, "Notes," *Theological Studies* 44 (1983): 87–94; and McCormick, "Notes," *Theological Studies* 45 (1984): 84–96.

10. Since the Second Vatican Council and the encyclicals of Pope Paul VI, church documents, while making no claim to being based exclusively on revelation, employ a natural-law approach in the context of an explicit Christian vision. The symbols of Christian faith—creation, redemption, and so on—are highlighted as the framework for discerning the demands of nature. See O. Williams, "The Catholic Teaching," *The Judeo-Christian Vision and the Modern Corporation*, Oliver F. Williams, C.S.C. and John W. Houck, eds. (Notre Dame: University of Notre Dame Press, 1982), 76–81.

11. For example, see Karl Rahner, "On the Theology of the Incarnation," *Theological Investigations IV* (Baltimore: Helicon Press, 1966), 105–20.

12. In terms of the classic analyses of the Christian approaches to culture by H. Richard Niebuhr, this account is some variant of "Christ Above Culture" and "Christ the Transformer of Culture." See H. Richard Niebuhr, *Christ and Culture* (New York: Harper & Row, 1951; Torchbook edition, 1956).

13. Edmund Pincoffs makes this same point in a philosophical context: "It does not follow that because my decision would have been right for anyone in the same circumstances it would have been right for me. It follows only that almost no one could rightly blame me for what I did: that what I did was permissible. But I can blame myself. Those persons close enough to me to understand and share my special moral ideals can blame me, too." See "Quandary Ethics," *Mind* 80 (1971): 552–71.

14. For an incisive argument that virtue, "the character of paradigmatic individuals," is the primary moral category, see Harold Alderman, "By Virtue of a Virtue," *Review of Metaphysics* 36 (1982): 127–53. See also James Gaffney, "On Paresis and Fundamental Moral Theology," *Journal of Religious Ethics* 11 (1983): 23–24.

15. *Nicomachean Ethics*, Bk. 11, Chap. 1, 1103a.

16. Ibid., Bk. X, Chap. 5, 1176a.

17. Ibid., Bk. II, Chap. 2, 1105a.

18. Ibid., Bk. II, Chap. 2, 1104b.

19. For one attempt at applying the insights of narrative theology to a philosophical business ethics, see O. Williams, "Business Ethics: A Trojan Horse," *California Management Review* 24 (1982): 14–24.

20. For example, the work of William Ouchi cites Hewlett-Packard as a model firm. See William G. Ouchi, *Theory Z: How American Firms Can Meet the Japanese Challenge* (Reading, Mass.: Addison-Wesley, 1981).

PART I

— ☉ —

The Moral Imagination

Some Models for Effective Teaching about the Good Life

1

"DOESN'T ANYBODY READ THE BIBLE ANYMO'?"

Illiterates at the Gates

— ◉ —

MICHAEL GOLDBERG

When I was an undergraduate at Yale in the late 1960s and early 1970s, I took a course in twentieth-century English poetry taught by Cleanth Brooks. Along with Robert Penn Warren, Mr. Brooks had founded the movement of literary analysis called the "New Criticism." More impressive to me, however, than his scholarly achievement was his gentlemanly manner. Hailing from Louisiana, he had a warm, Old-South, old-school, courtly way about him that made me, as his student, want to please him.

I am afraid, though, that my classmates and I often failed to please him. We would be discussing some poem in class, one for example by Eliot or Pound, and Mr. Brooks would take some phrase or image, and ask us to what it was alluding. We would just sit there like the great stone heads on Easter Island, silent and expressionless. To this day, I can hear Mr. Brooks breaking the long, awkward silence with a plaintive cry, "Doesn't anybody read the Bible anymo'?"

The answer, of course, was that we bodies, at least, did not. On the other hand, at least we had read other things that were then part of the standard literary fare served up on secondary school curricula: *The Scarlet Letter*, *Moby Dick*, and even *The Rise of Silas Lapham*, typically accompanied, of course, by generous portions of American history. Make no mistake: I am *not* putting out this menu as *the* right diet to build strong minds twelve different ways; I am only offering it to compare my own admittedly rather low-calorie regimen with the educational malnutrition plaguing today's business and professional school students as a result of the cultural anorexia they have suffered over the last decade or two.

In 1992 a team of professors at the Bowman-Gray Medical School of Wake Forest University in Winston-Salem, North Carolina, led by Dr. Richard Vance, published the results of a cultural literacy test taken by 210 first- and second-year medical students whose undergraduate work spanned 62 different institutions in 21 states.[1] If nothing else, simply by virtue of the very fact that they were medical students at a good school places them higher on the ladder of intellectual achievement than many other graduate and professional students in the United States. The test covered 22 subjects in the liberal arts, social sciences, and natural sciences, and its 250 items were reviewed, criticized, and finally approved by ten faculty members hailing from Wake Forest's Undergraduate College of Arts and Sciences and its medical school.

The average score was just a little over 28 percent. No statistical differences were discovered on the basis of sex, race, country of birth, political orientation, religious affiliation, type of college attended, college-class rank, grade-point average, plans to specialize, or the number and type of extracurricular activities. The only significant differences appeared with reference to (1) age—thirty- to forty-year-old students did better; (2) the number of books read per year; and (3) college major, i.e., liberal arts majors scored higher. The *highest* score was an anemic 69.2 percent while the lowest was 6 percent, made, by the way, by a white male.

The news gets worse. When the test was given to 144 law students, the average score dropped to 24 percent.[2] But here is what may be the worst news of all. When the test was given to one hundred MBA students, the already abysmal scores plummeted all the way down to 17 percent correct. Only 30 percent could identify, for instance, "Jehovah," only 20 percent the term "gulag," only 5 percent the name "Sir Thomas More," only 1 percent the notion "common law."[3] In a separate report, Vance and his colleagues gave examples of "some answers we did not expect": *Actuary*—"a home for birds"; *Aquinas*—"a Roman god"; *Stradivarius*—"as in 'Rex.'"[4]

The dreary news here is that it is not only, as poor Mr. Brooks opined, that nobody reads the Bible anymo', but that most bodies, and particularly most bodies in the business world, do not read anything much anymo'. Besides the scientific studies many of us already know about, let me share some first-hand knowledge gained from my own experience of working in different professional fields. As a university professor, I soon learned that the only sure-fire allusions and illustrations I could use with students were ones drawn from television sitcoms no more ancient than two or three years old, or taken from advertising campaigns of even more recent vintage. Later, as a special consultant to the Georgia Supreme Court and State Bar in professional ethics, I learned that designating most practicing lawyers as part of a "learned" profession was like calling Dan Quayle Hegel. But by far the most unlettered, the most poorly read group among whom I have worked have been business professionals. I say that with no glee but, on the contrary, with a sense of great sadness.

In my life, I have been fortunate to have been a member of the international strategic management consulting firm of McKinsey & Company which serves Fortune 500 clients. By any measure, the people at McKinsey were, as a whole, the smartest and nicest with whom I have ever worked. McKinsey consultants are typically drawn from the top 5 percent of Harvard MBA's—or from their equivalent at other select business schools—and usually they are chosen by McKinsey for their ability to work well in teams with others. Yet, during my years with McKinsey, I cannot remember even one consultant, from the most junior associate to the most senior partner, ever looking at or referring to one piece of literature or film that might be dubbed a classic.

So what? Just this: Without having ongoing, rich contact with narrative texts that continually invite them to envisage a world similar to, yet different from, our own, McKinsey consultants, like other business people, cannot help having impoverished *strategic* and *moral* vision. Powerful, compelling texts of this sort beckon us to imagine a world that is not yet, but *that might be*. The philosopher Martha Nussbaum, professor of law and ethics at the University of Chicago, has recently put it this way in her elegant book *Poetic Justice*:

> Literary works typically invite their readers to put themselves in the place of people of many different kinds and to take on their experiences. . . . [Such works] speak to an implicit reader who shares with the characters certain hopes, fears, and general human concerns, and who for that reason is able to form bonds of identification and sympathy with them, but who is situated elsewhere and needs to be informed about the concrete situation of the characters. In this way, the very structure of the interaction between the text and its imagined reader invites the reader to see how the mutable features of society and circumstance bear on the realization of shared hopes and desires.[5]

In short, contends Nussbaum, "Storytelling and literary imagining are not opposed to rational argument, but can provide *essential ingredients* in a rational argument."[6]

Although certain "hard-nosed" business types might initially balk at such claims, business-school education has implicitly granted their validity since its inception near the turn of the century. An old standby in the curriculum has always been the case-study method. Typically, students are presented with an engaging, often hypothetical, narrative displaying a problematic set of circumstances set within some business context, and then asked to offer ways of solving it. The students' analytical abilities are honed through their development of two key skills. First, they must be able to give a cogent account of the case, that is, they must be able to get the story straight. Having read the narrative text rightly, the students' second task is to *imagine* what possibilities, what options, might flow from it.[7]

There is, however, an even earlier precedent from the world of business and commerce, arguing for the need to develop the critical skills nurtured by the literary imagination. As Nussbaum points out, the venerable Adam Smith, "in many respects the founder of modern economics," emphasized the role of what he called "the judicious spectator" as indispensable to proper reasoning on economic policy matters. Smith's judicious spectator seems very like a person with the kind of vivid imaginative world narrative texts seek to create. Indeed, Smith himself gave considerable weight to literature as a source of moral guidance.[8] In his work, *The Theory of Moral Sentiments*, Smith writes (1.1.4.6):

> The spectator must . . . endeavour, as much as he can, to put himself in the situation of the other, and to bring home to himself every little circumstance of distress which can possibly occur to the sufferer. He must adopt the whole case of his companion with all its minutest incidents; and strive to render as perfect as possible, that *imaginary change* of situation upon which his sympathy is founded.[9]

Of course, we must remember that Smith's ideal rationalist is both *judicious* and a *spectator*. In that regard, moral reflection on the circumstances and options of the characters we read about, view, or hear must make some use of rational detachment so that there is not uncritical, whole-cloth identification with the characters' interests or our own. Hence, neither Smith and Nussbaum[10] nor I are arguing that the literary imagination *alone* can or should do all the work of moral, strategic analysis. But to those who would, Sergeant Friday-like, dismiss the role of narrative-shaped literary and cinematic texts in favor of the so-called "facts of the matter," our response is just as terse: Without the kind of imaginative, empathetic faculties literary and cinematic texts cultivate, our vision will be blinded, for we will be unable to discern, clearly and consistently, which facts matter—and how—and why.

Sometimes this lack of a cultivated imagination reveals itself in humorous, albeit minor, ways. I remember being at one of McKinsey's introductory training programs where new consultants from company offices all over the world were brought together to begin their immersion into the organization's strong corporate culture. Some of us "veterans" were stationed at each of the two dozen dinner tables to facilitate the newcomers' getting to know each other. So at my table, as an icebreaker, I asked people, "Suppose you could be anyone or anything other than who or what you are now, who or what would you be? Go ahead, let your imaginations roam free! How would you be different?" I turned to the consultant next to me and asked him to get the ball rolling. He looked up at me and said, "OK, what skills do I have?"

At other times, however, the lack of a cultivated, empathetic imagination appeared in not so humorous and far from minor ways which, as I said earlier, reflect an impoverished strategic and moral vision.

We were serving a client in the "forest-products industry"—what the rest of us call "paper." The client's enterprise spanned the globe, and McKinsey was called in to analyze the way in which the company's worldwide logistics operation could be improved. As was the McKinsey way, consultant teams worked with client teams to try to get "the answer."

At the outset, one needs to understand the difference between those on the McKinsey team and those on the client team. To repeat, McKinsey people typically come from the highest 5 percent of the top business schools in the country. They are courted like professional athletes and offered, besides high salaries linked to signing bonuses, incentives for high performance. In contrast, client team members are frequently middle-aged middle managers with far less talent and far dimmer futures, often working for poorly performing companies that may be in the midst of downsizing. In other words, there may be nothing "in it" for members of the client team, except the very real possibility that if all goes well in the study, the results may show that their positions are superfluous and that their jobs—and they—will no longer be needed.

The day-to-day work of the McKinsey team and its study or engagement is headed up by an "EM" or "engagement manager." Engagement managers are typically senior associates on the brink of becoming partners. They are under terrific pressure. When clients pay on average $250,000 a month plus 20 percent expenses, the stakes tend to be enormous. Therefore, at McKinsey, there is zero tolerance for failure. One botched engagement, and no one will rely on you again.

On the engagement for the paper client, I was working with an EM who not only headed up the McKinsey team, but who also ultimately bore de facto responsibility for the client team, even though, theoretically at least, the client team had its own manager leading it. A therapist friend of mine has a maxim, "Never work harder than the client." To McKinsey people, that kind of statement is just plain crazy. They take it as an article of faith that you always have to work harder than the client because if the client had worked hard enough in the first place, McKinsey would not have to be there to save the client's *tuchus*, to use the Old French term.

There are two immediate consequences of this view: (1) McKinsey people will typically work sixteen- to eighteen-hour days for days on end, and (2) McKinsey meetings with clients virtually always run over the time they are supposed to end. My EM certainly worked long hours, and he surely held overlong team meetings.

For his part, the client team manager struck me as a serious, responsible person. As far as I could tell, he always accomplished the tasks assigned him in a timely and effective way, thus honoring his commitments. For an upcoming team meeting, however, he had an additional team manager commitment to honor—he was also the manager of his nine-year-old son's baseball team. The McKinsey-client team meeting had been set for 4:00; his son's baseball team's game had been scheduled for 5:30. To make the latter in time, he would have to leave the former by 5:00. This deadline he repeated to the McKinsey EM several times before the day of the scheduled meeting as well as at least one more time during that day itself.

The meeting started promptly at 4:00. Things were going well, ground was being covered, progress was being made. The clock moved toward 4:30, then 4:45. I looked at the McKinsey EM. He seemed oblivious to the time. Then I looked at the client team manager who seemed increasingly oblivious to everything *but* the time. The clock edged up toward 4:50, then 4:55, then 5:00, with not so much as a pause, let alone a finale called by the EM. At 5:10 the client team manager got up and left. The rest of the meeting did not break up until somewhere around 6:00.

Afterwards, the EM pulled me aside and told me how upset he was with the client manager for leaving early. When I responded that the man had repeatedly told us of his prior commitment as Little League manager and that our meeting had nevertheless run way over time, my words simply did not register with the EM. Let me be clear. This EM was not some humorless ogre, but he simply and literally *could not imagine* anything being more important in someone's life than that person's job. To be even more specific, he could not imagine anything being more important in someone else's life than *his*, i.e., the EM's, job.

I hasten to add that I use the McKinsey EM only as an illustration of a certain all-too-familiar type I have encountered in business and, unfortunately, in the professions. I once heard a top-level executive of the same forest-products client say, "Employees are like trees. Easy to grow, easy to cut down." While he gets some cultural literacy points for using a simile, he gets lots of points off for the small-minded comparison he was trying to draw.

This was the same man who once remarked, "Trees in the ground have no value until we cut them down and make them into something." Either way, what this insufferable man suffered from most was a failure of imagination. Although he could have just as easily been talking about this executive, or about my EM, or about countless other people in positions of power and authority in business, Rousseau made a similar observation about the aristocracy: "Why does a noble have contempt for a peasant? It is because he will never *be* [and thus cannot imagine being] a peasant."[11] Without a cultivated imagination, even some relatively good people can do bad things.

As I said previously, an inability to imaginatively envisage another person's life can lead to deficiencies in strategic vision, and not just morally. After McKinsey completed the engagement component that analyzed the best way for the client to reorganize its global logistics operations, a new consulting opportunity developed regarding the implementation of the reorganized operation. The client CEO and his vice presidents decided to let their employees vote on which consulting group to use. McKinsey, although it had done the original analysis and that analysis was correct, lost the job—and with it perhaps millions of dollars in fees. There simply had been too many encounters between the client's employees and McKinsey consultants like my EM. There is one more chapter to this tale, however. The consulting firm the employees chose was frankly not as smart as McKinsey, and the implementation was bungled. With apologies to Kant—and acknowledgments to Nussbaum and Adam Smith—rational argument without imagination is blind; imagination without rational argument is empty.

As I said earlier, I cannot remember during my time with McKinsey hearing anyone discussing a literary or cinematic classic, much less seeing anyone reading or viewing one. Significantly, for most of the McKinsey people I knew, it was not a question during the course of their professional lives, of them becoming too burdened to read the books or see the films they once had. It was that *they had never done that at all.* In their undergraduate days, many had been business majors who were never required to wrestle with texts, whether literary or cinematic, that is, texts with complex, rich narrative textures. It was not simply that the value of the skill was lost to them. More drastically, more tragically, it was lost *on* them. So taking McKinsey people as a frame of reference for business's intelligentsia, and viewing McKinsey consultants within the broader context of the generally less intellectually able business clients whom they serve, I am prepared to answer the question of this conference in a straightforward manner. "How can literature and films stimulate ethical reflection in the business world?" *They cannot—it is too late.*

That does not mean, however, that the situation is hopeless. But it does mean that the focal point for reforming business ethics, i.e., the specific opportunity for using literature and film as sources of ethical reflection for business, must be located not among current practitioners, but among those in the early stages of becoming practitioners, namely, undergraduates. That means reforming the undergraduate business curriculum.

Let me be blunt. If I were president of one of the many colleges and universities in America that offer majors in business, business administration, accounting, and the like, I can think of no more important reform than to abolish them. At many schools across the country the most heavily enrolled undergraduate major is business, but there is no good reason why that subject should even be included in the liberal arts curriculum, or why in any way it should be considered as relevant to the life of the spirit and the life of the mind. If one can major in business, then why not in plumbing, carpentry, general contracting, or ROTC? In my view, students should be able to major in, e.g., economics, psychology, mathematics, that is, in courses of study that are genuinely intellectual pursuits and thus have a valid place in higher education. Although many graduate business and professional students come from the socioeconomic uppercrust, one might nonetheless say about them and their undergraduate education what is often said about those at the other end of the social ladder: A mind is a terrible thing to waste.

An acquaintance of mine teaches political science at a southern university. He also happens to be an alumnus interviewer for high school students applying to his alma mater, Princeton. Some time ago he conducted such an interview with a candidate for admission. At the end of the interview, he asked the candidate if she had anything to ask him. She inquired as to whether there was a business major. He said, "No." She asked, "Well, then, is there an accounting major?" Again, "No." With rising tension in her voice, she quizzed him once more: "Then what about any business or accounting *courses*?" Once more, his response was "No." Exasperated, the candidate at last cried out, "Just what kind of a school is Princeton, anyway?"

A real one. If I have not succeeded already in offending your sensibilities, permit me to continue. The frequency and size of business courses, programs, and majors in the undergraduate curriculum are signs to me of the university's corruption, i.e., of its decay, its adulteration, its falling away from its true mission. Corruption of mission and corruption of vision go hand in hand. Moral blindness becomes virtually inevitable. The academic world is forever lecturing the business and professional worlds about improving their ethics—a huge bibliography from the last ten years alone attests to that fact. But, strikingly, comparatively little has been written in the way of reflection about its own ethics by the academic world. One is reminded of what is sometimes said about consultants. They would lead you to believe they know everything there is to know about romantic love; they just do not know anybody to call up for a date on the weekend. Similarly, it would seem that academic ethics is for the most part just that—*academic.*

However, since I am not a college or university president nor am I likely to become one, let me make another proposal that is less draconian but no less modest. If, as seems likely, there are going to be undergraduate business programs and majors—as well as courses of study in other professional spheres such as pre-law and pre-med—then I propose that universities introduce some type of mandatory, interdisciplinary professional ethics program. Such a program would fit well within the liberal arts curriculum, for it would help students confront and answer the most basic question addressed by a liberal education: Who am I? Thus understood, the liberal arts curriculum does exactly what literary art is supposed to do, i.e., cultivate the imagination by presenting, from a variety of fields, different images of what it might mean to be human. The reason I would not want to be treated by one of the medical-student-cultural-illiterates in the Wake Forest study mentioned earlier is not because I seek a physician who could grow rich on *Jeopardy* by becoming a five-time champion, but because I do not want a doctor who has such an *impoverished vision of what it means to be human,* one who would most likely see me only as another case, or, in this age of managed (or mangled) health care, a DRG (diagnosis related group) offering him a potential economic incentive if he disposes of me efficiently. Instead, the kind of physician I want is akin to Adam Smith's "judicious spectator" who, we remember, must try "to put himself in the situation of the other, [bringing] home to himself every . . . little . . . distress possibly occur[ring] to the sufferer" while maintaining a prudent professional perspective wider than mine so as to have a broader field of vision regarding the appropriate course of treatment, of action, for someone with my complaint.

Why propose such a program for the undergraduate level? After all, business schools, like law schools and medical schools, already have ethics courses and programs in place. Prima facie, it would certainly seem easier to give a few tweaks to their present ethics curricula.

The problem is that the current professional ethics curricula themselves stand in need of more than just a few tweaks to be effective, as anyone who has ever been a student in or of them surely knows. Professional school ethics courses are often taught by instructors who possess little or no formal training in moral philosophy. Class discussions of moral issues frequently border on the superficial, leaving students with the impression that ethics are matters of individual preference and consequently lack the intellectual rigor of other subjects in the curriculum. Furthermore, because ethics courses many times do not count for as many credits as other, more traditional subjects, students come to regard the topic as an afterthought, "softer" than more "serious" courses in, e.g., microeconomics or torts. Against the typical professional school backdrop, ethics instruction achieves the opposite effect intended: instead of making students moral Solomons, it makes them moral cynics.

But where the professional school fails, the undergraduate liberal arts curriculum can succeed. While the former may only provide one or two un(der)trained instructors, the latter can offer a rich, interdisciplinary mix of faculty. Obviously, any program in professional ethics should naturally involve faculty well trained in philosophy and ethics. But because business and the professions come with their respective social histories and traditions, enlisting faculty who bring the perspectives and resources of a variety of disciplines such as history, anthropology, economics, and, of course, literature and film, is not only desirable but critical. In contrast to professional school students who may have become so socialized (read: jaded) by their specialized training as to dismiss the liberal arts out of hand, many undergraduates still retain—or can be forced to maintain for the moment at least—the openness, curiosity, and intellectual (and spiritual!) hunger that make moral education possible.

One could imagine, for example, a beginning course entitled, "Introduction to the Professions: From Athens and Rome to New York and Washington." Using faculty from philosophy, classics, history, and American literature, students could read materials arcing from Socrates' exchanges with Thrasymachus about what kind of power is really powerful, to Tom Wolfe's *Bonfire of the Vanities* about the so-called "Masters of the Universe" on the New York Stock Exchange. Or one could imagine a course called, "Confronting the Tragic: When Professionals Run Up against the Limits of their Professions." The value and values of such a course, taught by staff from the aforementioned departments as well as from film and drama, would provide a much deeper—and much healthier—conception of success than that currently abroad in the culture. One thing classical tragedy vividly displays is the limit of human power as well as the personal and corporate disaster awaiting those who go beyond that limit. It also holds out as well powerful images of what humanity writ large looks like in the face of tragedy. As Plutarch realized almost two millennia ago, such images give the young a rich store of self-images on which they can draw in later life.[12]

Thus, to repeat, this undergraduate, interdisciplinary program in business and the professions fits well within the mission of liberal education, namely, to throw up several different visions of what it means to be human, to give the young a liberal, generous supply of possible answers to the question, Who am I? thereby *liberating* them from the narrow confines of the answer: CEO, VP, or Middle Manager of International Widgets, Inc. After all, even one who would take the position that a business person's moral obligation extends no farther than his or her own self-interest would still have to admit that someone with a thinner notion of what it means to be a self, of what it means to be this particular self, stands in a significantly poorer position compared to someone with a more fleshed-out vision.

A self is something fragile. In a self's hope is also the potential for its despair. Because a self is capable of transformation, it is likewise susceptible to deformation. One way to misshape a self is to deny it the experience, the skill, *the practice*, of being alone with itself without distraction. Reading literature teaches that practice. As the literary critic George Steiner has keenly observed, "To read fully is to be silent and within silence. This order of silence is, at this point in western society, tending to become a luxury."[13] The little clips that run prior to the feature film in theaters these days, reminding audiences to be quiet, pointedly suggest that silence is increasingly difficult to find even in the darkened spaces of the movie house. Where silence is impossible, so, too, is reflection. Once more, therefore, talking about literature and film as sources for ethical reflection in the business world may well be only talk, because there is no time, no place, no prepared space in the business world for silent reflection and the grueling inner work that moral introspection requires.

One of the things that makes teaching professional ethics difficult in law school is that law school typically has everything except clients, that is, no opportunity for practicing lawyering, much less the chance for practicing legal ethics, and thus learning the kind of moral wisdom that finally comes only through being a practitioner. Clearly, even an interdisciplinary program of the kind I am suggesting cannot give and, in my judgment, should not give, students the experience of being a professional practitioner.[14] What it should give them, however, is deep experience at becoming reading practitioners, that is, at becoming practiced readers. I realize this task, as well as the task of developing a moral imagination, needs to be started long before the college years, not only in primary and secondary schools, but also in synagogues and churches, and above all, in the home. Nevertheless, firmly grounding the practice of imaginative reading, teaching the skill of sustained silent contemplation and critical reflection, is crucial at the one juncture in life which, for many people, is the only time they will have to lead a contemplative form of life focused on the development of the soul. That time of life is college, during the undergraduate years, the traditional nursery for such a life and such a soul.

For Jews, the nursery stories for animating that kind of life and soul have traditionally been found in the Bible.[15] One such Jew was Rabbi Israel

Meir HaKohen who lived in Lithuania during the nineteenth and twentieth centuries. As is the custom with rabbinic commentators, he is most frequently called by the title of his most famous work, the *Chafetz Chayyim*. The book is an extended disquisition on Judaism's prohibitions regarding slander and gossip, and its title, which literally means "desiring life," is taken from Psalm 34:13–15: "Who is the man who desires life, who wishes years of good fortune? Guard your tongue from evil, your lips from speaking guile. Shun evil and do good, seek peace and pursue it."

That is exactly what the Chafetz Chayyim did in his life. Mark Twain once said, "To do right is noble; to advise others to do right is also noble—and much less trouble." The reason that Jews still read what the Chafetz Chayyim wrote is that he did not only write about ethics; he *lived* ethics. The reason I am mentioning the Chafetz Chayyim here, in this context, is that he did not earn his living as a rabbi; rather, he earned it as a businessman.

When the Chafetz Chayyim was a young man, he opened a small store with his wife. He refused to keep in the store any goods that were not fresh or perfect. To make sure that he was giving good value he would always add a little to whatever was bought. Fearful that too many customers were buying at his store, thus depriving others of income, he would close his store at midday. Once, a non-Jewish customer left behind a herring he had bought, and the Chafetz Chayyim was unable to discover the customer's identity. Subsequently, the Chafetz Chayyim, to make sure that he himself was not guilty of theft, distributed a fresh herring to each of his non-Jewish customers on the next market day when they returned to buy from him.[16]

To many of us, indeed to many in the business world, conduct like the Chafetz Chayyim's is unimaginable. But that is exactly the point! For the Chafetz Chayyim, the moral conduct of many in the business world is what would be unimaginable. *His* imagination, a different imaging of what it meant to be human, was shaped, nurtured, and cultivated by a host of powerful texts, among them, the powerful literature found in biblical texts. I like to think that in the Chafetz Chayyim, Mr. Brooks, a genteel gentile, from half a world away, would nevertheless have found a *chaver*, a study-mate/soul-mate not so distant from his own imagination.

NOTES

1. Richard P. Vance, R. W. Prichard, C. King, and G. Camp, "Cultural Literacy of Medical Students," *Perspectives in Biological Medicine* 35 (1992): 281–91.

2. Richard P. Vance and R. W. Prichard, "Cultural Literacy of Law Students," *Journal of Legal Education* 42 (1992): 233–39.

3. Richard P. Vance, R. W. Prichard, and P. Peacock, "Cultural Literacy of Graduate Management Students," *Business Horizons* 35 (1992): 20–24.

4. Richard P. Vance, R. W. Prichard, and C. King, "Cultural Literacy of Professional Students," *North Carolina Medical Journal* 54 (1993): 415–18.

5. Martha C. Nussbaum, *Poetic Justice: The Literary Imagination and Public Life,* (Boston: Beacon Press, 1995), 5, 7. Although Nussbaum is speaking here of realistic novels, she acknowledges that her contentions could also be applied to certain types of films.

6. Ibid., xiii; emphasis mine.

7. It is also an important but often overlooked feature of the case-study approach that it is used in a *classroom setting*—that is, as a group, rather than individual enterprise, so that various readings of the case can be tested one against the other in an effort to get at the interpretation that is most adequate to all the salient elements.

8. Nussbaum, *Poetic Justice,* 75.

9. Quoted in ibid., 73; emphasis mine.

10. Cf. ibid., xvi, 74–77.

11. *Emile,* bk. 4, quoted in Nussbaum, *Poetic Justice,* 66. I suspect that some of the reason most of us human beings are so oblivious most of the time to the suffering we inflict on animals during the course of, e.g., medical experimentation is that we can never even rightly *imagine* being animals, let alone becoming one. A "smile" on a chimp's face is not a sign of pleasure, but of terror.

12. My friend, Professor Jack Sammons of the Walter F. George School of Law at Mercer University in Macon, Georgia, has remarked that the reading of classical tragedy ought to be a required part of every first-year law student's course of study since virtually every lawsuit might be seen as a tragedy insofar as it involves the conflict of (at least) two opposing rights. Law students might learn to see that a lawyer who loses his or her case is consequently not necessarily a failed or "bad" lawyer.

13. George Steiner, *No Passion Spent: Essays 1978–1995,* (New Haven: Yale University Press, 1996), quoted in *San Francisco Examiner & Chronicle,* 18 August 1996, Book Review Sec., 4.

14. The actual experience of a fine practitioner in any field can be gained only over a professional lifetime of experience; anything less than that—together with the moral judgment that goes with it—is therefore not only generally useless but can be dangerously misleading. Second, finding practitioners who can serve as the right moral models, the right mentors, for any kind of novice is notoriously difficult. There is only one kind of truly qualified practitioner/mentor to whom undergraduates have access and who can give them genuinely deep immersion into the experience of practicing the study of, and critical reflection on, the types of imaginative texts they will need to become expert ethical practitioners later on, no matter what professional field

they may eventually enter. That qualified practitioner/mentor is, of course, someone who is an expert undergraduate professor.

15. Cf., e.g., the statement of the second-century sage, Judah ben Tema, in Avot 5:21, that "at five, one is ready for the study of Scripture."

16. Dov Katz, *Tenuat ha-Musar*, vol. 4 (Tel Aviv: 1963).

2

FIVE EASY PIECES . . .
FOR ETHICAL REFLECTIONS
IN BUSINESS

— ◉ —

JOHN W. HOUCK

As I was reading Michael Goldberg's essay, particularly his suggestion that we eliminate three-fourths of our undergraduate population in the business school, I thought how amazing that you can turn an hour into an enemy.

What I want to do here, now that we have the thesis on the table from Michael Goldberg, is to suggest that the world of business education is not quite as grim, at least on the undergraduate level, as he has suggested. It may be an anti-thesis or it may only be a footnote.

Let me begin by being a little autobiographical. As I was reflecting on some of the classic films which I use in my MBA and undergraduate courses, I recall my days of film watching back in the 1940s. I had the distinction of being one of the early examples of a "latch-key child," that is, my parents, having been out of work for a long time in the Depression, were able to find, in war production, good-paying jobs, ten hours a day, six days a week. Now, what do you do with a ten- or eleven-year-old? Of course, today you would put out some cookies and a sandwich and suggest the TV but, in those days, all you could do was send this incorrigible eleven-year-old to films, to movies (we called them movies back then). I would sit in these films until my parents got home after school. I always remember that the worst thing was the intermission, because the lights would be on and, therefore, I could not indulge in the trip, or the high, of fantasy, imagining myself as the hero of *Four Feathers* (I would be the one to sneak through the enemy lines, or I would hear Gunga Din's call and I would turn the troops around). I was still too young to appreciate some of the romantic or even sexual escapades they showed in the film; in fact, I did not particularly like them. So I hated the lights going on at the intermission. The other thing I hated was the credits, because it seemed forever until we got to the action.

The first film I want to discuss is one that I think has a very skillful use of the time allowed for credits; I will outline some of the questions we talk about when I show the film to my students. To understand my approach to teaching, you should know that I do not believe it is appropriate to start a class without discussing some of the politics of that class—who has the power, different responsibilities, and how they should be expressed. In most classes, of course, there is just a detailing of the syllabus and a discussion of the grading process: your final grade will be 85 percent of this, 10 percent of that, 5 percent of this. Actually, to get a good grade, it is probably more important for a student to avoid taking a faculty parking spot—this is tantamount to failure! Seriously, I do not believe that grading is what we should emphasize. So to give the correct emphasis, I show Robin Williams's very fine film *The Dead Poets' Society*.

For some reason I find that the imagery in *The Dead Poets' Society* is remarkably similar to that of the university I am part of, and perhaps to that of most educational institutions—the heavy presence of parents, of symbols, banners, models, and all the excitement of the first days. So I ask my students to select one of two multiple choices that I give them. (They are all very good at multiple-choice questions because of their experience with the SAT tests.)

Interpretation A: This film is the story of the tragic consequences resulting from the subversion of our system: professional schools like law, business, and medicine need students who are prepared and well trained by undergraduate schools which need high schools to do their important, assigned role. Mr. Keating and the dead poets could spend their time better by prepping for the next exam!

Interpretation B: This film is the story of a hopelessly outmanned band of dead poets and their captain, Mr. Keating, confronting the society and its system of education. By their involvement and actions, they forced the high costs of our educational system to become visible: the acceptance of disguise as a necessity of life; the unconscious determination to manipulate others in the way one has been manipulated; the conviction that productivity is more important than character and "success" superior to satisfaction; the loss of curiosity, of a willingness to ask questions, and of the capacity to take risks.

I have done this now for several semesters, with five or six hundred MBAs and maybe a comparable number of undergraduates. Some people might suggest I am in a rut; I say, Why change a hit? The great majority, 95 percent, take interpretation B. They say this film is mainly about all these undesirable things, the bad things, and they have to write several paragraphs to justify their selection of this interpretation. But the shocker is that, of course, interpretation A is their own game plan, the one that got them here! Scenario A outlines what has been done to them and by them so they are, in essence, rejecting their own game plan. They went to a very fine prep school, much like Wharton Academy, did very well there, with good grades, and then 75 percent of them went on to an Ivy League university or Notre Dame (if they had heartier appetites). From college, they move on to some type of further program. I find it very interesting that they are rejecting their own game plan and I am pleased that they understand and can count these various costs they observed in the film.

This discussion of the *Dead Poets' Society* is about all I do when I explain what is expected in this class. I avoid relating any percentage breakdown for grades because I claim I lost the piece of paper on which I had such details and I do not want to confuse them.

The second film I show is selected primarily because I am educating future leaders—managers and business executives. It is a wonderful film that reveals much about where one might be going. It is Melville's *Billy Budd*. As you know, Melville began this short story and then hid it away somewhere because he could not finish it. (It reminds me of several novels I have been writing over the years.) What is rewarding about using the film is that I am often dealing with people who are not accustomed to reading books. I love the academic debates about reading the original text. Unfortunately, for many that is a lost art. The wonderful thing about this film is that Peter Ustinov, who wrote the script, produced it, directed it, and then starred in it, did something that is very rare—the written account is surpassed by the film. It is one of the few cases of producing a classic from a classic—which is not easy to do. It might be thought of as a takeoff on the old children's nursery rhyme "Three Men in a Tub." The time is circa 1800 and the setting is a British man-of-war. A major character is Captain Vere who, if you remember, is called "Story" Vere because he reads books. There is a master-of-arms, the disciplinarian named Claggart. As the story goes, there is a need to impress a sailor from another ship and they get this young, handsome sailor (I never knew if there were homoerotic possibilities here), Billy Budd. Billy Budd, Melville tells us, is the best sailor on the ship he is seized from, *The Rights of Man*. Now we are beginning to see what is really at stake here. This wonderful sailor is very popular with the other sailors; it makes for a happy ship where people laugh and enjoy doing their work. He is brought from *The Rights of Man*, under impressment, to this British man-of-war where the enforcer is Claggart. Claggart is played by Robert Ryan who, as you may recall, was typecast as a manic-depressive; he played the part brilliantly. That may be the only flaw in the film, as I will explain below.

It becomes obvious that we are going to have a struggle between Claggart (who represents that worldview that says people are no damn good), and Billy Budd (a simple man who cannot quite articulate exactly what he believes in). One suspects, that Billy, coming from *The Rights of Man*, believed people are basically good but that institutions hold them back. This theme is alluded to by the author. In any event, the two men are on a collision course.

This is a wonderful film for the education of future managers because Captain Vere is a manager, a leader, an arbitrator, the person in charge; and, of course, in our business schools we teach no followers—everyone is a leader. How is Vere going to handle this impending crisis? He gets warnings of the conflict from the other officers. His response: Give Claggart more slack, more rope, and we will see how he handles the problem. What we have here are clashes of the ideas of titans. How will Claggart respond?

What happens is that Claggart antagonizes Billy Budd. However, Billy Budd has one major defect; when he becomes overexcited, he stammers—he cannot get his words out. He becomes so frustrated that he throws a punch and knocks Claggart down. Claggart has an eggshell skull and is killed. You can imagine the ensuing problems on a British man-of-war, the avenger on patrol of revolutionary France.

The film gives only a brief segment on the trial. There are several interpretations of what this story is about, and each student is asked for his or her understanding of the matter. Some say that Billy Budd is the story of what happens when *good*, Billy Budd, conflicts with *evil*, the Master-at-Arms Claggart. Captain Vere is the hero-model in this view in that he struggles to preserve reasonable order and carry out the tradition he learned as a young midshipman. That interpretation does not get many adherents—about one in fifty students. Most students are critical of Vere in that he hides behind the tradition in which he was trained. Instead, the students argue, he should have been a better leader, he should have done a better job of monitoring what Claggart was doing, changing his methods or reforming them. Then, of course, they are perplexed by the fact that here is "Story" Vere, a man who is supposed to be a reader, one who has access to creative ideas from literature. This literary imagination that one hopes will inform all business leaders does not seem to have functioned in the life of Vere, at least not in his role as captain of the ship.

The interpretation I happen to be enthused about is this: *Billy Budd* is actually the story of Claggart, the brightest person on board the ship, who received his degree from a professional school that taught him how to run a ship most efficiently, a school not too unlike a university business school (a very prominent one in the Midwest, of course) which teaches that the goal of business is to maximize profit. Is it any surprise that Claggart, a good utilitarian for his time, supported a system of maximizing pain to obtain performance and compliance from the crew? I try to argue that this is *the* answer. The students object and dissent and are driven to riotous, mutinous talk. One of the problems students have with this interpretation is that it is a stretch, a reach; it is trying to take a situation from two centuries ago and give it a contemporary application. Of course, that is what one does with the literary imagination. Does it fit? There is no doubt my interpretation has the advantage of relevance, but maybe they are right, it is a reach.

One of the problems in the film is that Claggart, as played by Robert Ryan, is such a sick person. He really looks like a manic-depressive. He should be at a clinic. Students say he is sick. If the part had been played by someone else, perhaps the students would see more of Claggart in their own situations, in what we are doing to them and what has been done to them in forming them for the world of business.

The interpretation the students favor is the following: *Billy Budd* is the story of a rotten social system with both Claggart and Billy Budd as victims. Claggart says in the film, "I am what you made me." That is a pretty good defense. Further, it is the story of the bankruptcy of leadership in the person of Captain Vere and the other officers. Then I ask the students to name some of the actions necessary to reform the system and to revitalize leadership. This is the most popular interpretation and has much to be said for it; it also elicits some spirited debate.

The final film is one about which the students are very knowledgeable. They have either read the book or seen the film in junior high or high school. I refer, of course, to Harper Lee's *To Kill a Mockingbird*. I like it because it is a classic, both as a book and a film. There is no debate about it. You might even argue that they improved the film because they eliminated the aunt. I think she fouls up the works somewhat.

It is splendid film. Gregory Peck plays Atticus Finch. The film explores the qualities of character in Atticus Finch and, indirectly, the qualities of a good person. Discussion flows easily from this focus on character. There is a lot of discussion about whether he is a good parent. He listens. He is kind.

He is the best person, best lawyer, he could be. He has a will no one can break. He is also very competent.

We move on to discuss what his strongest quality is, and that, of course, opens much debate. Bearbaiting is a wonderful technique or strategy in university teaching. I like to do a lot of bearbaiting, especially in a Catholic university with its medieval history, because that was the leading sport in medieval times. I like to point out that Finch's chief quality is that he is a truth speaker. Who makes Tom Robinson say the one thing that will surely condemn him for the charge of rape? We also have much discussion about the struggle to find the most important virtue. Atticus Finch says that what the town needs is to start telling the truth. The truth must be spoken. They have been lying to each other about the terrible question of race and racism.

Finally, what I do is to show the last few minutes of the film. Up to now we have met a hero and dissected his character and his qualities, and we thought we had it all figured out. We had the description of this character, why he is so good and why he should be honored and why we should perhaps model our lives on his. But when the sheriff says that Bob Ewell "fell on his knife," Atticus Finch, the truth speaker, says that Jem was defending himself and that there has to be a hearing. Then, all of a sudden, we find out that it was Boo Radley who was shadowing this event and saw what Bob Ewell was going to do. Boo Radley is the quiet, simple, strange person living down the street. Suddenly now, do we have to have a hearing for Boo? The truth speaker, if he is going to be faithful to his beliefs, has to speak the truth. The sheriff—and it is wonderful to explore the qualities of the sheriff because he does not come off very well—says that they can't do that, because they would have to take him to jail and then the women will bring cakes and he won't be able to survive all of this attention because he is a recluse and a loner. Then, we are left with the question: Do we have a flawed hero because Atticus Finch accepts the fabrication? To young people (I am used to fabrications) he should have been consistent. But wait a minute—to be consistent, to be of top value, as Scott says, is to kill another mockingbird.

We go back and forth with these questions and people argue. The point has to be made again and again: How do you see this working out in your career over the next forty or fifty years in business? Thus, the students are led to examine how this wonderful story might shed light on their own lives.

I hope these brief remarks provide evidence that some of us are excited about the prospects of business education today and even more hopeful about the quality of many of our future leaders.

3

THE BROTHERS KARAMAZOV

Responsibility and Business Ethics

— ◉ —

TIMOTHY L. FORT

One might not think of Fyodor Dostoyevsky's masterpiece, *The Brothers Karamazov,* as a resource for business ethics. Even in the significantly less complex film version of the novel, the themes extend far beyond business. For instance, while it is true that one might ask whether particular characters behave morally in their financial affairs, deeper themes portray recurring issues in business ethics: the need of a good that restrains human actions and the responsibility of individuals in exercising their freedom. These themes are perennial, and Dostoyevsky portrays them in general terms of human nature.

I want to demonstrate the applicability of Dostoyevsky to business ethics through what is essentially a teaching note. My hope is that by relating what I do with the film in my classroom, readers can understand the relevance of Dostoyevsky to business ethics and have a model for making *The Brothers Karamazov* accessible to students and others.

Making Dostoyevsky's themes accessible to students requires some preparation.[1] In teaching *Karamazov* (and in reading this chapter) one must be prepared for the fact that although the scenes at first seem to be disassociated with each other, the overall picture finally emerges. This approach makes the film more complex but also more rewarding because it is more realistic. The elements for making good use of *The Brothers Karamazov* are in the timing of the film in the course, a prefatory handout, and discussion after the showing.

THE BROTHERS

Dostoyevksy gives us many complex characters interacting in a quite disjointed way. To avoid beginning this chapter with a distracting summary of this complex film, I will limit myself to brief descriptions of the four "brothers Karamazov." (For a summary of the plot, see Appendix 1.) Dostoyevsky paints the brothers as "extreme types" who gradually become more individually complex and balanced as the film progresses.

Alexey is the youngest of the brothers. A priest, he is very nonjudgmental, seeking to meet his family's needs as best he can. In particular, he tries to mediate between his father, Fyodor, and his brother Dimitri who are at serious odds with one another and who, at least at the beginning of the film, share a debauched lifestyle. Alexey believes his father has embezzled the sons' inheritance from the estate of their deceased mother. At the end, Alexey assists in arranging for Dimitri's escape from prison.

Ivan is the intellectual journalist who philosophizes that there is no God and, therefore, crime is not only lawful but inevitable. He is attracted to Katya, the pretty fiancée of his brother Dimitri. When he learns of his half-brother's (Smerdyakov) plan to arrange for his father's death, at first he refuses to leave his father's side. After Smerdyakov points out the possible inheritance they will all receive, he changes his mind. When he learns of his father's death at the hands of Smerdyakov, Ivan believes that he (Ivan) is really responsible for the crime because Smerdyakov believed Ivan's philosophy that all is lawful since there is no God. When Dimitri is unjustly convicted of the crime, Ivan also assists in arranging for his escape from prison.

Dimitri is full of life. He struggles to be good but continually fails because of his passion. Yet, he always picks himself up and tries again. He falls in love with the same woman his father pursues. The tension between Dimitri and his father is so intense that Dimitri almost kills him and threatens to kill him "next time." It is, therefore, easy to frame him for Smerdyakov's actual killing of the father. At the beginning of his escape, Dimitri insists upon stopping at the house of a man whom he has insulted, thus restoring the man's honor in the eyes of the man's son.

Smerdyakov is an allegedly illegitimate son who serves as his father's butler. Smerdyakov deeply admires Ivan and his philosophy and, therefore, arranges to kill his father and blame Dimitri for the crime because "all is lawful." However, when Ivan fails to endorse Smerdyakov's action and goes to the police, Smerdyakov commits suicide.

PLACEMENT IN THE COURSE

It is dangerous to show the film early in the course. To business students, many of Dostoyevsky's rich and deep themes may be obscure. If students have not thought, for instance, about how organizational incentives can lead to unethical behavior, the portions of the film that tease the viewer with the question of who is responsible for the crime can fly right past them.

I prefer to show the film at the end of the course. The film's themes capture much of the course, and its dilemmas become touchstones for further reflection. Placing a film at the end of a term comes as a welcome relief for exhausted students as well as being a memorable, visual reinforcement of the course's themes. However, the danger in placing it at the end of the course is that it can be tempting for students to skip the class. If the film is shown during the class, students may promise they will just watch it on their own. If students are required to see it on their own, it is tempting for them to avoid a 150-minute film. At the same time, the story is so intricate that showing excerpts significantly detracts from the film's power.

For six years, I showed the film in class during a ten-week course. A fourteen-week course should obviously also be able to accommodate showing the film in class. If one has a seven-week course, the film can be shown at a separate time in lieu of assigned reading. Then the film can be discussed, and a quiz given to assure attendance, during the next class session.

THE PREFATORY HANDOUT

Appendix 2 is a copy of the handout I give to my students in advance of the film, to prepare them to look deeper than the entertainment value of the film. There are four important items to stress.

The Existence of the Good

First, one must address the religious notions in the film. Dostoyevsky was quite clear that, without belief in God, everything is permitted. In Smerdyakov's words, "crime becomes not only lawful, but inevitable." Dostoyevsky's argument can make some students uncomfortable. Recognizing that fact, I caution them that if they find the reference to "God" problematic, they should think in terms of "good." I hardly think this would satisfy Dostoyevsky, who was far more theistic. One can, however, still follow a great deal of his argument that, unless there is a firm belief in the existence of some transcendent good, then crime is permitted. I have yet to see any student express discomfort with the film, given this prefatory caution.

One focus of Dostoyevsky's attack is the "sensualists" or "hedonists" for whom life is a quest for pleasure to satisfy individual wants. Such a philosophy will be on the lips of more than a few ardent free-marketers who argue that the good is the choice of individuals to do whatever they want. If all is free contracting, however, and there is no good other than choice and pleasure, "crime" really does become inevitable. Ivan professes this too, but he, like most students, is appalled at what this justifies. Smerdyakov's murder of the father shows that there must be some good that prevents crime. Thus, at a threshold level, *The Brothers Karamazov* demonstrates that free choice, individual gain, and relativist morality can lead to troubling consequences. Whether students follow Dostoyevsky's belief in the need for "God" or "good," the point still has significant force.

Freedom and Responsibility

The second critical element is that of freedom itself. Unrestrained freedom is, of course, the antipode of what Dostoyevsky has in mind. To understand Dostoyevsky's point fully, one must relay to the students "The Legend of the Grand Inquisitor." That legend stands for the human reality that while human beings demand freedom, they also easily and voluntarily relinquish it in favor of someone telling them what they ought to do. Business students are no exception. While professing the wonders of the "free" market, they are also often willing to do what they are told to do at work.

Further, business people and students often express frustration at the refusal of business ethicists to tell them what is right and wrong. (Of course, they often do not like it if one does suggest what is right and wrong.) Some find ethical theories "hard" and, therefore, "not relevant"; they are the people most tempted to ask what the "right" answer is. They prefer rules or economic efficiency to hard thinking and, like the subjects of the Grand Inquisitor, are quite happy to relinquish their freedom. If business students really want their freedom, there is hard work ahead. Ethics is not simply a list of new commandments but a commitment to wrestle with hard issues.

Separating Responsibility from Consequence

The third related issue is that of separating responsibility from consequence. Smerdyakov kills the father because he believes in Ivan's theory about "no God" and "all is lawful." Ivan knows of Smerdyakov's admiration of him and his thinking. He also knows that Smerdyakov is "arranging" for his father's death, although Ivan thinks Dimitri will be the agent of the death.

In spite of knowing this, Ivan leaves on a trip. The murder occurs while Ivan is gone.

When he returns and discusses the murder with Smerdyakov, Ivan realizes his responsibility; he is implicated, perhaps not legally, but morally. He created Smerdyakov's modus operandi and, knowing where it could lead, deliberately "looked the other way."

This is a perennial question in a corporation. Executives give orders and set expectations. They nurture a culture of behavior. But if an action consistent with that culture results in behavior that creates outrage, then the blame is apportioned to various underlings. LaRue Hosmer has demonstrated this problem in his article on the wreck of the *Exxon Valdez* and subsequent problems in the cleanup of the oil spill, caused by the culture of Exxon—the funding and firing decisions made by the company—and minimalist notions of ethics.[2] In a bureaucracy that separates responsibility from consequence, there are too many layers under which an executive can hide, just as Ivan did.

The Characters

Finally, the fourth level of analysis applies to the particular characters. Dostoyevsky draws the brothers as extreme character types early in his book and seeks to make each of them into an integrated, whole person toward the end. The sterile, intellectual Ivan becomes a passionate, accountable pursuer of the good; the rebellious Dimitri acknowledges his culpability for many blameworthy actions and commits to a life of integrity; and the consistently nonjudgmental Alexey organizes Dimitri's escape in direct violation of an unjust law. Each becomes a more "balanced" character.

The danger of extremism is also seen in other characters, such as the suffering little boy, Ilyusha, whose unturned commitment to honor nearly destroys his father. The "virtuous" Katya eventually turns bitter. The "free" father, Fyodor, meets his just deserts.

One can conduct a complete class simply in terms of the characters. By writing a prefatory note (Appendix 2), I help prevent students from being caught up in the (highly entertaining) drama of the story and thereby missing the subtle philosophical challenges occurring throughout. For the same reasons, it is also worth repeating these challenges in summary form just before the students see the film. Appendix 3 is a handout I give to the students before showing them the film; it provides space for them to write their reactions to the four questions. Having this sheet in front of them further prevents the film from being viewed purely as entertainment.

DISCUSSION OF THE FILM

In the discussion, I allow students to offer any thoughts they might have about the film. This often brings questions to clarify points about the film they did not understand. Beyond that, the first set of comments usually are directed at the characters, in particular the Karamazovs themselves. Students nearly universally dislike the slovenly father because he has connived to obtain others' money and seems to be happily living an extravagant life of gluttony and promiscuity. Encouraging the students to express why they dislike him results in questions regarding limits and freedom from restraints.

The discussion of Alexey's character has surprised me over the years. While many students identify with his peaceful, nonjudgmental, compassionate nature, others find him cowardly. Some have argued that he is a person who really does know right from wrong but yet he does and says nothing to prevent some enormously destructive behavior. The interesting feature of this argument is that often, early in the class, ethics students are very cautious about "imposing values" on others as they resent having values imposed on them. Most students, however, believe Alexey should stand on moral principle to prevent destructive behavior.

The carryover of that response to business is obvious. What should Alexey have done earlier to prevent his father's death? Asking students how they react to Alexey's approval of Dimitri's (clearly illegal) escape is an interesting point because they understand that a virtuous person must balance many goods and that cultivating those judgments on an ongoing basis is necessary to make good decisions at a time of crisis.

Few students admire Ivan; they find him arrogant, aloof, haughty, and irresponsible. Are executives like Ivan? Do they accept responsibility for the culture they foster? This is a suitable time to discuss the responsibilities of leaders in a corporation.

Finally, there is Dimitri. Students usually identify with him because he "has a great thirst for life." Although he regularly falls on his face, he gets up and tries again, demonstrating how hard it can be to do the right thing. When Dimitri's actions are "public relations," as when he is "gallant" toward Katya, they eventually prove empty. But when he tries to be "straight" and "clean," he discovers how difficult it is to live a life of which he can be proud. But he is determined to do so. His character is an excellent example of the kind of determination necessary to be an ethical business person.

Some students ask if we are supposed to feel sorry for him. Some find him hopelessly weak and that forgiving him will only exacerbate his problem. Generally, I direct students not to judge whether he merits forgiveness but whether his determination merits respect.

I usually end the discussion by letting it take on its own dynamic. However, I prefer to end with Dimitri, as his character is a great sendoff, although Alexey and Ivan are also worthwhile. In any case, I make sure that each of the Karamazovs is discussed, along with reinforcing the four points of the prefatory handout.

Determining whether or not the discussion has been good is not very difficult. To the extent one is able to move from characters to their message, one has accomplished a great deal. I use the film because it encourages deep questions of human nature that have enormous implications in business. Human beings tend to think in terms of stories rather than philosophies, and the telling of a rich story tends to provoke questions that are still being asked after the class ends.

Of course, the final test is years down the road. Do students, in fact, remember *The Brothers Karamazov* and, if so, do they find it compelling? Does it "stick" with them? To some extent, the jury is still out on that question. I have talked with students who were in my class six and seven years ago, and one of the most common remarks is how well they remembered this film.

CONCLUSION

The Brothers Karamazov is one of the great stories of human literature. The film can do only partial justice to the novel, but it does ask many hard questions that directly relate to any life, including a life in business. Showing it to a class takes time, and the length of the class may determine whether one is justified in spending the time to show it. If the class is long enough, however, the film ties together many of the themes discussed in a business ethics class and provides a touchstone for student identification with the class and its themes for years to come.

APPENDIX 1

Summary of the Plot of *The Brothers Karamazov*

The plot itself is interesting and needs to be remembered as a backdrop to the philosophical material. One must also know that the film differs in several respects from the novel. Some of the names are different: the novel's Karamazov priest, Alyosha, becomes Alexey Karamazov; the Grand Inquisitor never appears.

The film opens with Alexey asking his debauched father to give him money for Dimitri, Alexey's bother. His father demands that Alexey obtain Dimitri's signature on a promissory note to repay the sum. Alexey takes this money to (the also debauched) Dimitri, who, instead of paying his bills, gives the money to an attractive officer's daughter, Katya, whose father has embezzled money from the military. Without Dimitri's money to replace the missing funds, the embezzlement will be discovered and her family will be disgraced. Although she offers her body to him, Dimitri simply gives her the money (as he later describes it) to be "gallant."

The money changes Katya's life. Shortly after the money replaces the embezzled funds (and thereby hides the embezzlement), her wealthy aunt dies, leaving Katya an heiress. Had the embezzlement come to light, the aunt would have disinherited her disgraced relatives. In gratitude, Katya accepts Dimitri's previous, insincere proposal of marriage and sets out to win his love, but they are never married.

Instead, Dimitri becomes enchanted with the innkeeper, Grushenka, who has also attracted the attention of Dimitri's father, Fyodor. To get his money back from Dimitri, Fyodor convinces Grushenka to buy Dimitri's notes at half their value. Their plan is that Dimitri, without money to repay the debts now owed to a nonfamily member, will marry Katya, who will provide the money to repay the notes.

Grushenka sends a retired officer, Captain Snegiryov, to buy Dimitri's notes. Eventually, Dimitri confronts Snegiryov and publicly humiliates him in front of his son. The captain refuses Dimitri's challenge to a duel because of his responsibility to his family that, apparently, has no other means of financial support. This humiliation is too much for Captain Snegiryov's son, Ilyusha, who becomes very sick as well as deeply depressed by the shame of the loss of family honor. Because of the depth of that shame, Captain Snegiryov refuses Dimitri's later offer of money to obtain the family's forgiveness. Honor prevents the acceptance of money that would buy medicine for Ilyusha and for the family to live out its dreams.

Dimitri's fascination with Grushenka also emboldens his father. Fyodor invites Grushenka to visit him in return for a "gift." The mutual antagonism between Dimitri and Fyodor becomes acute; Dimitri physically attacks his father and threatens to murder him. Dimitri is convinced that Grushenka will go to his father for a conjugal visit and goes to intercept them. Tapping

Grushenka's prearranged signal on his father's window, Dimitri finds his father expecting her. Dimitri runs away rather than kill his father, but injures a servant on the way out of the premises.

The allegedly illegitimate brother, Smerdyakov, who serves as Fyodor's butler, uses Dimitri's visit as the opportunity to kill Fyodor. This is a plot that had been hatched by Smerdyakov out of loyalty to Ivan, the intellectual third Karamazov brother. Smerdyakov believes Ivan when he writes that there is no God and, therefore, no impediment to crime. Knowing that Ivan and Smerdyakov would benefit from Fyodor's death, Smerdyakov intimates to Ivan that he would feign an epileptic seizure when Dimitri comes to kill Fyodor. If Ivan were absent from the house, no one would be present to stop Dimitri. Ivan leaves for Moscow, starting the chain of events that leads to Fyodor's death. Smerdyakov does fake a seizure, but when Dimitri does not kill Fyodor, Smerdyakov frames Dimitri by killing Fyodor himself, in devotion to Ivan and his philosophy.

Dimitri is arrested for (and subsequently tried and convicted of) his father's murder. After the arrest, Ivan returns from his trip to Moscow and, upon learning that Dimitri is innocent, confronts Smerdyakov with their mutual culpability. Feeling betrayed by Ivan's newfound belief that there is something called crime, Smerdyakov hangs himself. Ivan attempts, with no success, to take the blame for having inspired Smerdyakov to murder Fyodor. A major reason for Ivan's failure is Katya's bitter condemnation of Dimitri. She produces a note Dimitri sent to her in which he rejects her and indicates that he will kill Fyodor.

At the trial, the prosecutor asks Ivan if there were witnesses to the crime and whether anyone could corroborate the fact that Smerdyakov was the agent who killed Fyodor. After thinking for a moment, Ivan responds that the witness is inside each one of us—the devil. If there is evil, says Ivan, then there must also be good, and if there is good, then all is not lawful.

After Dimitri's sentencing, Ivan and Alexey arrange for his escape by bribing his prison guards. Grushenka, whose love Dimitri has won, will accompany him. Before crossing the border, however, Dimitri insists on visiting Ilyusha, Captain Snegiryov's little boy who is ill. After another unsuccessful attempt to buy the boy's forgiveness with toys and medals, Dimitri asks the forgiveness of Snegiryov. In front of Ilyusha, Dimitri says that when he proposed the duel, he knew Snegiryov was an expert marksman who declined to duel because of his own self-restraint and mercy toward Dimitri. Thrilled, Ilyusha instructs his father to forgive Dimitri and spare his life. Freed of his burden, Dimitri escapes.

APPENDIX 2

Notes on *The Brothers Karamazov*

Many critics have claimed that Dostoyevsky's novel *The Brothers Kara-mazov* is the greatest novel ever written. If you have time, I highly recommend it. You will need a lot of time, though, since, depending upon the edition, it can run up to one thousand pages. Obviously, even a two-and-one-half-hour film cannot do justice to such a piece of literature, but the film itself is a good one. It is, at heart, a commentary on human nature and the integration of aspects of human nature into individual persons. You will not necessarily see a great deal of "business ethics," but you will see perennial moral issues described in the film that are also manifested in business.

A word about religion. Dostoyevsky uses Christianity as his moral foil and it certainly was his intent that it be viewed in those terms, but there is not much that is exclusively "Christian" about the film. If one considers God at all, or if one simply considers the idea of good when the film refers to God, one can see the same points being made. The central use of the concept of "God" or "good" (although Dostoyevsky would have been very uneasy about a secularized "good") is whether one can prevent anything if there is no concept of "God" or "good." However, one aspect of religion, unfortunately, is not in the film. It is the most famous part of the novel, the story of the Grand Inquisitor. Because it serves as a useful backdrop to the film, I will briefly recount the story.

One of the novel's characters, Ivan, is reviewing an essay he had written many years previously. In that essay, situated at the time of the Spanish Inquisition, Christ returns to earth. The people joyously welcome him, except for the Grand Inquisitor, who is the local priest. He is not so happy. His concern is that to practice the kind of freedom and individual ability to make moral choices—represented in the story by Christ—people will be confused. Therefore, they need to rely on someone who can tell them what is right and wrong. The Inquisitor orders Christ's imprisonment and exile to prevent this exercise of freedom among the people, not because the Inquisitor wants to control them, but because he genuinely cares for them. He simply believes they are incapable of actually exercising moral freedom and choice. Oddly enough, the people are overjoyed at this new incarceration, too, because—and this becomes a central point—people claim to want to have the freedom to make moral choices but, in the end, are very willing to relinquish that freedom in favor of the commands of someone else.

That story is directly applicable to much (although not all) of business and ethics. Often business people look at business ethicists as those who are supposed to come up with specific answers to questions. While professing a love of freedom, they really do not wish to struggle with the responsibilities of freedom to make moral choices. Thus, when an ethicist provides a schema to analyze a business problem without providing an answer, the ethicist is criticized for being too fuzzy and inexact. But then the question is: Do we really wish to have the responsibility entailed by freedom?

The Grand Inquisitor's insight is even more dramatically evidenced in business. In lieu of the freedom to decide how actions affect a community, a default decision-making process relies on economic efficiency. In this way, for business people, moral choice often gets thrown out the window and the safety of efficiency becomes the commandment to obey.

At this point in the class, you should have guessed that I see a vital role in economic efficiency: Business's existential justification is its ability to use resources efficiently to meet social and consumer needs. The point, however, is to recognize that business people risk their freedom in cloaking themselves with the commands of economizing just as the people did under the rule of the Grand Inquisitor.

This dilemma surrounding moral freedom leads to many other dilemmas in the film. It is set in nineteenth-century Russia and we are immediately confronted with the predominant group that Dostoyevsky calls "the hedonists" which include the father (Fyodor) and the son (Dimitri). It also describes the primary female protagonist, Grushenka. For these folks, happiness is about pleasure and self-interest narrowly conceived. They are like the Gordon Gekkos of the world, to whom the pursuit of pleasure and utility are the only things to be valued. For them, greed is surely good; it is the only thing that makes sense. Dimitri has some misgivings about this, but only some. At times, he wants to be "gallant," but he soon recognizes that his "gallant" actions are a sham so he could appear to be morally superior. There is no depth to his actions; they are simply public relations.

He finds also that after one's pleasures have been satisfied, it becomes difficult to pay for them. Money then becomes something needed "to be free." If Dimitri could only "settle some debts" he could be free. But, at least at the beginning of the film, that is not enough to enable Dimitri to restrain his instinctual desires. Dimitri's need for money to pay for his hedonism runs directly into his father's own hedonism and greed, and even that of Grushenka.

Dimitri's dilemma, of course, is replicated throughout society. It is the basis of overused credit cards and of well-paid business people being unable to be comfortable with the considerable incomes they make. (It also applies outside of business.) The question of the hedonist is, What is enough? For such people, there is never enough because the pleasures always outstrip the ability to pay for them. The result is a voracious, never-ending and never-fulfilled attempt to meet an insatiable appetite.

The hedonist position is not the only extreme position portrayed in the film. If it were, we could simply content ourselves with *Wall Street*. Dostoyevsky is also worried about the opposite of hedonism. Throughout the film, Dostoyevsky presents "pure" people like Alexey, the brother/priest, the young boy, Ilyusha, and Katya. They are so pure, one wonders if they really are good, not to mention real. Alexey is so concerned about everyone getting along without being judgmental that he lets an enormous amount of self-destructive behavior continue. He never takes a stand on anything. Ilyusha is so bound by notions of virtue and honor that he nearly destroys his father. Katya's eternal devotion eventually becomes mean. These figures are "greedy" too and, in the extreme, their greed can be as devastating as that of the hedonist. They can be compared to those who call for a very "pure" (noncompetitive, no layoffs, environmentally clean) form of business that might not be business at all. Just how realistic are they? Do they have any gumption?

What really happens in the film is the maturation of the characters so they become more balanced; they move from being archetypes to being human. (Dostoyevsky was also using characters to portray social ideas related to Russia herself but, for our purposes, we can look at the film in terms of the development of the individual characters.) Theirs is a central lesson for business ethics, one most aptly articulated in our readings by Greenleaf, Solomon, Hosmer, and Chappell: Greenleaf's notion of integration, Solomon's Aristotelian notion of virtuous balance, and Chappell's use of the Buddhist's middle way. No one virtue, whether greed, honor, or hedonistic pleasure, ought to be practiced or pursued in isolation from other, complex realities of life. The pursuit of one singular virtue or role can be very destructive.

Then there are the critical characters who wrestle with the central philosophical dilemma: Ivan and his allegedly half-brother Smerdyakov. Smerdyakov quotes Ivan: "There is no God. Without God, nothing is unlawful, even crime. Crime is not only unlawful, it is inevitable."

This quote returns us to the first assignment. Whether one uses the notion of "God" or "good," if there is no vision of it is it not true that any other thing, even crime, becomes not only lawful, but inevitable? If there is no good, is any business activity unethical? This is where the notion of economics being "value-free" and "business being business" runs into trouble because, without a notion of the good, nothing is really outlawed. Business affairs inevitably become what one can get away with. It is also why many contemporary theories of business ethics fail: they never address the nature of the good, largely in fear that it will take on too many religious overtones. But the issue is unavoidable and it need not involve any particular institutional approach; instead, it may reflect the inherently relational nature of life.

Ivan must struggle with this question of whether the absence of a God or a good inevitably and justifiably leads to crime. Does he really believe it? Smerdyakov does. If Ivan no longer agrees with it, upon what basis can he disagree? You might be surprised with his answer and you need not accept it: What your good or God *is* defines how you will conduct your business affairs. Without your embrace of a set of "affectionate" relationships that inspire a person even within the confines of business, the only restraints against negative business behavior are those actions that get one into trouble.

The notion that one can get in trouble underscores the ultimate relationality of human beings. Relationality undermines relativity, because people react to the actions others take. So on one level, being ethical—that is, concerning oneself with the satisfactory character of relationships with others—is important. Many of the theories we have studied describe why others may react negatively to the affairs of business and ultimately constrain the behavior of business.

But at the deeper level, the level beyond "getting caught," is where a person would consider internalizing moral principles. That is the level where Ivan struggles, trying to balance internalized notions of the good with the realities of life: There is a good that must be part of our lives if they are to be in balance, but there are other realities of life that, if we ignore them, can make our virtue destructive.

So Dostoyevsky offers us no clear moral rules but, instead, leaves us with a schema, a call for balancing multiple concerns. Life consists of struggling with a package of concerns; it is not the pursuit of a single objective. Therefore, Dostoyevsky calls upon those who ask for freedom to accept the responsibility for considering what that freedom means.

APPENDIX 3

Topics to Consider While Watching *The Brothers Karamazov*

1. The notion of good and what is lawful: Without a notion of the good, is everything lawful?
2. The notion of freedom: How does one decide what is the right thing to do? Is obedience enough? How do the characters balance competing goods and competing choices?

3. The relationship of responsibility and consequences: Who is responsible for the crime? Why?
4. What do you think of the following characters?
   a) Alexey
   b) Ivan
   c) Fyodor
   d) Ilyusha
   e) Katya
   f) Dimitri

NOTES

My thanks to Nancy Nerad, LeRue Tone Hosmer, and Tanya Kopps for their critical assessments of this paper.

1. I have had four students over the past five years who had taken courses on Dostoyevsky in college. Those students, to whom I owe a great deal, forced me to look much more deeply into *The Brothers Karamazov* than I had previously done.

2. LaRue Tone Hosmer, *Ethical Issues in Business*, 3d edition, (Burr Ridge, Ill.: Irwin Publishing, 1995), 136–57.

4

MALICE IN WONDERLAND

American Working-Girl Scenarios

— ☉ —

EILEEN T. BENDER

A woman should be good for everything at home, but abroad, good for nothing.

> Euripides, *Meleager* (circa 400 B.C.)

You may tempt the upper classes
With your villainous demi-tasses,
But heaven will protect the working girl.

> Sung by Marie Dressler (*Tillie's Nightmare*, 1930)

Early this summer, a news group colleague posted a provocative query on the Internet. She asked fellow subscribers to recommend American literary texts which "talk about the intersection between manhood and work." The posting engendered a stream of suggestions, ranging from Ben Franklin to Jay Gatsby; from Alger's "Ragged Dick" to Dreiser's "Financier"; from Whitman's roustabouts to Frost's hired men; from men who survived the hazards of Sinclair's slaughterhouse to those who suffered the indignities of Updike's car dealership; doctors from Rappacini to Arrowsmith; organization men like Madison Avenue's *Man in the Gray Flannel Suit*; loners like that itinerant photographer in Madison County.

Indeed, in American literature the workplace has been viewed, whether negatively or positively, as a proving ground for American manhood; the forge of identity and character. The ability to define oneself gracefully under its pressures has been a perennial index to masculine worth. But what works for the American Adam does not always sustain the American Eve. Not surprisingly, Listserv "lurkers" neither sought nor volunteered suggestions for texts dramatizing an intersection of work—the struggle for a viable identity in the arena of the marketplace—and the development of *womanhood*. Defining women's character through their work rather than through their personal lives seems somehow at odds with prevailing cultural and artistic norms.

Similarly, in "Business and American Literature," a course I taught at the University of Notre Dame in the early 1980s as part of a national interdisciplinary project, "Creating Connections" (with welcome counsel from John Houck), the texts we used characterized the U.S. workplace as a "wonderland" *minus* Alice—a male-dominated, often vertiginous "eat or be eaten" realm, where problematic mentors advised the aspiring entrant to jump aggressively over pawns, to capture his competitors' space, to move toward the executive row.

The contemporary literature we discussed reflected a dystopic looking-glass vision of the American dream, a critical and often cynical variation on the "strive and succeed" theme of Horatio Alger. At the same time, these works continued to reify, even if by ironic contrast, an ethic of manly work, rooted in native ground. But while it was no secret that in contemporary American society women were pursuing careers in ever increasing numbers, we encountered no text which suggested that *woman's* true worth might be measured and validated by her success in the workplace. In U.S. society as well as in U.S. literature, a rhetorical gulf yawns between the historically masculine narrative of private enterprise—the "business plot"—and the narrative of woman's private life—the "marriage plot."

Persistent cultural attitudes about the relationship of work and gender, constructed and reconstructed by society over time, are registered in this absence. In the collective imagination, whatever their actual roles, women are assigned to the domestic sphere (since Euripides!), a private, circumscribed, demilitarized zone sharply distinguished from the combative "wonderland" of commerce. "Home" as a safe haven and "sisterhood" as woman's essential source of power are cherished myths—in the double sense that they are widely held and frequently false. Enshrinement in the domestic sphere for the woman seeking self-expression may be equivalent to house arrest. Under the mask of sisterly benevolence and care may lie the perverse grimace of the sibling rival.

This fundamental division of gender roles in the workplace also enforces an axiological discordance. The virtues and values traditionally associated with the feminine—empathy, capacity for nurturance, spirituality, and self-sacrifice—are set *against* and undercut by the self-promoting, assertive, and competitive values associated with success in business. As women's experience seeks to write itself into the American narrative of success, it is constrained by the very structures it would reformulate. In consequence, woman's story has been repressed and marginalized in the quintessentially American narrative of business. This oppositional script has not written itself but has been and is being socially constructed, part of an ongoing dialectic, open to revision. It remains for us to determine whether—or how—we should follow it.

I suggest it is not only possible but important to describe the *woman's* story which threads its subterranean way through the American myth of success. Indeed, when we interrogate that myth, reproduced both in fiction and film, we find it reflects not one but two plots, which employ the same language and inhabit the same narrative, but lead to very different outcomes for male and female characters. This, in turn, challenges the tacit assumption of an ineluctable U.S. business script which reads women's story *out*. Instead, I suggest that women's search for character and identity is repeatedly frustrated by America's historically masculine strive-and-succeed Alger-ian mythology. The resulting tangle of values and confusion of goals are reflected in a dialogic tension visible in literature and film.

Attempting to steer clear of reductive essentialist arguments, I will re-enter the workplace "wonderland" with several literary and cinematic texts as guides, to trace *"Alice's"* itinerary. In the process, I hope to uncover and describe the ambivalent ethic of work which often misdirects woman's passage; an ethic also at odds with the American ideal of principled enterprise.

AMERICAN LITERATURE: MANLY WOMEN AND MIRTHLESS MAIDS

Let us review the images of working women in American literary "success" narratives. From the first, they are shaped by an unspoken but powerful assumption that women, removed from domesticity and its presumed sexual and moral constraints, become wantons, unfit for marriage. Once she crosses the boundaries of the workplace, in the words of the Marie Dressler ballad, only heaven can protect the working girl. In this view, man is bravely bound to go to work just as he, if called, would go to war, and thus is defined by his public endeavors. But woman's public value is set by others: her ability to sustain the twin cornerstones of U.S. society, home and family.

Interestingly, these implicit and influential cultural values have literary consequences. First, the narrative of "success" follows the trajectory of self-actualization. Self-sacrifice, that essential "feminine" virtue, leads instead to

narrative erasure. Second, "woman's work" receives no material compensation, has no remarkable consequence, and thus has little or no dramatic value. Because it is essentially communal, there can be no pride of authorship. Work done for the welfare of others provides spiritual satisfaction—as in the saying, "virtue is its own reward," an axiom rarely equated with business success.

Third, woman's work, in the words of the old adage, "is never *done*." It follows a predictable and inexorable repetitive rhythm, always already in process, whose ending is simultaneously a beginning rather than culminating in a triumph or reaching a climax. Trapped in the relentless coils of domesticity, working women are often depicted as victims or accomplices rather than independent moral agents. Even when literature provides us with images of women at work, it is to demonstrate, both overtly and subliminally, that women themselves have little choice in the matter. The individualistic and self-motivated struggle to achieve a "brilliant career" has only recently become part of woman's plot (largely in popular culture and contemporary "women's films"). In "classic" American literature the workplace has been seen consistently as a dynastic realm in which the fittest of individual men find empowerment and women as a "species" are fatally imperiled.

Melville's "The Paradise of Bachelors and The Tartarus of Maids" (1855) provides a stunning picture of this male/female tension. Following a scornful account of a privileged male-only "temple" of British gentlemen, the narrative scene shifts from old to New England. Seeking homespun and "democratic" writing materials, the narrator travels to a Massachusetts paper mill, only to find himself in a twisting, nightmarish, wonderland descent, leading through a "Dantean gateway" to the "great whited sepulcher" of the "Devil's Dungeon" paper factory. Clearly, he has also passed through a metaphorical looking glass into the bachelors' antiworld, where rows of female "maids," old before their time, "pale with work and blue with cold," serve the implacable paper machine, their faces as "blank" as the foolscap fed through their stiff fingers. It is the very obverse of domesticity as well. The terms of women's employment require them to be single and childless. Their work, though like traditional woman's work repetitive and endless, nurtures no family nor brings even spiritual satisfaction; their very lives are at risk from the harsh climate and relentless assignments.

Strangely moved by these women and appalled by their dire working conditions, Melville's narrator, with an oddly chivalrous gesture, doffs his hat in "homage to their pale virginity" and beats a hasty retreat. Ironically, Melville has himself exploited the maids by turning their mute suffering into moral allegory, perhaps inadvertently underscoring the inevitability of their fate (*The Heath Anthology*, 2480–97). For female characters in nineteenth-century American fiction, work apart from what Carol Gilligan, in *In a Different Voice*, calls the "ethic of care," provides neither self-actualization nor economic advancement. It can even be seen as a life sentence, as in the penitential piecework of Hester Prynne's *The Scarlet Letter*.

In contrast, Melville's contemporary, Margaret Fuller, called upon women to redefine themselves through work, asking them to leave their trivializing and irrelevant assignments to play more significant public roles. In *Summer on the Lakes* (1844) she rages at her sisters who dutifully practiced the piano and dancing but "have not learned to ride, to drive, to row, alone," and urges their daughters to develop "bodily strength." In *Woman in the Nineteenth Century"* (1844) she goes further, holding up for highest praise a new model, the "manly woman" (*The Heath Anthology*, 1620–55).

For this "immoral" suggestion Fuller was savagely excoriated, and she lived up to public expectations when she entered an "illicit" liaison and bore a child out of wedlock. After her death, her Transcendentalist friends sought to rehabilitate her reputation by assigning her a marital surname, Fuller Ossoli, in her posthumous "memoirs." In Hawthorne's *Blithedale Romance* (1850) Fuller is regarded more ambiguously in his portrait of Zenobia, a vibrant woman and passionate feminist. Despite her vaunted public role, Zenobia is condemned by Hawthorne to follow the conventional woman's plot. Unlike her real-life model, who drowned in a shipwreck within sight of the American shore on her way home from Europe, Zenobia drowns herself because of unrequited love.

As it might well be today, the concept of the manly woman was considered a threat to the social fabric in nineteenth-century America, as reflected in male rhetoric and public invective. It was also associated with *working* women. Thus, journalist Robert Bonner could argue in the *New York Ledger* in 1859 that a woman "transplanted" from the home to the marketplace becomes "a monster, a *man-woman*," who "advocates the 'largest liberty' in the indulgence of her passions."

The misrepresentation of working women, still embedded in a fable or fantasy of domesticity, is even more visible in realistic fiction of the early twentieth century, influenced by the influx of women into the workplace. We can perhaps best see the resulting dialogic tension between the success and marriage plots in the heroine's poignant scenario as seen by Theodore Dreiser and Edith Wharton.

The journey from rural America to the bustling urban marketplace—the *Bildungsroman* itinerary—is the route to degradation for the young woman from the country. Tellingly, Dreiser's *Sister Carrie* (1900) loses her virginity to

Drouet, a brash traveling salesman she meets on the train to Chicago. Unable to survive on a working girl's low wages, she moves in with him and then is easy prey for the more sophisticated philanderer Hurstwood, who runs off with Carrie on a supposed wedding trip. All is not lost. Through Hurstwood's influence and Carrie's very modest talent, surprisingly she achieves fame and fortune as an actress—a profession in which saintly virtue would be an encumbrance. Carrie thus is no longer the victim of exploitative sexual relationships and is saved from the life of drudgery and hardship that is her respectable sister's lot. Dreiser also contrasts her success with Hurstwood's failure. At the end of the novel he has lost everything and we see him literally in the gutter, below Carrie's window. Yet, despite her material success, Carrie's story does not have the happy ending of the rags to riches plot, as Dreiser's final passage confirms:

> Oh, Carrie, Carrie! Oh, blind strivings of the human heart! . . . Know, then, that for you is neither surfeit nor content. In your rocking chair, by your window dreaming, shall you long, alone. In your rocking chair, by your window, shall you dream such happiness as you shall never feel. (*Carrie*, 465)

Limited, able to sense but not possess the vision of the artist, and surely not destined for marriage, Carrie experiences the career woman's double bind. Locked into a lonely, repetitive, aimless rhythm, she neither savors nor senses her triumph over adversity. Rather, she is suffused by a sense of futility and ineffable longing.

For Lily Bart, trapped in the social machinations of Old New York in Wharton's *The House of Mirth* (1905), a woman may seek economic security through a good marriage but not economic independence. Possessing the manners of the upper classes but not their means, resisting loveless engagement, Lily can survive only as a social parasite, in effect giving away her only commodity, herself. Without crumbs from her friends' tables, Lily has no life support. Literally on the street, she seeks a milliner's job but finds only humiliation in the marketplace, an arena in which her greatest assets, grace and charm, have no commercial value. Ironically, Lily dies with a vision of lower-class domesticity—the memory of her brief visit with a woman who has survived an exploitative workplace seduction and, though still poor, has found a workingman to serve as loving husband and father of her baby.

Thus, American writers from Melville's time to our own have dramatized the struggles of the individual caught up in the relentless machinery of the modern workplace. But while men survive and frequently succeed, it is *woman* who is perpetually frustrated, her narrative of self-fashioning arrested or co-opted by an unrealistic cultural mythology. Even when women do reach a position successful in masculine terms, they are considered failures, under the terms of woman's implicit subterranean domestic plot.

SISTER ACT AT THE MOVIES:
ALL ABOUT THE WORKING GIRL

To invite further reflection on these value conflicts, we turn to film—both the mirror and the maker of mass culture. Film is also a particularly appropriate medium for the exposure of these intersecting and often competitive cultural narratives. Indeed, the movies not only document who we think we are—and were—but also reflect the inconsistencies in our self-image. In turn, they help us negotiate shifts in our collective identity over time, registering the impact of social and ideological change.

As we shall see in each film as well as through their intertextual resonance, *All About Eve* (Joseph Mankiewicz, 1950) and *Working Girl* (Mike Nichols, 1988)[1] dramatize the tension in woman's success story between a traditionally masculine ethic of dominance, competition, and self-promotion, and an ethic of sisterhood, care, and self-abnegation. The success plot, radically at variance with woman's counterplot, creates a crisis of character and identity for the "working girl." Played out in both the public arena and on the private stage of women's experience, this results in a curiously duplicitous discourse. These two Hollywood presentations of the working-girl scenario, filmed almost four decades apart, also dramatize the beginnings of a new discourse: the potential transformation from one kind of America to another.

How have American motion pictures represented the U.S. workplace? Indeed, they tell us a story we want to hear: that the individual man *can* make a difference, even within industrialized society. The hero can resist corporate forces and defeat them. Even the corrupt world of insider trading can be redeemed by the efforts of one man who prizes his integrity more than profit, as in Oliver Stone's *Wall Street* (1987).

Yet there has also been a change over time in the qualities we associate with business success. As John Belton suggests in *Movies and Mass Culture*, once they were epitomized in the character of George Bailey (played by Jimmy Stewart) in Frank Capra's *It's a Wonderful Life* (1946): industry, honesty, common sense, good-neighborliness, and devotion to home and family. But as Belton also points out, "these innocent and homespun virtues associated with Capra's rustic heroes have tended to give way in American films of our own era to more worldly and cynical scenarios. . . . character types from the past persist today but in surprising and parodic ways: take, for instance *Forrest Gump*" (Belton, 12–14).

Other revisions are visible Hollywood representations of the American scene. Today, as women assume traditionally masculine prerogatives in the business world, once-stable indices of male identity begin to seem arbitrary and unstable, as in the recent film *Disclosure*, in which a male executive (Michael Douglas) is subjected to sexual harassment by a predatory female executive (Demi Moore).

If the male business hero is undergoing a curious metamorphosis, what have American films shown us about *women* in the workplace? Carolyn Galerstein, in her filmography, *Working Women on the Hollywood Screen*, points out that working women are familiar character types in the movies. Of the nearly 12,000 American feature films made between 1930 and 1975—from the silents to the advent of feminism—she finds that in about 4,500 the leading female role is that of a working woman, usually fitting the prevailing stereotypes of nurses, teachers, boarding-house owners, and secretaries.

What constitutes success for movie career women? We find duplicitous scenarios once again, as suggested both by Galerstein and Ann Kaplan (*Women and Film*). In the 1930s, for example, a favorite genre involved the rise and fall of the female journalist. In a telling reversal of Alger's "strive and succeed" formula, the newswoman is cast in a "succeed and retreat" scenario. The workplace—in these films, the newsroom—proves to be a coercive moral environment, masculinizing the high-achieving woman and threatening to foreclose her "ideal" narrative, the marriage plot, if she remains there too long and "succeeds" too well.

Thus, in *Front Page Woman* (Curtiz, 1936), a reporter, played by Bette Davis, proves to her male colleagues what a "good newspaperman" she really is, only to give up her profession (eagerly) in favor of marriage. In another Capra film, *Mr. Deeds Goes to Town* (1936), an unethical and opportunistic reporter (Jean Arthur) turns into a simpering ingenue and is literally carried out of the public arena in the arms of the man she has been exploiting for front-page copy. In her idyllic country cottage, she presumably will not be bothered again by such ethical temptations. An even more exaggerated version of this script features Barbara Stanwyck In *Meet John Doe* (Capra, 1941). She almost drives her front-page subject to suicide—before allowing *him* to rescue *her* from the evils of work. While seeming to glamorize the pursuit of a career, these movies caution working women to reconsider their ambition to succeed in business rather than in marriage.

Such messages became more bewildering with the start of World War II, when women both in society and in the movies moved out of the home and into the workplace. Despite their vital role in the war effort, women were expected to retain their femininity. Thus, in the often-cited *Rosie the Riveter* (Santlee, 1944), the indefatigable but improbable Rosie not only learns how to rivet (with some difficulty), but puts on musical shows at the war plant! As Mary Anne Doane points out in "The Economy of Desire":

> "Rosie" was conceived from the beginning as a temporary phenomenon, active only for the duration. . . . throughout the war years, the female spectator-consumer was sold a certain image of femininity that functioned to sustain the belief that women and work, outside the home, were fundamentally incompatible. (Doane, 127)

But even Rosie's modest career options were soon to be sharply curtailed. After the war, Hollywood directors and producers dramatized the threat that working women posed to "family values." This fear surfaces in the form of movie femmes fatales, destructive career women like Bette Davis (*The Little Foxes*) and Joan Crawford (*Mildred Pierce*)—ruthless, domineering, and repellent (particularly to male spectators). Thus, a seemingly irreconcilable conflict between marriage and employment sends the celluloid female worker, like many a real-life sister, into early retirement.

Cinema may thus have sustained, more than it challenged, the ideology of the dominant culture. It has also perpetuated a vision of a workforce that never was, as Galerstein suggests. The working woman is increasingly outnumbered by her domestic celluloid sisters, belying workplace statistics. Interestingly, in one film category, the working woman is represented far out of proportion to any estimate of her presence in the actual workplace: the prostitute. Galerstein also finds that an inordinately high percentage (about 30 percent) of working women in films of the 1930s, 1940s, and 1950s are entertainers—actresses, singers, dancers, chorus girls—again falsifying reality (Galerstein, xiii).

Why? Obviously, movies are an ideal vehicle to showcase artistic performance. But more importantly, as we have seen in *Sister Carrie*, show-business heroines epitomize the American success scenario, rephrased in a feminine idiom. Something very significant is lost in the translation of the Alger myth into "the-star-is-born" narrative—woman's agency. The show-business heroine rarely attains stardom by virtue of her own talent and industry. More often, she is the beautiful object of a lascivious, masculine gaze; the aspiring ingenue is lifted out of a journey to nowhere by a male talent scout or director who fashions her into a movie queen.

All About Eve (Mankiewicz, 1950) may seem a new and even emancipated version of this star-is-born narrative, since it involves an actress working her way up through her own efforts. But we soon realize that in woman's scenario, such industry is typically subversive, underhanded, and unethical. The film opens on the occasion of the presentation of Broadway's most coveted drama award to a brilliant young actress, Eve Harrington (played by Anne Baxter). This would seem to qualify as "success" in the American business plot. But the camera, panning around the less-than-delighted expressions of the onlookers, suggests that another plot is also waiting to be disclosed.

This "inside" story about Eve is told by several of those present at the award dinner, a multi-refracted technique reminiscent of *Rashomon* (which, interestingly, was released in the same year). Each character has played a different role in and has a different "take" on Eve's history: a success story—Eve's rise to stardom—but undermined by woman's plot—her fall from grace. If we expect an entertaining, show-business spectacle, we will be disappointed. Instead, as voyeurs, we peer behind the scenes. There, the aspiring actress, Eve, stands in the wings, watching the curtain call of a star seemingly at the peak of her career, Margo Channing (played by Bette Davis). From the beginning, the envious and ambitious Eve displays her most extraordinary acting skills *off-stage* through multiple acts of deception. The first comes after that curtain call. Eve offers to return the star's costume to wardrobe. Margo surprises Eve in her first masquerade, as described in the screenplay:

EVE: *Near the wings. She stands before a couple of cheval mirrors setup for cast members. She has Margo's dress held up against her body. She turns this way and that, bows as if to applause—mimicking Margo exactly.* (*Eve*, 65)

At this stage, Margo misreads Eve's impersonation as adulation.

It is important to note that Eve is meant to represent not only a particular type of working woman, the actress, but any working woman seeking top billing and willing to defy any ethical or social proscription in the process. Joseph Mankiewicz, the director and screen writer, in *More About All About Eve* (1972), shows how little sympathy he has for such professional ambitions: "Eve is essentially—in the theater, *Harper's Bazaar*, *Vogue*, IBM, whatever—the girl unceasingly, relentlessly, on the make." Thus, he uses the already problematic star-is-born formula to subvert it still further. Progressively superimposed upon the rags-to-riches plot is an insidious narrative which rewrites the "happy ending" of the success-story script.

How does Eve, a young woman with dubious credentials, displace a famous and successful actress? First, Margo has just turned forty, a chilling milestone for a woman in a youth-oriented 1950s culture. Flattered by Eve's seemingly worshipful adulation, Margo takes the young woman in and is taken in herself—at first. Once "adopted," Eve insinuates herself into Margo's life, arranging her finances, keeping her calendar, and even planning a surprise birthday party for Bill, Margo's director and lover. This proves a most unpleasant surprise to Margo, who realizes that her street-wise housekeeper, Birdie (Thelma Ritter), is right: Eve has set her sights on everything Margo possesses: Bill and her place in the American theater.

Too late, Margo attempts to fight back, cajoling her producer to hire the young woman as a secretary. In a devious double cross, however, Eve is hired as Margo's understudy instead. Next, taking advantage of Margo's inevitable and unbecoming rage, Eve wins the cooperation of Margo's best friend, Karen, who thinks she is teaching Margo a needed lesson. In an act of sabotage, Karen ensures that the car taking Margo back to the New York theater after a weekend in the country will run out of gas. Interestingly, this scene of sisterly perfidy becomes the occasion for poignant lament. Margo confides to Karen her own misery, not because of Eve's treachery or because she will miss a performance for the first time in her acting career, but because of her status as an accomplished professional woman:

> Funny business, a woman's career. The things you drop on your way up the ladder so you can move faster. You forget you'll need them again when you go back to being a woman. That's one career all females have in common—whether we like it or not—being a woman. Sooner or later we've got to work at it, no matter what other careers we've had or wanted . . . in the last analysis, nothing is any good unless you can look up just before dinner—or turn around in bed—and there he is. Without that, you're not a woman. You're something with a French provincial office or a book full of clippings—but you're not a woman. (*Eve*, 157)

As Margo begins to retreat, Eve's career begins to advance. She arranges that the suave and villainous *Times* critic, DeWitt (played by George Sanders) will be present at her unscheduled "debut," in an audience which also includes other appreciative New York drama critics. Eve is picture-perfect in her role. The star, it would seem, is born. But as she reaches for stardom, the "woman's plot" begins to surface, trapping her in its inexorable patterns.

In the process, Eve's stage accomplishments are minimized. Significantly, we never see her actual performance; the focus is again backstage. A vibrant, triumphant Eve is occupying Margo's dressing room, attractive in Margo's wig and costume. Bill drops by with congratulations. Flushed with victory, she turns to him seductively, only to face a major defeat, not as an actress but as a woman. Bill pledges his fidelity to Margo and scornfully rejects Eve's sexual invitation:

BILL: I'm in love with Margo. Hadn't you heard?
EVE: You hear all kinds of things . . .
BILL: I'm only human, rumors to the contrary. And I'm as curious as the next man . . .
EVE: Find out.
BILL: (*Deliberately*). Only thing, what I go after, I want to go after. I don't want it to come after me. (*Tears come to Eve's eyes. She turns away slowly.*) Don't cry. Just score it as an incomplete forward pass. (*Eve*, 162–63)

Turning professional triumph into personal humiliation, this scene provides an index to the film's double consciousness. The aspiring starlet does achieve the highest level of recognition—the Siddons award. But, like Sister Carrie, Eve Harrington finds that public success for a woman is loveless, lonely, and frustrating.

Perhaps even more forcefully, the film also dramatizes the perversion of sisterhood into something malicious and destructive on the public stage. Not one but three powerful women fall or fail in the film, victims as well as perpetrators of acts of feminine betrayal. A fourth woman, a lovely but ungifted would-be starlet (played by a young Marilyn Monroe), is derailed when she is upstaged at her audition by Eve's first reading as Margo's understudy. The terms of women's bitter competition are only intensified by the presence of so many "queens" on the board.

All About Eve, like the front-page-woman scenarios of an earlier day, ultimately suggests the only terms a woman can negotiate successfully are those of surrender, followed by a retreat to the domestic sphere. In a move foreshadowed by her earlier lament to Karen, Margo Channing accepts those terms and Bill's once-rejected proposal, testifying to the make-believe quality of the working girl scenario. Luminous in a Mankiewicz closeup, Margo tells the adoring Bill and her stunned playwright that she is soon to be "A foursquare, upright, downright, forthright, married lady . . . that's for me. And no more make believe. Off stage or on." She insists, lightheartedly, that she has outgrown childish things; marriage is a game "for grown up women only." If she should again work in the theater, she jokes, she would "play a mother." Finally, to her playwright's surprise, Margo relinquishes her claim on the starring role in his next play. When he protests, "What's you're being *married* have to do with it?" she answers, "It means I've finally got a life to live! I don't have to play parts I'm too old for—just because I've got nothing to do with my nights!" (*Eve*, 201–3). As suggested earlier, withdrawal from the public role is tantamount to self-erasure. Margo becomes little more than a silent spectator in the film once she becomes a suburban housewife.

Margo's reversion to female stereotype is an ironic resolution of the dialogic tension in *All About Eve*. Barbara Leaming suggests this in her biography of Bette Davis:

> Unexpectedly, Margo appeared to accept and even to recommend the retrograde sexual politics of the 50's. . . . At one fell swoop in admitting that yes, a woman must choose between happiness and a career, Margo seemed to undo all that Bette's gutsier characters had proved about a woman's capacity to function bravely and effectively on her own. (*Bette Davis*, 225–26)

Leaming calls this "Mankiewicz's quintessential postwar male fantasy," for the woman to choose ambition and career over the man in her life is to condemn herself to the barren, pathetic, lonely life of Eve Harringon.

Eve's fate is a potent caveat for would-be career women. She loses her chance for love or marriage in her upward climb: DeWitt threatens to blackmail her if she tries to enter any other relationship. Even winning the Siddons award is a hollow victory; Eve carelessly leaves it in the taxi after the ceremony. As the film moves to a close, it is clear that Eve herself will be the next victim of false sisterhood. Phoebe, a self-styled "president of the Eve Harrington fan club," has found her way into Eve's hotel room and is preparing to insinuate herself into Eve's life and usurp her place. She offers to pack for Eve who is bound for a destination demeaned by the characters in this film—Hollywood. When Addison DeWitt arrives to drop off the Siddons trophy which Eve has left behind, the girl accepts it on Eve's behalf, and, the script tells us, "holds it as if it were the Promised Land" (*Eve*, 243). The final scene is meant to remind us of our first view of Eve backstage, underscoring the eternal duplicity inherent in women's success scenario. In the writer-director's words:

> *She takes the award into the bedroom, sets it on a trunk. As she starts out, she sees Eve's fabulous wrap on the bed. She listens. Then, quietly, she puts on the wrap and picks up the award. Slowly, she walks to a large three-mirrored cheval. With grace and infinite dignity she holds the award to her, and bows again and again . . . as if to the applause of a multitude.* (*Eve*, 245)

The message for women in *All About Eve* is clear, dramatizing the precariousness of success in contrast to domestic bliss. Mankiewicz also presents an uncompromising view of women's "frailty" and workplace ethics.

Ruthlessness is rewarded; the talent needed to succeed in business is used perversely by women for sabotage. Eve's performance brings down the house; but the house, this scenario tells us, is where the successful woman really belongs.

HEAVEN HELP THE WORKING GIRL

On January 22, 1988, the *Chicago Sun-Times* ran a feature about the reaction of an audience of working women to a movie playing at the Chicago Theater:

> Most of the women have come right from work, in the company of other women from the office. . . . Throughout the theater, as the film progresses, women take to elbowing their seatmates and exchanging meaningful looks as, up on the screen, an ambitious secretary makes an end run around her dastardly female boss in a scramble for love and success. . . . What's this?

"This" is *Working Girl*, Mike Nichols's revisioning of the *All About Eve* scenario almost forty years later. In his hands, this 1950s theme becomes the framework for social satire, revealing the persistence of a flawed ethic of success and the unresolved dialogic tension generated by the growing presence of women in the U.S. workplace. His film also suggests, albeit ironically, the possibilities of an alternative scenario. The opening footage of *Working Girl* sets out the terms of a wonderland passage to "a new Jerusalem"—as the rousing background chorus suggests—and a new and improved model of sisterhood. After an aerial view of the Statue of Liberty, we see the Staten Island ferry—a comic image of transition which is used throughout the film— bearing crowds of workers, including working girl Tess McGill (Melanie Griffith), to the shores of Manhattan. As if to reinforce these "rebirth" images, Tess is celebrating her birthday on board with her affectionate girlfriends and a makeshift cake. (We may also recall that it was a surprise birthday party that alerted Margo to Eve's sabotage.)

While this opening exuberantly promises a new passage, we soon understand that Nichols is steering his heroine into a modern but still duplicitous workplace. There, women are commodified. When Tess asks her male supervisor for assistance in getting into a management seminar, he sets her up with a boozy and predatory manager who tries to "interview" her in the back seat of the corporate limousine. Disgusted, Tess walks home in the rain, skipping night school, only to find her boyfriend in bed with someone else. The stage is set for her passage into a new wonderland: a supposedly "woman-friendly" workplace, where she has been hired as secretary to a female executive, Catherine (Sigourney Weaver).

Nichols seems to have moved a considerable distance from the claustrophobic interiors of *All About Eve*; both the similarities and differences between the two films help us measure that distance. Tess McGill is in many senses an "Eve," seeking to rise to the top of her profession—and soon modeling herself after her new boss, Catherine, who is not older—both are thirty—but far wiser in the devious ways of the business wonderland. But Tess herself also represents a new kind of working woman, possessing both "manly" attributes—which she describes as "a head for business," and "feminine" qualities, "a 'bod' for sin." Nichols gives this visual emphasis as we frequently catch glimpses of "Victoria's Secrets" beneath her crisp and tailored business suits.

In *All About Eve*, the ambitious starlet betrays the curiously naive star. In *Working Girl*, it is the aspiring upstart who is overly naive and trusting. Eve Harrington operates in secret, provoking Margo's unseemly frustration and rage. Tess at first is as open, guileless, and enterprising as any Alger hero. She comes up with a brilliant new business strategy and brings it to her new mentor, expecting that, as a woman, Catherine will extend a sisterly hand to assist her in climbing the corporate ladder as no male boss ever would. Her mistaken assumption makes Tess an easy mark for her boss's exploitative and malicious subterfuge.

When Catherine leaves town on a skiing trip, and breaks her leg at the resort, delaying her return, Tess agrees to check on her apartment. She is inspired by what she sees there: visible signs of success, including a Warhol-like panel of multiple Catherine images. Like Eve Harrington who has spent months perfecting Margo's every inflection and gesture, Tess attempts to parrot and emulate her polished boss, riding her exercise bike, trying on her costumes, trying to repeat her "lines" recorded on her dictaphone. But as she listens, she receives an unexpected message. Sitting in front of Catherine's dressing table mirror, attempting literally to remake herself in her mentor's image, Tess hears in Catherine's own voice on dictaphone tape that she not only has stolen Tess's idea but is planning to take credit for it herself.

It is a critical turning point for Tess, suddenly freed by Catherine's ugly example to trespass over ethical boundaries herself. She uses her boss's office as the staging ground for her masquerade. Dressing for success works as well in the workplace as on Broadway. Costumed in Catherine's power suits, changing her hairstyle from a blowzy bob to an elegant twist, Tess convinces Jack (unbeknownst to her, Catherine's most recent beau) to serve as her partner in implementing her idea. Her business deal takes shape not only through

Jack's know-how, but through Tess's intentional use of duplicitous "feminine" strategies. Dragging a reluctant Jack behind her, she crashes a reception hosted by their prospective client, and presents her case seductively and convincingly in his arms on the dance floor.

All the parties soon reach an agreement "in principle," although Nichols is quick to underscore the hypocrisy of that phrase. One of the prospective investors sums up the ethically bankrupt situation. "Of course, there is an agreement in principle," he remarks. "What constitutes *principle* in this day and age I'm going to leave to you barracudas to squabble over." For the "barracudas" of modern business, making a deal becomes a potent aphrodisiac. When the corporate merger seems set, Jack and Tess, wild with elation, rush out of the office and into bed.

But Catherine returns sooner than expected, bursting into the boardroom at the final closing, crutches and all, to play her own game of countersabotage. She can overlook a lover's infidelity ("I forgive you, Jack") but not a rival woman's victory. Moving to recapture her advantage, she exposes her secretary's imposture and shamelessly claims that Tess has stolen *her* idea. Were this the 1950s era, Tess, like Margo Channing, might have left the field, retreating to domesticity. Jack, risking his own future, persuades the client to give Tess a second hearing, and Tess checkmates Catherine decisively. In the aftermath of Catherine's humiliating defeat, Tess wins Jack's admiration and her career goal—the offer of a management job from the CEO she had wooed and won on the dance floor.

Working Girl sets off in comic relief the multiple revisions both the business scenario and marriage plot have undergone since the 1950s. The mutually dependent ideals of workplace ethics and virtuous domesticity have become difficult to imagine or sustain, except in farce. Nichols reveals other gender-related shifts in society as well as in cinema. To complement a newly enfranchised woman, we have a "sensitive" hero, who practices "feminine" virtues of sacrifice and care. The final image we have of Jack is mockingly domestic: in his apartment kitchen, he solicitously hands Tess her lunch box as she goes off to her first day on her new job.

The last scene demonstrates the extent of the imaginative distance between *All About Eve* and *Working Girl*. Again, we witness a repetitive cycle of betrayal set in motion by a woman's ambitions. Sent to "square one," her new office at the end of a long corridor, Tess finds it occupied—her future secretary is using the telephone.

In the ironic coda of *All About Eve*, the young actress Phoebe has invaded Eve's territory and has already begun to usurp her space. But in *Working Girl*, the embarrassed secretary and the surprised boss circle each other warily, exchanging places. Her secretary (hoping to be called "assistant") asks for guidance about how to operate. Tess makes it clear that she will not adopt the hierarchical strategies that once betrayed her, nor will she offer a false promise of sisterhood. But neither does she have a new script at hand. She asks with obvious sincerity to be called by her first name; she suggests she can get her own coffee. But in the film's last line, Tess simply tells her half-disbelieving assistant, *"The rest we'll just make up as we go along."*

The modern workplace, it seems, is open to the woman who knows and can play by the rules of the game.[2] But the ending of *Working Girl* also suggests that she may have the potential to change it. Tess McGill, a woman who has recognized and even demonstrated her own capacity for malice, may indeed be invited to take a seat at the corporate businessman's mad tea party. But the challenge facing women seeking a yet undiscovered "new Jerusalem" is how to keep from being pawns in a game lacking ethical coherence, in which "principle" is merely a figure of speech.

In his essay, "Postmodern and Consumer Society," Fredric Jameson describes the "failure of the new," the "frustration" of contemporary filmmakers at not being able to say anything that has not already been said. But if *Working Girl* is "postmodern" in its reinvention of an earlier scenario, it is not because everything we need to know about women and work in America has been said. Rather, it is because, despite decades of social, political, and demographic change, the culture remains ambivalent about the ethic of "success"—an ambivalence threaded through American fiction and made especially visible in these film scenarios of working women. As Nichols translates this story into a comic mode—brassy instead of tragic, open-ended instead of fatalistic, the effect is not to repeat but to overwrite the plots of the past. It is as though there were another text laid over the first, a text with an altogether different outcome; the film becomes a palimpsest. The desire and need for a different but equally valued narrative of success, expressed in *Working Girl*'s final montage of images and voices, begins to displace the duplicitous scenarios society has scripted for women in U.S. business.

NOTES

1. The films discussed in this essay: *All About Eve* (Joseph Mankiewicz, 1950) and *Working Girl* (Mike Nichols, 1988), are available on videocassette. The screenplay of *All About Eve*, which differs slightly from the film scenario, is also available in a 1951 Random House edition.

2. Indeed, in a 1991 text, *Sisterhood Betrayed*, the authors warn career women against succumbing to what they call the *"All About Eve* Complex," their label for a pattern of unsisterly conduct prevalent in the modern workplace.

BIBLIOGRAPHY

Barber, Jill, and Rita Watson. *Sisterhood Betrayed*. New York: St. Martin's Press, 1991.

Belton, John. *Movies and Mass Culture*. New Brunswick: Rutgers University Press, 1996.

Doane, Mary Ann. "The Economy of Desire." In Belton, *Movies and Mass Culture*, 119–34.

Dreiser, Theodore. *Sister Carrie*. New York: New American Library, 1961.

Fuller, Margaret. "Summer on the Lakes," "Woman in the Nineteenth Century." In *The Heath Anthology of American Literature*, vol. 1, Lauter et al., eds. (Lexington, Mass.: D. C. Heath, 1994), 1620–54.

Galerstein, Carolyn. *Working Women on the Hollywood Screen: A Filmography*. New York: Garland, 1989.

Gilligan, Carol. *In a Different Voice*. Cambridge: Harvard University Press, 1982.

Jameson, Fredric. "Postmodernism and Consumer Society." In Belton, *Movies and Mass Culture*, 185–202.

Kaplan, E. Ann. *Women and Film*. London and New York: Routledge, 1983.

Leaming, Barbara. *Bette Davis: A Biography*. New York: Ballantine, 1992.

Mankiewicz, Joseph. *All About Eve, A Screenplay (based on a short story by Mary Orr)*. New York: Random House, 1951.

———. *More About All About Eve*. New York: Random House, 1972.

Melville, Herman. "The Paradise of Bachelors and The Tartarus of Maids." In *The Heath Anthology of American Literature*, 2480–96.

5

OTHER PEOPLE'S MONEY

A Study in Self-Deception

— ☉ —

OLIVER F. WILLIAMS, C.S.C.

To argue that most evildoers do not know what they are doing when they are doing it is to argue that most evildoers are victims of self-deception. Often people assume that the decisions in the business world which cause great harm to people are made by people *fully aware* of their misdeeds but intent on some goal which seems to justify their behavior. For example, when we read about the Archer-Daniels-Midland Company (ADM) price-fixing scandal which cost major companies hundreds of millions of dollars in fines, we imagine that the executives involved were consciously and deliberately re-flective about all the harm price fixing may have caused but were moved to act out of fear for the survival of the company or some other such crisis. Is this indeed the case? The self-deception hypothesis argues that the executives understood what they were doing as keeping a firm safely in the black—no more, no less; they really never adverted to the harm their price-fixing prac-tice may have been causing.

Self-deception is the subject of an insightful analysis by the philoso-pher Herbert Fingarette; in that study he cites a passage from O'Neill's *The Iceman Cometh* as a classic example of the phenomenon.[1] In the passage, Mr. Hickey, a traveling salesman who is a gambler and heavy drinker under constant pressure from his wife to mend his ways, tells us why he finally killed her. In the very telling of his story, Hickey comes to see that he was lying to himself.

> That last night I'd drive myself crazy trying to figure some way out for her. I went in the bedroom. I was going to tell her it was the end. But I couldn't do that to her. She was sound asleep. I thought, God, if she'd only never wake up, she'd never know! And then it came to me—the only possible way out, for her sake. I remembered I'd given her a gun for protection while I was

71

away and it was in the bureau drawer. She'd never feel any pain, never wake up from her dream. So I—

So I killed her. (There is a moment of dead silence.)

And then I saw I'd always known that was the only possible way to give her peace and free her from the misery of loving me. I saw it meant peace for me, too, knowing she was at peace. I felt as though a ton of guilt was lifted off my mind. I remember I stood by the bed and suddenly I had to laugh. I couldn't help it, and I knew Evelyn would forgive me. I remember I heard myself speaking to her, as if it was something I'd always wanted to say: "Well, you know what you can do with your pipe dream now, you damned bitch." (He stops with a horrified start, as if shocked out of a nightmare, as if he couldn't believe he heard what he had just said. He stammers). No! I never—! (Fingarette, 59–60)

In the spelling out of his story, Hickey came to see his self-deception. In the business world, the problem is even more complex, for while we seldom have outright murder at issue, life in business is controlled by role expectations. Self-deception may allow one to do something in a corporate "role" that would be unthinkable otherwise. The challenge is to be able to step outside the professional role and assess what the limits of that role might be. One must have a story that can encompass the professional story and put it in perspective. For example, had the executive in the ADM price-fixing case seen himself primarily as a husband-father-citizen-Christian/Jew/religious person, he may have had the resources to step outside his professional story and see that price fixing violated the limits of his professional role.[2]

One way to help students grasp what is at issue in self-deception is through the use of film. Here I will describe how I use the film *Other People's Money* to illustrate self-deception and how it operates in a life.[3]

My first experience with using *Other People's Money* in a class setting was as part of a seminar I moderated for the Aspen Institute in Aspen, Colorado. Founded over fifty years ago by the Great Books guru, Mortimer Adler of the University of Chicago, the Aspen Institute conducts numerous seminars usually of a week or two in length, for senior executives. Unlike most of the contemporary "how-to" seminars, however, the Aspen Institute focuses on developing the underlying vision of the manager. What sort of person do I want to become? What sort of organization am I shaping and what sort of community am I forming by my decisions? Using some of the classic readings from authors such as Aristotle, Plato, John Locke, Hobbes, as well as from contemporary authors, the seminar strives to lead the students to these foundational questions.[4]

An Aspen seminar usually has the students read and act out one play. The play *Other People's Money* by Jerry Sterner was selected for the seminar

I moderated in the summer of 1986.[5] Each seminar participant is assigned to take the role of one of the characters in the play, and the play is read aloud. In reading the play and taking a role, you begin to see (feel, think and perceive) the world as the person would whom you are playing. How does it feel to be a blue-collar worker losing your job because of a takeover artist? How does it feel to be a financial wizard who can engineer a takeover? The CEO of a company being taken over? How does each of the key characters envision the proper role of business in society? Who is correct? How can we as managers avoid serious ethical failures in our professional lives? These and other questions offer much material for serious discussion and debate.

When the class gets much beyond the fifteen to twenty members normally in an Aspen seminar, viewing a film and writing a reflection paper and then discussing in a large-class context, has been a much more effective way to lead the students to examine the basic questions. Some outline of how one might use the film *Other People's Money* may be helpful.

The film, directed by Norman Jewison, is, on the face of it, a story about a hostile takeover. It presents, in dramatic form, the arguments for and against the thesis that takeovers are in society's best interest. These arguments follow closely those made by leading business scholars, for example the management guru Peter Drucker[6] (arguing against takeovers) and the renowned economist Michael Jensen[7] (arguing for takeovers). Upon deeper reflection, however, the film portrays some very vivid examples of that human phenomenon of self-deception. Arthur Miller, in *Death of a Salesman*, captures the essence of the problem when he has Bif, the son of the salesman, Willy Loman, speaking of his father, say: "He had the wrong dreams. He never knew who he was."

I will outline the arguments for and against takeovers as presented in the film and then highlight some of the ethical strengths and failures demonstrated in the lives of the major characters. Rather than simply focusing on how the ethical violations might have been avoided by a better analysis of the situation, however, I argue that at root these ethical failures stem from the lack of an adequate vision of what constitutes a good life—a vision of the kind of persons we want to be and the kind of communities we want to form. For it is the images of the story of this vision of what constitutes the good life which attune us to recognize obligations. The images of ill and dying children, for example, arouse our moral sensibilities. The role of moral obligations is to preserve a way of life, and without some coherent notion of the desired way of life there is little sense in speaking of moral obligation.

First, let us view how Andrew Jorgensen and Lawrence Garfield, the antagonists in the drama, each view the hostile takeover. Jorgensen, sixty-eight years old, is the current chair of the board of New England Wire and Cable, having followed his father who founded the firm some eighty years ago. Garfield, about forty, is the financial expert who is about to take over the firm by winning a proxy vote with his slate of officers.

The setting is at the annual shareholder meeting and the shareholders are about to vote on the Garfield takeover proposal. First, Andrew Jorgenson, played by Gregory Peck, speaks (his arguments are not too unlike those of Peter Drucker).

> It's good to see so many familiar faces and many old friends. Some of you I haven't seen in years. Thank you for coming. Bill Coles, our able president, in the annual report has told you of our year, of what we accomplished and need for further improvements, our goals for next year and years beyond. I would like to talk to you about something else. I want to share with you some of my thoughts concerning the vote that you are going to make in the company that you own. This proud company which has survived the death of its founder, numerous recessions, one major depression, and two World Wars, is in imminent danger of self-destruction. On this day in the town of its birth, there is the instrument of our destruction. I want you to look at him and know all of his glory: Larry the Liquidator. The entrepreneur of post-industrial America, playing God with other people's money. The Robber Barons of old at least left something tangible in their wake—a coal mine, a railroad, banks. This man leaves nothing; he creates nothing; he builds nothing; he runs nothing. And in his wake lies nothing but a blizzard of paper to cover up the pain. Oh, if he said, "I know how to run the business better than you," that would be something worth talking about. But he's not saying that; he's saying I am going to kill you because at this particular moment in time you are worth more dead than alive. Well, maybe it is true but it is also true that one day this industry will turn. One day—when the yen weakens, the dollar is stronger, or when we finally begin to rebuild our roads, our bridges, the infrastructure of our country. Demand will skyrocket and when those things happen, we will still be here. Stronger because of our ordeal, stronger because we have survived and the price of our stock will make his offer pale by comparison. God save us if we vote to take his few dollars and run. God save this country if that is truly the wave of the future. We will have then become a nation that makes nothing but hamburgers, creates nothing but lawyers and sells nothing but tax shelters. And if we are at that point in this country, where we kill something because at the moment it is worth more dead than alive.
>
> Well look around, look at your neighbor! Look at your neighbor! You won't kill him, will you? It's called murder and it's illegal. Well, this too is murder on a mass scale. Only on Wall Street they call it maximizing shareholder value. And they call it legal. And they substitute dollar bills where a conscience should be. Damn it!! A business is worth more than the price of its

stock. It's the place where we earn our living, where we meet our friends, dream our dreams. It is in every sense the very fabric that binds our society together. So let us now, in this meeting, say to every Garfield in the land: Here we build things, we don't destroy them. Here we care about more than the price of our stock. Here we care about people.

Following Jorgenson's address, Bill Coles, the president of New England Wire and Cable and the moderator of the meeting, introduces Lawrence Garfield. Garfield, played by Danny Devito, is portrayed as an obese and cunning New Yorker with a Bronx accent. While during the introduction Garfield is greeted with catcalls, by the end of his address he has mesmerized many in the audience.

Amen and Amen and Amen! You have to forgive me, I am not familiar with the local custom. Where I come from, you always say Amen after you hear a prayer. Because that's what you just heard, a prayer. Where I come from that particular prayer is called the prayer for the dead. You just heard the prayer for the dead my fellow stockholders and you didn't say Amen. This company is dead. I didn't kill it, don't blame me. It was dead when I got here. It's too late for prayers for even if the prayers were answered and a miracle occurred and the yen did this and the dollar did that and the infrastructure did the other thing, we would still be dead. You know why? Fiber optics, new technologies, obsolescence. We're dead all right; we're just not broke and do you know the surest way to go broke, keep getting an increasing share of a shrinking market. Down the tubes, slow but sure. You know at one time there must of been dozens of companies making buggy whips, and I bet the last company around was the one that made the best goddamn buggy whips you ever saw. How would any of you like to be a stockholder of that company? You invested in a business and this business is dead. Let's have the intelligence, let's have the decency to sign the death certificate, collect the insurance and invest in something with a future. Ah, but we can't, goes the prayer; we can't because we have responsibility. A responsibility to our employees, to our community. What will happen to them? I got two words: Who cares? Care about them? Why? They didn't care about you. They suck you dry; you have no responsibility to them. For the last ten years this company bled your money. Did this community ever say "We know times are tough, we'll lower taxes, reduce water and sewer." Check it out. You're paying twice what you did ten years ago. And our devoted employees who have taken no increase for the past three years are still making twice what they made ten years ago and our stock is one-sixth of what it was ten years ago. Who cares? I tell you: me! I'm not your best friend, I'm your only friend. I don't make anything? I'm making you money. Unless we forget that the only reason why any of you became stockholders in the first place. You want to make money. You don't care if they manufacture wire and cable, fried chicken or grow tangerines. You want to make money. I'm the only friend you got; I'm making you money. Take the money, invest somewhere else, and maybe you may get lucky and it will be used productively and, if it is, you create new jobs and provide a service for the economy. Even—and God forbid—make a few bucks for yourselves. If anybody asks, tell them you gave at the plant. And, by the way, it pleases me that I am called Larry the Liquidator. You know why, my fellow stockholders, because at my funeral you will leave with a smile on your face and a few bucks in your pocket. Now that's a funeral worth having!

As mentioned above, the basic structure of the arguments of Jorgenson and Garfield are not too unlike those of Drucker and Jensen, both highly respected scholars. To argue, as Jorgenson does, that economic rationality must have a social conscience if we are to maintain the sense of fairness and justice in the American ethos is not an unfamiliar line of thought to scholars of business ethics. As mentioned above, Peter Drucker, a professor at the Claremont Graduate School, is well known for this position. Lest the viewers come to believe that Andrew Jorgenson is our model ethical business leader, however, the author of the film script has made it clear that he leaves much to be desired in the way of business competence. Is not Garfield correct when he says that the wire and cable business has become a victim of obsolescence? Why was not Jorgenson developing new products ten years before Garfield came on the scene? The film ends with some Japanese businesses contracting with a newly restructured, employee-owned wire and cable company to manufacture airbags made from stainless steel wire cloth. Why did not Jorgenson think of that?

Jorgenson, unfortunately, typifies the sort of business leader with a strong ethical sensitivity but marginal business competence. While he clearly demonstrates great respect for the dignity of his employees, the fundamental change that is constitutive of capitalism—what Schumpeter called the "creative destruction" of business—seems to elude him. Perhaps no one has said it better than Peter Drucker.

> Society, community, family are all conserving institutions. They try to maintain stability and to prevent, or at least to slow, change. But the organization of the post-capitalist society of organizations is a *destabilizer*. Because its function is to put knowledge to work—on tools, processes and products; on work; on knowledge itself—it must be organized for constant change. It must be organized for innovation—and innovation as the Austro-American economist Joseph Schumpeter (1883–1950) said, is "creative destruction." It must be organized for systematic abandonment of the established, the customary, the familiar, the comfortable, whether products, services and processes,

human and social relationships, skills or organizations themselves. It is of the nature of knowledge that it changes fast and that today's certainties become tomorrow's absurdities.[8]

On the other hand, to argue, as Garfield does, that a market for corporate control leads to a restructuring that is essential for competitiveness of business is a common position of top scholars of finance. Perhaps the best proponent of this position is Michael Jensen, a professor at the Harvard University Graduate School of Business. What is surprising if not shocking, however, is that Garfield sees absolutely no responsibility to the employees of New England Wire and Cable and to the community which it called home for some eighty years. As he says in the passage quoted above, when referring to the future of the employees and the community, "Who cares? Care about them? Why? They didn't care about you."

Garfield's position here is unfortunately one held by others influential in the world of finance. To single-mindedly focus on economic rationality to the detriment of any advertence to social values is not clarity of purpose, as some claim; in the eyes of many it is sheer folly. John J. Phelan, Jr., a leader in Wall Street and the former chairman and chief executive officer of the New York Stock Exchange, expressed this position well.

> Anyone who owns a corporation has a certain number of obligations. The poorest management occurs when fulfillment of these obligations is neglected and somebody, either existing management or a new management, comes in and "throws people out the window." It may be necessary over time to retrench that company, to begin a shifting and sorting process, but throughout, the management has an obligation to those people who have worked there. Management has an obligation at least to sit down and find some way to try to work out some of the problems, and not just "dump people out the door" and say it is in the economic interest of the company and the shareholders that half the work force be eliminated. One might argue that the company cannot afford this sort of obligation to its employees; for if half the workers are not let go, the company might well go bankrupt and all would lose their jobs. Yet any new buyer of a company should have worked out before he or she took over that company what was going to happen with the redundancy force, how the new management was going to treat the employees in some decent way, particularly with regard to the handling of pension funds. We are talking about people's futures; pensions are the cushions for employees when they get to an age where they are not as productive. There ought to be a legal obligation that protects the pensions of employees when moves are made to increase efficiencies of companies. We must respect our employees and part of that respect is to treat them decently whether one is an old owner or a new buyer.[9]

Ethicists, in agreement with Phelan, make the argument that there are implied contracts with employees and that the moral manager is obliged to consider them in the calculus. Other developed countries have legislation requiring some minimal standards for treating employees and communities in takeover situations.

It would be easy to dismiss Garfield and those in the financial world with similar views on responsibility to employees in takeover situations as simply moral midgets. We all know people who are tone deaf to ethical issues and apparently Garfield is one of these. Yet, upon further analysis, the problem is not so simple. Lawrence Garfield has some high ethical ideals which are in evidence in the film. For example, when Jorgenson's lawyer, Kate Sullivan, offers a "greenmail" package to Garfield, he is offended. Kate responds that greenmail is not against the law and that Garfield could make considerable money. But Garfield says greenmail is unethical; it is unfair to all the other shareholders and therefore he will have no part in it.

Another example of Garfield's moral self-image is demonstrated in the scene where Jorgenson's secretary and long-time love, Bea Sullivan, comes to see Garfield. She offers him all the proceeds of a trust fund she has, some one million dollars, if only Garfield will cease his efforts to take over New England Wire and Cable. Again, Garfield is insulted, responding that he makes money *for* widows and orphans, he does not take it from them. Bea responds with anger, saying: "Before or after you put them out of business?" There is a moment where one wonders if Bea might have pierced the armor of Garfield, but he quickly recovers and brushes her remarks off as those of an emotional woman.

Garfield does not really believe that he has any responsibility to workers or the community or any stakeholders other than the stockholders. He seems to be kidding himself; he seems to be an example of what the philosopher Herbert Fingarette described so well in the book mentioned above called *Self-Deception*. When Garfield agrees to a "stand-still agreement," an agreement not to buy any stock for a certain period of time, with lawyer Kate Sullivan, he has no qualms of conscience in immediately violating the promise. Somehow promise-keeping in the world of finance seems to mean nothing to Garfield.

This self-deception or insincerity with oneself is only a requirement for one who has high ideals, otherwise why bother with the deception. What the self-deceiver lacks is not integrity but the courage to spell out what is really going on. The insincerity with himself is made possible by the story or narrative which guides Garfield's life. What is life all about for Garfield, what is his master story? What are his hopes, fears, aims, and guides for his conduct? In the film he provides several glimpses of what he is all about.

The film opens with Garfield engaging in a monologue.

> I love money. I love money more than the things it can buy. Does that surprise you? Money—it don't care if I snore or not. It don't care which God I pray to. There are only three things in this world with that kind of unconditional acceptance: dogs, donuts, and money; only money is better. You know why? Because it don't make you fat and it don't poop all over the living room floor. There's only one thing better: other people's money.

Garfield tells us he loves money more than the things it can buy. He tells us later that he understands himself primarily as a capitalist and he spells out what that means for him.

> You make as much money as you can for as long as you can. Whoever has the most when he dies wins. Look, it's the American way. I am doing my job. I am a capitalist; I am simply following the law of free enterprise—survival of the fittest. Since when do you have to be nice to be right? They can pass all the laws they want. All they can do is change the rules, they can never stop the game. I don't go away, I adapt.

Garfield, like many today who justify what they do in the name of capitalism, seems to misunderstand the basic features of the system outlined so clearly in the "bible of capitalism," that eighteenth-century work authored by Adam Smith. Smith, a moral philosopher, captured the basic dynamic of what has become known as capitalism in his classic work, *An Inquiry Into the Nature and Causes of the Wealth of Nations*, published in 1776.[10] The fundamental question that Smith sought to answer was why some nations were beginning to accrue wealth and have a higher standard of living while others were remaining poor. The answer, said Smith, is that what characterized those places that were creating wealth was a system of exchange relationships, where each person, while motivated by self-interest, contributes to the common good. What we now call the market economy, when left relatively free, said Smith, will gradually enable more and more people to enjoy the good things of creation.

When Smith said that where each person pursues his or her own self-interest, the common good is enhanced, he was simply observing what was going on around him in England. If the baker wanted to build an addition to his house (his self-interest), he knew that to have the resources to do this he had to bake a bread of higher quality and/or lower price than his competitors. The net effect was that the community got a better bread and resources were used efficiently (the common good was enhanced).

The genius of the market mechanism was that everyone did not have to *intend* to enhance the common good in order for it to be achieved. The baker's *motivation* for baking a higher-quality bread and perhaps finding the technology to sell it at a lower price is irrelevant, for the common good will be enhanced even if his only real interest is to add to his house. In this regard, Smith spoke of a "hidden hand" achieving the common good.

As I have argued elsewhere, however, Smith's position is only understood in the light of his earlier work, *The Theory of Moral Sentiments*.[11] The assumption there is that "self-interest" would not be equivalent to selfishness or greed, but rather that the self would be shaped by the moral forces in society, especially the family. Thus, a person so shaped would have a conscious care for the dignity of persons and would not lightly fire them from a job. Garfield seems to believe that his only obligation as a "capitalist" is to make money and, as long as he does not violate any laws, he has no moral obligations to employees and the community. In this regard, he misunderstands Adam Smith.

To accrue wealth for its own sake would be totally foreign to Smith. He envisioned the market as only viable within the context of a moral community. This is certainly not to say that a merchant would not be unethical on occasion, for Smith was not naive about the flaws of human nature. He did, however, assume that most people would have moral ideals and that the basic virtues of the Judeo-Christian vision would perdure. The Garfields of our time, should they dominate the business community, would be the downfall of capitalism as Smith envisioned it.

All of this digression into the "bible of capitalism" is simply to point out that the cover story under which Garfield works, that greed is good, is an aberration of capitalism. Garfield seems to have persuaded himself that greed is good and that he has no need to advert to the implications of the plant closing. For him the "hidden hand" will make all turn out for the common good, and thus he has no qualms of conscience as long as he is pursuing wealth. In this, Garfield is a victim of self-deception. Managers must *consciously* and *deliberately* work for the common good when the dignity of the person is at stake. No "hidden hand" will excuse unethical behavior.

How is it that some people are more attuned to recognize wrong-doing and moral obligations than others? Our reasoning is shaped by our convictions. One acts in a way to be true to oneself.

Moral personality is formed first in the family and then in the community, and a community is defined by its story. In any community we are schooled in the virtues required to be a certain sort of person. For example, Christians through their language, habits, and feelings construe the world in a certain way. Character traits such as compassion, generosity, and forgiveness are highlighted. The intellect is affectively qualified in that it is attentive to certain features of experience that it might otherwise miss or undervalue. When efficiency and productivity are the only values reinforced, people are slowly molded to do whatever will "get the job done." Treating people functionally dulls their sensitivity and constricts their perspective so that their "world" becomes basically functional.

Without compassion, justice, loyalty, and the other moral virtues, the right moral dilemmas will not even arise in one's life. Moral virtues so shape a person that the world is seen truthfully. While the Garfields of this world clearly have some moral ideals, they need to be actively involved in a moral community (religious, philosophic, civic, and so on) to keep their vision clear and overcome the continual tendency to self-deceive. Making money and making the world a better place are not the same thing; only one involved in self-deception would claim they are.

NOTES

1. Herbert Fingarette, *Self-Deception* (New York: Humanities Press, 1969).

2. For an account of how the Christian story provides a context for a professional story, see Oliver F. Williams and John W. Houck, *Full Value: Cases in Christian Business Ethics* (San Francisco: Harper & Row, 1978).

3. *Other People's Money*, a Norman Jewison film (Burbank: Warner Bros., 1991).

4. For a good example of the content of an Aspen Institute seminar, see the book by the seminar director of Aspen, James O'Toole, *The Executive Compass: Business and the Good Society* (New York: Oxford University Press, 1993).

5. Jerry Sterner, *Other People's Money: A Play in Two Acts* (New York: Samuel French, 1987).

6. See, for example, Peter F. Drucker, "To End the Raiding Roulette Game," *Across The Board* (Conference Board, 1986), 30–39.

7. See Michael C. Jensen, "Takeovers: Folklore and Science," *Harvard Business Review*, November–December 1984: 109–21.

8. Peter F. Drucker, *Post-Capitalist Society* (New York: HarperCollins, 1993), 57.

9. John J. Phelan, Jr., "Ethical Leadership and the Investment Industry," *Ethics and the Investment Industry*, Oliver F. Williams, Frank K. Reilly, and John W. Houck, eds. (Savage, Md.: Rowman & Littlefield, 1989), 31–32.

10. Adam Smith, *The Wealth of Nations*, Edwin Cannan, ed. (Chicago: University of Chicago Press, 1976).

11. Adam Smith, *The Theory of Moral Sentiments* (Indianapolis: Liberty Classics, 1976). This work was originally published in 1753, twenty-three years earlier than *The Wealth of Nations*.

PART II

— ⊕ —

The Moral Imagination

*Toward a Better Understanding
of Ourselves and Our Times*

6

"IF POWER CHANGES PURPOSE"

Images of Authority in Literature and Film

— ⊙ —

TERESA GODWIN PHELPS

I want to tell two stories about power: the familiar story about the corrupting influence of power, a story that plagues all organizations and governments, and a not-so-familiar alternative story about the effective use of power. To tell these two stories, I will enlist the help of my fellow storytellers, Shakespeare and the contemporary American filmmakers of *Working Girl, Wall Street, Disclosure,* and *Mr. Holland's Opus.*

In the initial scene of Shakespeare's play *Measure for Measure,* Vincentio, the Duke of Vienna, deputizes Angelo, his most virtuous citizen, about whom he later remarks, "Hence we shall see, / If power changes purpose" (III, ii, 51–54). Thus, Shakespeare sets the scene for the dramatic analysis of a still pressing question: What becomes of people when they are given power over others? Will the Duke's delegation of his power to the upright Angelo change Angelo? What will become of Angelo's renowned virtue? The central question in this most puzzling of Shakespeare's plays might be stated, What does power do to us?

Do we in our culture believe that power changes us for the worse? Unfortunately, the answer is a resounding Yes! From the overly familiar "Power corrupts. Absolute power corrupts absolutely"[1] to images in contemporary film, power has a bad reputation. Yet for businesses to function, leaders must both delegate power and be able to entrust others with authority. In other words, authority must be *given* and *taken* appropriately or problems result. Yet authority and its concomitant power is so frequently misused that the very word *power* has negative connotations. (One writer has called it the last dirty word in management.)[2] In light of this ubiquitous misuse, business leaders must nonetheless risk delegating authority on a regular basis. How do they, how should they, make choices? What qualities are desirable in a person to whom one delegates power?

Before suggesting answers to that question, I want to explore our cultural stories about power. Examining popular cultural images found in film gives us some idea of how communities define themselves by the kind of stories they tell about themselves. Films, in particular, use a kind of shorthand that depends upon the viewers' own shared stories; they rely on what the viewers already know. Film images thus both rehearse known narratives and reinforce those narratives.

What are our contemporary cultural narratives about power in business? What commonly held stories do films reenact and depend upon for meaning? The story put forth in Mike Nichols's *Working Girl* clearly depends upon some shared knowledge we have as viewers. In the initial meeting with Tess's (Melanie Griffith) new boss, Catherine Parker, we see how Catherine manipulates her and uses the rhetoric of equality and shared power. Tess is Catherine's image to the outside world and thereby is a *version* of Catherine. Catherine's "You are on time, you never make a promise you can't keep" quickly shifts into "I." Tess's identity becomes subsumed into that of her new boss. They are a "team": "I consider us a team, Tess. . . . It's a two-way street on my team; do I make myself clear?" The minute Tess acts on Catherine's version of equality and team spirit by calling her by her first name—Catherine—Catherine looms up over her. The scene is brilliantly directed and the bodies and faces of the two women sharply contradict all of Catherine's words.

Later, Tess, with ambitions and no power, goes to Catherine with an idea. Despite Catherine's repeated, "It's a two-way street, remember?" we *know* what will happen when Tess leaves Catherine's office. We supply the story that power is never beneficent and sharing, that Catherine's avowed "two-way street" is a dead end for Tess. Catherine will take Tess's idea and claim it as her own.

We are offered a competing narrative in a brief scene that follows. Tess is on her knees, buckling Catherine's ski boots. Catherine once again looms over Tess. Tess's naive women-helping-women story is undercut and even mocked by the film's juxtaposition of images. The film maker can use subtle cues, confidently relying on us knowing and believing the other, more predominant, story: a person with power in a business setting, like Catherine, will take advantage of the person over whom she has power, Tess. We *know* Catherine will steal Tess's idea. Catherine's power is power *over*. We are right. The filmmaker depends on our shared cultural story about the corrupting influence of power.

We see a similar misuse of power in Oliver Stone's *Wall Street*. Young investment broker Bud Fox (Charlie Sheen) telephones Wall Street wizard financier, Gordon Gekko (Michael Douglas) over and over until, finally, he is granted a meeting. Seconds before entering Gekko's office for the first time, Bud adjusts his tie in a mirror, the last time we or he will see the naive and innocent Bud Fox. The camera gives us Bud's perspective as he walks into Gekko's cavernous office. Gekko's words and body language portray unmitigated and unmerciful power over others. He is constantly on brief telephone calls, using language like "block anybody else's merger efforts," "lunch is for wimps," "Christmas is over, business is business," "I want every orifice in his body flowing red," "rip their throats out." Seduced by all of this and impressed by the aggressively successful Gekko, Bud uses inside information—he betrays his father—to give Gekko a stock tip.

In a later scene, Gekko's character becomes chillingly clear and Bud's desperation to be like Gekko is poignantly portrayed. Bud's fresh face in the mirror is replaced by his face in Gekko's limo window. The pause as the camera stays on Gekko's face is dramatic rather than suspenseful, as Bud's subsequent knock on the car window comes completely expectedly; his Jekyl-to-Hyde transformation has begun: "You've got me."

Despite these cultural narratives about the evil inherent in power, power is an integral part of our lives; we all use it and we are all subject to it. Power is both ethically neutral and necessary; it organizes and rationalizes human behavior. "Power admits to no simple definitions. It is part of the complex nature of human relations. It is central to life as we know it. It is critical to human interactions."[3] Quite simply, power is the means by which we get others to do things, it is how we get our way in a group. We can use power to control the actions of others and we can use power to change attitudes, ideas, beliefs, and opinions. Leadership, a much less negative word than power, is actually only the abstract notion of power seen in action.

Our myths and religions are "saturated with concerns for power"[4] and the philosophers have been far from silent on power. Plato and Machiavelli both instructed us on its use; Hobbes claimed that power was the measure of our social status. Nietzsche saw power as the essential and irreducible prime motive for action; humankind's prime desire is for power.[5] Yet all our philosophy somehow falls short of being of any real help in discussions about power in the workplace. Philosophy cannot compete with our cultural story about the abuse of power, a story that underlies our responses to film images of power. We need to deconstruct and rehabilitate our notions of power so we may use authority more profitably. Where can we turn for help? Well, perhaps to literature. While philosophy engages our intellectual selves, it leaves untouched our emotional sides. Images and stories capture us in ways that philosophy cannot. Stories, whether in books or films, concretize a dilemma. They do not allow us to think about a problem abstractly; if the story is good, we are drawn into it and forced to takes sides. We must make choices; we like one character and despise others; the ending pleases us or depresses us.

By using Shakespeare's *Measure for Measure*, I hope to deconstruct our cultural story about the corrupting influence of power and to analyze what qualities are dangerous and what are valuable in a person to whom one delegates power. In so doing, I will set forth an alternative story about power, one in which power is used wisely and well.

In *Measure for Measure*, Shakespeare analyzes the misuse of power. As the play unfolds, power does change Angelo. He commences his reign by upholding a long unenforced fornication law and condemns one Claudio to death for fornication with his betrothed (and pregnant) Juliet. When Claudio's sister, Isabella (a cloistered nun), comes to Angelo to beg for her brother's life, Angelo becomes smitten with Isabella and offers her brother's life in exchange for her chastity. In a scene not unlike Demi Moore's remark in *Disclosure:* "Come back and finish what you started or you're dead!" Angelo abuses the authority the Duke has lent him to further his own ends. This cool, dispassionate upright man, this "angel" who is better than, and removed from, the regular citizens, metamorphoses into a lustful, abusive lecher. Angelo offers Isabella something only he with his power can do—free Claudio—in exchange for sex from Isabella. While this kind of quid pro quo sexual harassment is chillingly contemporary and of particular interest to many of us, it is but a specific, gender-related example of the misuse of power. (In *Disclosure*, Michael Douglas's lawyer says, "sexual harassment isn't about sex, it's about power.")

Authority has two facets worth examining: the giving of it and the taking. What is the Duke's role in Angelo's subsequent transformation? What mistake did the Duke make in giving Angelo his power? At the outset, the Duke explains that he has "Elected him our absence to supply; / Lent him our terror, dressed him with our love, / And given his deputation all the organs / Of our own pow'r" (I, ii, 19–21). The Duke, a wise man (despite what many readers see as ill advised actions in the play), correctly delineates the dual aspects of power: "Lent him our *terror*, dressed him with our *love*." Terror and love, the two means by which we may exercise power and authority over others. In other words, we can make people do things by threatening them with violence, by using their fear, or by showing love and concern for them. I suggest that *Measure for Measure* is really about this dualism. Which is the more effective way to exercise power and to act with authority: terror or love?

The Duke explains that Angelo believes him gone to Poland, but the Duke will be disguised as a friar and will return to observe Angelo's rule. The Duke's motives in transferring his authority to Angelo and then spying on him are puzzling. On the one hand, the Duke confesses that he (the Duke) has let laws go unobserved and his stern authority over his people is impotent—"in time the rod becomes more mocked than feared" (III, ii, 26–27); people have made a "scarecrow of the law." The Duke is counting on Angelo to uphold and reinforce the dead laws. In more contemporary terms, the Duke wants Angelo to play the heavy, to do what the Duke cannot do: enforce his own strict laws.

On the other hand, the Duke seems to be testing the cool, dispassionate Angelo: Angelo "scarce confesses / That his blood flows, or that his appetite / Is more to bread than stone" (III, ii, 51–52). Here we have a clue as to what goes wrong with Angelo's rule. The Duke selects Angelo to rule in his absence because Angelo seems to have the right individual qualities. Escalus (the Duke's wise advisor) confirms this: "If any in Vienna be of worth / To undergo such ample grace and honor, / It is Lord Angelo" (I, i, 22–24). Angelo is virtuous; he is a man of "stricture and firm abstinence" (I, iii, 12); he is "a man whose blood / Is very snow-broth; one who never feels / The wanton stings and motions of the sense, / But doth rebate and blunt his natural edge / With profits of the mind, study and fast" (I, iv, 57–61); he is disciplined, intellectual, and unemotional. What could go wrong?

What the Duke and Escalus both miss is that Angelo's dispassionateness and coldness will make him a bad governor. Angelo is all mind and no heart. Good judgments are not made with dispassionate logic alone.[6] In fact, because Angelo's emotional side is so undeveloped, it appears as shadow[7] in his response to Isabella. He does not know his emotional side, it is "dark, unlived, and repressed," so he loses control when his emotions are called forth in his response to the beautiful and chaste Isabella when she begs for her brother's life. Isabella beseeches Angelo to be less rational and to "go to your bosom, / And ask your heart what it doth know" (II, ii, 137–38).

But Angelo is accustomed only to consulting his head. This is demonstrated most clearly in the story of his earlier betrothal to Mariana: "She should this Angelo have married; was affianced to her by oath; and the nuptial appointed" (III, 1, 217–18). Before the wedding, however, Mariana's brother, who was supplying her dowry, is lost at sea. Thus, Mariana lost both her brother and her husband-to-be, Angelo. Angelo "[l]eft her in her tears, and dried not one of them with his comfort; swallowed his vows whole, pretending in her discoveries of dishonour. . . . and he, a marble to her tears, is washed with them, but relents not" (III, ii, 329–34). It is the Duke who relates this information to Isabella about Angelo. The Duke's definition of virtue is a narrow one; one who is "marble to her tears" may still be virtuous.

After Isabella's initial meeting with him, Angelo sends her away until the next day, saying he will think about her request. In tortured soliloquies as he awaits Isabella's return, Angelo feels strong emotions for the first time: "Ever till now, / When men were fond, I smiled, and wond'red / how" (II, iii, 185–87). He has no idea what to do with them: "O heavens, / Why does my blood thus muster to my heart, / Making it both unable for itself, / And dispossessing all my other parts / Of necessary fitness?" (II, iv, 19–23). Angelo has never learned to handle strong emotions and they overwhelm him and make even his thinking unclear. He falls in love with Isabella, but instead of acting on that love and granting her brother's life his love takes a perverse form: "And now I give my sensual race the rein. / Fit thy consent to my sharp appetite, / Lay by all nicety and prolixious blushes, / That banish what they sue for; redeem thy brother / By yielding up thy body to my will, / Or else he must not only die the death, / But thy unkindness shall his death draw out / To ling'ring sufferance" (II, iv, 160–67). If Isabella does not have sex with Angelo, he will not only execute her brother but will prolong the death with torture. Angelo freely uses the terror component of power lent him by the Duke, but he has not also donned the garment of love that the Duke recognized as necessary for the moral wielding of power.

In addition, Angelo's isolation from the community also makes him a bad governor. Angelo is virtuous but he leads a solitary life. His worth as a member of a community has not been tested. He sees himself as morally superior to his subjects; he has what is recognized in the management texts as an "attitude of superiority that [will] naturally lead to the righteous abuse of power."[8] Angelo does not consult others and he repeatedly refuses to listen even to wise counsel. Isabella tells him to "consult his heart"; Escalus, the Duke's wisest counselor, beseeches him to have mercy on Claudio: "Ay, but yet / Let us be keen, and rather cut a little, / Than fall, and bruise to death" (II, 1, 2–4). But Angelo stays rigid, refusing to listen or compromise. He keeps his own counsel.

One contemporary version of Angelo is Meredith Johnson (Demi Moore) in *Disclosure*. Meredith seems to have all the right qualities for success. She has ideas, she closes deals, she "cleans up messes," she saves mergers, she takes no prisoners. A telling scene is when she gives her acceptance speech when she is made vice president. The lights go out, putting her colleagues into darkness while she stands in the spotlight. She is completely analytical; she does not really talk but resorts to a kind of business spreadsheet babble; she advocates relating to each other as "pure consciousness"—

her perverse notion of community, entailing "freedom" from everything that defines us as individuals. It is not until she fails that this coldness is seen as detrimental to her leadership. In fact, even after her downfall, she claims there are at least ten headhunters after her, within an hour, for comparable jobs. Yet her emotional side is unintegrated. She takes sex where she pleases, without love involved. She is an autonomous woman, isolated from the community, immune to real emotion.

Another contemporary version of Angelo in his lack of emotional depth and in his isolation from the community is our old friend Michael Douglas's Gordon Gekko in *Wall Street*. "The lesson in business," he tells Bud Fox, is "don't get emotional about stock, it clouds the judgment." Bud, the character we are watching to see if he becomes a clone of Gekko, begins to cut himself off from his emotional caring self. To a friend and colleague, he shouts, "I'm sick and tired of playing wet nurse to you." The problems with isolation from the community are many, of course, but an insidious outcome is that the isolated individual may recreate a perverse community in which values are subverted and redefined. In a famous scene, Gekko redefines greed. "Greed is good, greed is right, greed works. Greed clarifies, cuts through, and captures that essence of the evolutionary spirit." The impulse toward community is strong and necessary; yet, if a person like Gekko, who is self-alienated from the preexisting community, acquires enough power to create his own community, it may well be dominated by a 1984-ish "newspeak" of values.

Any characters in *Wall Street* who care about other people, who let emotions "cloud" their judgment (Bud's father, his coworker, Gekko's adversary), are shown as weak semifailures, dim lights next to Gekko's flash and dazzle.

Despite the cultural narrative that shows such people as ultimately bad users of power and authority, our model for power remains a hierarchical one; we have power *over* others. The delegation of power thus seems to call for choosing a person who is autonomous and dispassionate, for choosing an Angelo. Yet, if we are to be instructed by the disaster of Angelo's rule in *Measure for Measure*, we need another image of power, one that represents not power *over* but power *with*. We need a benevolent and effective story about power. We need authority that emanates from love instead of terror.

In a far-reaching and influential book, *In a Different Voice*, psychologist Carol Gilligan puts forth two models for describing and arranging relationships. She roughly equates these with women's and men's perceptions, but I do not want to pursue the gender differences here. Rather, I think the two models are useful ways of thinking about power. The one model is hierarchical; Gilligan likens it to a ladder, a hierarchy of rights, rules, and ranks. Its counterpart is based on interconnectedness, a web of relationships based upon responsibilities, a nonhierarchical vision of human connection.

In his lifelong study of the power motive, David McClelland discovered two quite different fantasies that people have about power. Some fantasies of power equate it as assertion and aggression. Other fantasies of power, however, equate it with giving and caring; acts of strength are acts of nurturance.[9] "In relationships of temporary inequality, such as parent and child or teacher and student, power ideally is used to foster the development that removes the initial disparity. In relationships of permanent inequality, power cements dominance and subordination."[10] Power *with*, then, is temporary and its goal is to empower and free the other. Power *over* seeks permanence and a disempowering of the other through fear.

The second model that McClelland and Gilligan put forth gives us an alternative version of power, power *with*. It is what Tess believed Catherine would do for her in *Working Girl*. It is the way good parents exercise power over their children, the way good teachers exercise power over their students. All the requisite elements of power are present. Both parents and teachers must get others to do things, must control and channel behavior, and must influence and even change ideas and attitudes. Their power, though, emanates from love and concern, rather than from terror and fear. They are unlike Angelo in that they are influenced by their emotions as well as their minds, and they build community rather than taking a position that is superior to others. The best authority is an invitation to community.[11]

Do we have any film images that look like this? I think we do, but most of them come not from films about business but from films about teaching. Teachers, unlike business leaders, have a cultural narrative of power that actually empowers the other. In a scene from *Mr. Holland's Opus*, Mr. Holland (Richard Dreyfus) empowers a shy and insecure student, one who later becomes governor of the state. Mr. Holland has an "organization," his orchestra, and he could more easily exclude this untalented clarinetist. Instead, he helps her get in touch with her own emotions in a profound way—"play the sunset"—to give her power over her own talent.

In a business setting, we do have images of this sort. In *Wall Street*, Hal Holbrook, in a minor role, plays a boss who sees what he and his workers do as part of a larger project; they are all part of a community. Finally, *Disclosure* is not so much about sexual harassment (despite a powerful advertising campaign that tried to convince us it was), but about two models of power: that of Meredith Johnson and that of her counterpart, Stephanie Kaplan (Rosemary Forsyth). In the final scene of *Disclosure*, we are shown what qualities we should seek in a person to whom we delegate power. In earlier scenes we have discovered that Stephanie is a devoted mother; she is spending time at the Seattle operation because her son is a freshman at the University of Washington. Before giving her acceptance speech, she hugs her son who is by her side. Her first words—a sharp contrast from Meredith's—thank others, the department heads, the very people Meredith explicitly neglected to mention in her analytical acceptance speech. She introduces all the department heads, empowering them and indicating immediately that they will keep their jobs; she does not need fear to keep things in line. The camera cuts back and forth from Stephanie to her son and the next words we hear clearly from Stephanie are, "We all work so well together; it's exciting." Herein lies her passion—working with others. Michael Douglas says to her son, "Your mother's an extraordinary woman." In her defining moment, Stephanie is shown as mother, as parent, as one who empowers through nurture. The film's final scene shows us what Michael Douglas has learned—a screen image of an E-mail from his daughter, signed "A Family." He has a chance to become like Stephanie.

NOTES

1. Lord Acton, letter to Bishop Mandell Creighton, April 3, 1887. I have given the familiar, slightly misquoted version; his actual words were, "Power tends to corrupt and absolute power corrupts absolutely."

2. Warren G. Bennis, *Changing Organizations* (New York: McGraw-Hill, 1966).

3. Gilbert W. Fairholm, *Organizational Power Politics: Factors in Organizational Leadership* (Westport, Conn.: Praeger, 1993), 13.

4. David C. McClelland, *Power: The Inner Experience* (New York: Irvington, 1975), 3.

5. See, *The Will to Power: An Attempted Transvaluation of All Values*, vol. 2 (London: Russell and Russell, 1964), 161ff. Nietzsche defines power as meaning self-overcoming; the antisocial uses of power come as people experience powerlessness, the antithesis of self-overcoming power. Thus, power used to dominate others is an expression not of self-overcoming power but its absence.

6. Antonio R. Damasio, *Descartes' Error: Emotion, Reason, and the Human Brain* (New York: Putnam, 1994). Damasio "propose[s] that reason may not be as pure as most of us think or wish it were, that emotions and feelings may not be intruders in the bastion of reason at all; they may be enmeshed in its networks, for worse *and* for better" (p. xii). Damasio, a neurobiologist, suggests that the absence of emotion and feeling in the reasoning process can be as damaging as an overabundance of it.

7. I borrow this term from the psychologist C. G. Jung. In Jungian psychology the shadow is defined as the "personification of certain aspects of the unconscious personality. . . . [T]he dark, unlived, and repressed side of the ego complex." In M. L. von Franz, *Shadow and Evil in Fairytales* (Zurich: Spring Publications, 1974), 5.

8. Charles M. Kelly, *The Destructive Achiever: Power and Ethics in the American Corporation* (Reading, Mass.: Addison-Wesley, 1988), 151.

9. McClelland, *Power*, 102ff.

10. Carol Gilligan, *In a Different Voice: Psychological Theory and Women's Development* (Cambridge, Mass.: Harvard University Press, 1982), 168.

11. James Boyd White, *Acts of Hope: Creating Authority in Literature, Law and Politics* (Chicago: University of Chicago Press, 1994).

7

STORIES OF LEGAL ORDER IN AMERICAN BUSINESS

— ☉ —

THOMAS L. SHAFFER

My interest here is in stories about business people and their lawyers—stories that show the social, economic, and legal order introduced by lawyers to the conduct of business. I also hope, as I go along, to appreciate the art of the people who tell such stories, especially writers of American lawyer fiction and modern American investigative reporters who, as we know from *All the President's Men*, are the minstrels, muckrakers, and court jesters of the late twentieth century.

Barbarians at the Gate is an example of the art. That story appears first in a book written by two dogged, insightful reporters, Bryan Burrough and John Helyar. Then it becomes a movie. Both the reporters' story and the movie are like and unlike a Wall Street lawyer story told by Louis Auchincloss. The reporters' story is like and unlike the movie. The storyteller's art and the filmmaker's art complement one another. If you love stories as much as I do, you will agree with me that Ross Johnson looks like James Garner. He is Rockford at the country club. It is as true to say that as it is to say that Atticus Finch looks like Gregory Peck. Images are that powerful, even if, in both cases, a Hoosier academic wants to go back to the written account to find out whether the actors got it right.

I suggest, on the main agenda, that stories of American business and its lawyers differ according to the sorts of order lawyers bring to business. Consider three possibilities:

1. Lawyers over business
2. Lawyers against lawyers' order
3. Lawyers serving business order

The first order that lawyers bring is, as Toqueville noticed, a manifestation of American civil religion. American lawyers are the priests in what Thomas Jefferson called "God's new Israel." David Hoffman, father of American legal ethics, told his law students they were called "to vindicate the laws of God and man," to be "ministers at the altars of justice."

This first legal order in business is thus a patriotic display. Before the plumbing-industry antitrust cases came to court, management at the Kohler Company—long identified with union-busting conservative rectitude in Wisconsin—imposed an "anti-fraternization" rule. Those managers were characterized by Allan T. Demaree, writing in *Fortune*, as "tough and puritanically independent" when they forbade employees to have casual drinks with employees of competitors. The mood Mr. Demaree was after in his story is that, in Sheboygan, the Sherman Antitrust Act is to business what standing for the Star Spangled Banner is to basketball teams.

Louis Auchincloss made fun of this sort of rectitude in his lawyer-character Abel Donner and his arrogant business client Simeon Thorne (of *Fellow Passengers*), with regard to the "jurats" of notaries public, the two or three lines of archaic symbolism that are at the end of legal documents. Mr. Donner would not allow the notary to fill in those blanks under Mr. Thorne's signature if Mr. Thorne was not present. He required Mr. Thorne to come to the law office, to be present for the notary, even though that cost Mr. Thorne a trip to Wall Street and a lost day at the race track. Mr. Thorne found Mr. Donner scrupulous and oppressive. He threatened to hire a different law firm, but Mr. Donner did not seem to hear him: "Mr. Donner . . . took not the slightest notice of his client's grumbling or of his impatient gestures, simply explaining points of law to him in his dry monotone and pointing out the places where Thorne was to sign," as the notary looked on. "A thing to [Mr. Donner] is either right or wrong, and there's no decision to be made about it! He's like an early Christian, before they started squabbling about the coexistence of the Trinity."

Mr. Donner's partner, Dan Ruggles, said of Mr. Donner: "I could not make out that he believed in anything but the application of the brace of law to the support of a fleshy boneless society that without it would have flowed idly over the ground like some viscous liquid."

Reflecting on her or his stories on the electrical industry price-fixing cases, *Fortune's* editorial writer said: "Business has become so complex that many of its ramifications have got beyond the understanding of our moral instructors, the clergy, and the moral understanding of businessmen themselves. There is a 'gray' area where there are no written rules of conduct."

A first-order business lawyer would say that the editorial writer missed the point: The problem those managers got into started when they began ignoring their lawyers. Lawyers are the clergy of the first legal order.

The second legal order I am looking for in these stories is oblique and subversive, as if the business and its lawyers were doing what teenagers do, or the mental patients who gave Erving Goffman his theory of secondary adjustment.[1] In the electrical equipment price-fixing case, the president of Allen-Bradley Company, a more flexible Wisconsin business than Kohler, said that fixing prices "is the only way a business can be run. It is free enterprise."

The second order is not anarchic, although, like the spirit of teenagers, it has a taste for rebellion. One of Auchincloss's antitrust trial lawyers thus rebelliously complained about the way the government proves price-fixing: "Will you deny, . . . that there's something radically wrong with a system that requires a defendant to prove himself a son of a bitch to beat a criminal indictment?" His moral distaste was implemented judicially in the plumbing industry price-fixing case, when the conspirator who informed on the others ended up with the heaviest sentence.

The second order *is* an order. It does not aspire to chaos. Sometimes it is what the theologian Walter Brueggemann calls "prophetic destabilization." It even brings to mind the fact that America's rebellion against Britain was devised by lawyers.[2] It is a legal order—as much as any other legal order. In the electrical-equipment cases, a manager at General Electric conceded that bid rigging violates the antitrust statutes. "But it wasn't . . . any more unethical than if the companies had a summit conference the way Russia and the West meet. Those competitor meetings were just attended by a group of distressed individuals who wanted to know where they were going." That business manager made a moral argument that, to a second-order lawyer, would suggest a legal defense: It is not illegal for competitors to meet in trade association and professional organizations to discuss economic trends and conditions for doing business. If the government is to sustain a price-fixing case, it has to prove more than that the competitors had a meeting.

Thomas Osgoode, corporate chief executive officer, wrote a letter to the editor about the first-order *Fortune* editorial I quoted: "Certainly, laws were violated. But it is now fair to ask whether the Sherman Antitrust Act is applicable to our present-day economy any more than the prohibition of liquor was in the late 1920s. It is my contention that the Sherman Antitrust Act is a cosmetic law that no longer applies or works in our present international competitive economy. . . . There is no such thing as reasonable competition under such circumstances, and the Sherman Act is about as useful as a balloon with a hole in it." Mr. Osgoode's is as an argument for legislators, as it is also an argument to regulators who vary widely, from administration to administration, in their zeal for enforcing the antitrust laws. It is about what the law should be.

Second-order lawyers and their clients make an analogous move when they make common cause with the bureaucrats who are supposed to make rules for business, that is, when they create or exploit a version of what President Eisenhower called the military-industrial complex. For example: At one point in the plumbing industry price-fixing case, those who were commissioned to sell bathtubs noticed that much of their competitive pressure came from low-priced tubs covered with ordinary enamel, rather than from more expensive tubs covered with acid-resistant enamel. They and their lawyers devised an overture to the Department of Commerce, aimed at a new commercial standard that would require acid-resistant enamel for all tubs.

The third legal order in business rises out of, celebrates, and highlights what is distinct in a particular business culture. Third-order lawyers are sometimes like Amos and Micah, who show up in Israel and remind Israel of its memory and its commitment. They are sometimes like Clement Ludlow, one of Auchincloss's New York lawyers: "His whole life . . . had been premised on his ability to get on with people, to hear their problems, to find *their solutions*, to assist them by the very impersonality of his sympathy, by acting as a calm voice from the dark silence of the confessional box" (emphasis added).

Jeff Furman, lawyer and accountant, was for years both priest and prophet in the hippie-entrepreneur business culture of Ben and Jerry's Homemade Ice Cream. Like the Hebrew Prophets, Mr. Furman did not create the culture; he saw it and proclaimed it; he expressed it in legal order. From time to time, he reminded his clients of how they had set out to do business: He devised Ben and Jerry's business-charity partnerships; he came up with the five-to-one salary ratio between managers and the people who put the ice cream in the pint cartons; he negotiated with the rock musician a flavor called Cherry Garcia.

Mr. Furman drafted the offering circular for Ben and Jerry's first effort to raise investment capital. A person needs to pause over the memory of the lyrics in a typical stock prospectus to appreciate what Mr. Furman brought to that otherwise solemn liturgical moment in the early history of a company. The last page of the circular gave the prospect five boxes to check:

____ Yes, Ben, I don't have anything better to do with my money. . . .
____ Sorry, Ben, if I had it I'd do it, but I don't so I won't.

___ You've got to be kidding.
___ I've got some questions. . . .
___ Other: _____

These three legal orders represent the hope for a peripheral awareness of the fact that we are in the hands of storytellers who tell their hearers about themselves as they tell stories about lawyers and businesses. Allow me, in closing an introduction to this little adventure, to offer a bit of prepositional simplification:

The three orders I am talking about can be labelled as (1) lawyer power *over* order—imposing order on business; (2) lawyer power *against* order—resisting order imposed on business; and (3) lawyer power *with* order—discerning and then serving the order in business.

Think of Toqueville's picture of America in the 1820s, and of early nineteenth century American gentleman-lawyers—Daniel Webster, Joseph Story, David Hoffman. They were, Toqueville said, our only aristocrats; they represent the first order, law *over* order.

Think of the civil-rights lawyers of the 1960s, who were said to practice "law *against* order" (Charles Morgan's phrase), as representing the second order.

Louis Highmark, a corporate lawyer under whom I once practiced, represents the third. Mr. Highmark would listen to what his business client had in mind, and then say: "That's a *good* idea. There has to be some way we can do it."[3]

LAWYERS OVER BUSINESS

Lawyers who bring civil rectitude to business are, in some ways and when they are at their best, like the rabbis of the Talmud, who devised a legal order for Jews in the Diaspora—a detailed, ponderable, complex legal order that was developed as if scattered, stricken Israel were still prospering in the Promised Land. Lawyers of the first legal order, like the rabbis, claim authority and impose sanction. Their authority is maintained with presence, like one of Agatha Christie's family solicitors who reads the will after the funeral. (Lawyers as the presence of order are more interesting in serious English lawyer fiction. It is a striking thing, for example, that Lewis Eliot, the central character in C. P. Snow's ten-novel *Strangers and Brothers* series, written by a physicist become bureaucrat, is a lawyer.)

The dean of Wall Street takeover lawyers, Joseph Flom, said that the lawyer in Wall Street deal-making is the presence of *credibility*. Mr. Flom might add something about etiquette, which is critical in the provincial business law he and his partners practice (as *Barbarians at the Gate* demonstrates). He might repeat a passing remark he made, on the importance of excluding bad actors from Wall Street: He would advise corporate managers not to talk to "outlaws." T. Boone Pickens and Sir James Goldsmith were present to hear that.

American lawyers tend to admire and even copy the style of English lawyers, but American business lawyers are not like English business lawyers. We Americans do not have a dynastic aristocracy to protect our class system. We have lawyers for *noblesse oblige*; that was Toqueville's point. Auchincloss's Oscar Fairfax said of his lawyer-father, who wrote a history of his law firm, that "a reader might have wondered whether [those lawyers] had not been working as much for the public good as for the interests of their clients. It was certain, anyway, that Father equated the two." Another difference is that American lawyers have practiced a level of personal involvement with their clients that would be improper for, say, Mr. Rumpole of the Old Bailey. In the United States the two things—priestly service in the temples of American civil religion and attention to the interests of clients as lawyers understand them—go together.

The danger for those who practice law in this first order is power. Lawyers impose with power—and power corrupts. The danger sometimes shows up as arrogance, and sometimes as self-deception without arrogance, as in the law-firm history written by Oscar Fairfax's father, where the American gentleman-lawyer identifies self-interest with community interest. Examples abound in lawyer professionalism and in the price-fixing stories told by investigative journalists. Judge J. Cullen Ganey sentenced business managers to prison in the electrical-industry case and then made them a captive audience for a homily on American civil religion. He sounded like a twelfth-century bishop pronouncing excommunication by striking the floor with the lighted end of his candle: "This is a shocking indictment of a vast section of our economy, for what is really at stake here is the survival of the kind of economy under which this country has grown great, the free-enterprise system." Robert A. Bicks, who prosecuted those defendants, was an acolyte for the ceremony. "These men and companies have in a true sense shocked the image of that economic system which we profess to the world," he said.

Lawyer arrogance in the first order becomes what the Marxists came to identify as hegemony. There was touching evidence of this in the testimony of Ralph Cordiner, CEO of General Electric and cabinet secretary in the Eisenhower administration, before Senator Kefauver's subcommittee, after the judge sent several of Mr. Cordiner's colleagues to jail—touching because Mr. Cordiner was a true believer in the first legal order and had suffered because of the second-legal-order impudence of his subordinates.

Mr. Cordiner and his lawyers had imposed stern antitrust guidelines on their decentralized conglomerate corporate business, as they also and at the same time sent down severe, single-minded demands for increased profits. The issue, Mr. Cordiner told the senators, was what Aristotle would have called formation: "Unless you can get a deep conviction of individuals through teaching, through exposure that this is the proper thing to do, and that they will never meet with their competitors or talk to their competitors or do anything that is contrary to law . . . I don't know how you get it."[4]

The executive editor of *Industry Week*, meditating on the electrical cases, was not so docile. He said, "[T]he essence of good management is concern for the stockholders, customers, and employees. Unfortunately, however, there is another group, another force, that has moved up front in more and more managerial minds in recent years—especially in the U.S. That group is lawyers, and that force is the law." Some of what the editor complained about has to do with expertise, with "professional" access by lawyers to mysteries not available to mere managers. In Arthur Miller's play *A View from the Bridge*, Marco defends himself against the stern judgment of his lawyer, Mr. Alfieri, and says, "All the law is not in a book." "Yes," Mr. Alfieri says, "in a book. There is no other law." But the power I am talking about here is more than a matter of access to secrets. Toqueville was right: It is an aristocracy. As my colleague Teresa Godwin Phelps demonstrates in chapter 6 of this volume, the moral question is not whether one has power; it is what one does with the power one has.

LAWYERS AGAINST LAWYERS' ORDER

Practitioners of lawyer power *against* order understand that law is power in the United States, and most of them believe that law is politics. In the price-fixing stories, sales managers, caught between demands for profits from the higher echelons of their decentralized corporations, and a self-righteous, first-order prohibition against talking to competitors, needed lawyer power against order. Sometimes the sales managers apparently ignored their companies' lawyers and responded, as Goffman would have predicted, with communal systems of adjustment and defiance; however, like the civil-rights lawyers, sometimes they responded with the law.

An example is the uncertain and halting attempt to educate judges on the realities of doing business. Aron, Moulton and Owens, left-wing critics of the project, say that "corporate contributors and business-friendly funders in a handful of foundations [have] invested billions of dollars in a multi-faceted, comprehensive and integrated campaign to mold a new American jurisprudence that favors protecting and enhancing corporate and private gain over preserving social justice and individual rights." The campaign is said to have eliminated much federal regulation of business, to have persuaded academics to do "research" on free enterprise, and to be the source of conservative public-interest think tanks and law firms.

Direct, defiant subversion of the first legal order may not be more successful, but it is more interesting. Sometimes the salespeople who were caught up in the price-fixing conspiracies come across like Hebrew prophets railing at priestly power. These business people pointed to the truth of what was going on when corporate rulers virtually ordered their subordinates to fix prices as they righteously promulgated memoranda full of antitrust morality. An interesting example is the evidence in the electrical-industry case that the price fixers saw no need to tell their bosses that they were making anticompetitive deals—because their bosses *knew*. But they warned their co-conspirators *not to let the lawyers know*. I think of my Southern Baptist grandmother snuffing out her cigarette and fanning the air in our living room with both hands when she heard the minister coming up the front walk.[5]

Among many second-order episodes at Ben and Jerry's Homemade one of the most vivid came in their early days, when they got into a losing legal battle with a broker over a failed attempt to merge their company with the maker of M&Ms—Mars. Lawyers for the broker twice attempted to seize Ben and Jerry's money. Ben and Jerry moved their funds from bank to bank in Vermont and, as the plaintiff's lawyers came closer, finally withdrew all their funds and took them in a sack to Jeff Furman's bedroom in Ithaca, New York. I suppose they ultimately paid the judgment against them, but at the time their lawyer figured out a way to preserve their cash flow.

The principal danger in a second legal order in business is that it is weak, vulnerable to defection, subject at every moment to breakdown. The bathtub sales managers succeeded in getting the product protection they wanted from the Commerce Department, but their deal with the government turned out to be not deep enough to eliminate destructive competition. They did not proceed to sell expensive, acid-resistant bathtubs according to the criteria of free enterprise under the Sherman Act; they met and fixed prices anyway—"higher ones on the average," according to Mr. Demaree's account, "to be announced almost simultaneously with the switch to acid-resistant enamel." That conspiracy fell apart, as such arrangements often do, when one of the conspirators defected and became an informer to the government.[6]

LAWYERS SERVING BUSINESS ORDER: *BARBARIANS* AS A QUIZZICAL CASE

I suspect Jeff Furman designed Ben and Jerry's 1992 annual report to shareholders. The report has a section, unusual for that sort of art form, devoted to what the company called its "social assessment." The calculus for measuring progress in the company's social mission is a drawing of the device you see at county fairs, where strong people strike a pad with a sledge hammer and try to make a puck hit the bell at the top. If the hammerer (the company) is not doing well, the puck rises to a section marked "bottom feeder." As the hammerer does better, the puck moves up to sections marked "Scrooge," "regular Joe," "June Cleaver," "sainthood," and, finally (the bell) "Mother Theresa."

The statements themselves are orthodox, but they are accompanied by a running cartoon strip in which a cartoon character who looks like a cross between Tinkerbell and Wonder Woman urges the reader along and explains what the numbers mean: "Here's the test," she says. "Flip through the financial statements . . . & take a hard look at them. Read the management's discussion & analysis & the footnotes. Go ahead—You can do it. Then think of the questions you want to ask. Call or write our investor relations staff. See if you can stump 'em. I dare you."

When I returned to *Barbarians at the Gate,* Burrough's and Helyar's splendid story on the R.J.R.-Nabisco leveraged buy-out (LBO), and remembered my own experience with some of the same Wall Street lawyers and bankers, I hoped to find an example of third-order business lawyering to compare with Mr. Furman's. I think the comparison can be made. But, finally, *Barbarians* presents a quizzical case—not quite what I had hoped for but, for all of that, instructive, and instructive in a way I had not expected to find in that story.

A Hoosier academic reads *Barbarians* as if it were an episode from *Star Trek.* The props are faintly familiar, but the story could never happen in Indiana. It does, though, involve some impressive business lawyering, and if even a Hoosier academic is to theorize on business lawyering, he has to take *Barbarians* into account.

The first thing to notice is that *Barbarians* occurs in an insular, provincial business and legal culture. The oligarchy in this business culture—which has no counterpart in Indiana—calls itself "The Group." The Group invents and presides over virtually all large financial reorganizations of American business. Members of the Group are not primarily differentiated by conventional function, nor by role, nor by profession. They do what they do as if they were actors in a repertory company: One of their number is today Lady Macbeth, tomorrow Desdemona, and next week will be pulling the rope to raise the curtain.

What holds the Group together—as in "the play's the thing"—is skilled attention to the transaction at hand and a remarkable level of mutual trust. Their term for the transaction at hand is "The Deal," often (as in *Barbarians*) the conversion of a publicly held corporation into a private business.[7]

Members of the Group observe high standards of competence which is measured by success in deals, which is measured by income from deals for themselves and their clients. The Group shows only formal concern for regulation from a formal, law-school, legal account of business entities: They do not rebel against it; they adapt to it.[8] Except in a ritualistic and occasionally public way, what law students learn about corporate finance does not reveal much about the Group, and members of the Group do not reveal much about themselves.

The operative order of the Group rises out of its theatrical culture, which has reduced its implicit morality to limits that are virtually regulatory, to etiquette,[9] and to routine. The legal order excludes from the stage those whom Mr. Flom calls outlaws, and keeps at bay all from the government or the left who would otherwise intrude upon its performance.

There comes a time, of course, when lawyers emerge from the Group to be lawyers. With that development in the drama—in the R.J.R.-Nabisco case it was the auction of the company in response to competing bidders—comes the manifestation of a distinctly legal order. In *Barbarians*, the law was announced, presided over, and at critical points dictated by the lawyer for the board of directors, Mr. Flom's partner Peter Atkins who was like the good witch in The *Wizard of Oz*. The legal order he manifested was derivative not from formal legal principles and rules but from the sacred importance of the Deal. These lawyers are faithful less to the interests of their clients than to the Group's *understanding* of clients' interests (and so, as a third-order story, *Barbarians* is quizzical). They manifest their power by successful control of the galloping egos of corporate managers who are both their subjects and their audience; but, given that qualification, the law here could be third-order law.

Derivative Legal Order

In *Barbarians*, Ross Johnson's emotions got the Deal started. He wanted to make more money, of course, but he also wanted his company to be among the giants of industry—"to be the hero of a Harvard Business School study." He resented the disdain visited on the tobacco industry, the low public price of its stock, and the possibility that he would lose his position and his power in a hostile takeover. Possibly more than anything else, he wanted to be a player in the largest deal in Wall Street history. That is, I think, typical of the way a company comes to turn its fate over to the Group.[10] Once the initial step is taken, though, the client's emotions become irrelevant and the manager who thought to be a player finds himself in the audience. The task of the legal order is to keep emotions—anyone's emotions—from threatening the Deal, as repertory actors could not bear an outburst from someone offstage. "Johnson's problem was that he insisted on thinking in terms of the real world, real money, real investments," a lawyer member of the Group said. "This wasn't the real world. This was Wall Street."

An example was the auction in *Barbarians*. The stage set for the third act of the drama was a conference room in Mr. Atkins's law office: Bids were sent in; requests for information were denied; bidders waited in waiting rooms—the eminent and powerful Henry Kravis and his advisors for two days at one point—and directives were dispatched. Early in the play Mr. Atkins set a deadline for bids; in the third act, he moved the deadline, then moved it again, as he interpreted and reinterpreted what "deadline" meant. As a result, the Shearson Lehman team was denied an opportunity to revise its bid. Its lawyer and Mr. Atkins argued in the hall. After the Kravis team prevailed in the auction, there was talk of litigation, but nothing came of it. Nothing came of it because nobody outside the Group had law from a law book for deciding the deadline question. There came to be law for that, but it was third-order law. Mr. Atkins discerned it, announced it, and imposed it. The Group accepted it and, I suspect, the Group treats it now as useful legal precedent.

Clients' Interests

The culture of the Group says that the Deal, like a drama, runs in only one direction. It cannot be reversed or, if that should happen, it will be a business and professional and aesthetic failure as if a play were canceled halfway through the second act. Lawyers in this legal order are as eloquent in their faithfulness to the interests of their clients as any lawyers are, but their faith is a faith that says that clients want the Deal as much as the Group does. There are several points in the *Barbarians* story at which Mr. Johnson would have given up, but neither his lawyers nor anyone else in the Group paid any attention to that possibility, and he did not give up. When he tried to act on his own, his lawyer brought him back to the Deal. When his behavior toward the board of directors threatened the Deal, Mr. Atkins told Mr. Johnson's lawyer to speak to Mr. Johnson—and the lawyer did as he was told to do. At the end of the story Mr. Johnson merely lost.

Ego

If it were possible, in these "financial restructuring" cases, to think of *the Deal as the client,* the conduct of lawyers such as Messrs. Flom and Atkins would be as clear an example of third-order business lawyering as is Mr. Furman's work for Ben and Jerry's. I suggest that the splendidly told tale in *Barbarians* on what third-order lawyering is like is instructive when that assumption is made.

With that assumption—that the Deal is the client—the law that orders the transaction is, as the Atkins-made law on bidding deadlines was, third-order law discerned and imposed by lawyers who understand the purposes and commitments of their client. The law that is in the books—first-order law—is not as important as factual circumstances that threaten the Deal. Among these circumstances (on the account in *Barbarians*) nothing is more threatening than the egos of the business barons who have employed lawyers to obtain ownership and control for them.[11] What has to be pondered, from beginning to end, is not so much "the law" (in a first-order sense, as in the price-fixing cases) as the human clients' continued adherence to the Deal. When the Deal is the client, these lawyers are third-order lawyers operating under third-order law.

The prologue to an LBO, before managers and directors take themselves to New York City, is the formal separation of management from the control of the business. This is an awesome moment, particularly so in a company such as R.J.R.- Nabisco was, where the ruling position in the company, the position of chief executive officer, is a barony and, until the moment of LBO divorce comes, the board of directors is an aggregation of subbarons who were chosen and commissioned by the chief executive officer.

The opening scene in *Barbarians* is the visit of Steve Goldstone, come from his law office in New York, where he is a trusted member of the Group, to Mr. Johnson's corporate headquarters in North Carolina. The next scene, also in North Carolina, is the ritual expulsion of management from the board, as the board takes control of the company. Burroughs and Helyar pay particular attention to this second scene because, on their account, the Group regarded Mr. Atkins's neglect of it, in another case, as an episode in which first-order law threatened the Group's third-order law.[12] It illustrates, on the present point, the second of two initial steps through which lawyers from the Group take early control of managerial ego.

Repeatedly, then, throughout the story, lawyers from the Group (whose client, I am assuming, is the Deal) have to discipline their (human) clients, to prevent managerial ego from interfering with the progress of the drama. The *denouement* in *Barbarians* is an almost comic example (as Burrough and Helyar tell it), an episode that illustrates the difference between a business lawyer who represents her clients' interests and a business lawyer who represents what she supposes her clients' interests to be. It is that difference that makes *Barbarians*, as a business-lawyer story, quizzical.

Mr. Johnson and a small group of managerial allies began by offering to buy the company from the shareholders. That required those offering to make the purchase relinquish control of the company to the remaining members of the board of directors. From the middle of the drama, and thence to its climax, the controlling board members entertained other bids to purchase the company from the shareholders. One of those other bids was ultimately successful, when the board accepted Mr. Kravis's bid and rejected Mr. Johnson's.

What remained was a momentary, ultimate reunification of the board of directors, the return of the unsuccessful management bidders, and particularly the return of Mr. Johnson as chairman of the board. The business of that meeting was formal approval of the corporate merger that followed from Mr. Kravis's success. The board which, of course, been meeting and acting without Mr. Johnson, understood the difference between the two kinds of board meetings and asked its lawyer, Mr. Atkins, whether Mr. Johnson was to be invited to take his once and never-more-to-be place at the table. I suppose what the question really meant was whether Mr. Atkins could think of any way to keep Mr. Johnson from attending the meeting. Mr. Atkins, at that point not about to allow a first-order ritualistic requirement to interfere with the Deal, consulted his trial-lawyer partners while the board waited for an answer. No doubt these trial lawyers told Mr. Atkins that Mr. Johnson had a "right" to be present.

But Mr. Atkins came up with a third-order alternative: He quietly asked Mr. Johnson whether he planned to come—a routine question for a host (the meeting was in Mr. Atkins's office) who might as well have been asking whether Mr. Johnson wanted cream for his coffee that morning. Mr. Johnson said he "did not plan to come. No one bothered to ask Johnson whether he *wanted* to attend his final board meeting" (emphasis added). No one talked to him about his rights.[13]

NOTES

1. Goffman: A secondary adjustment is "any habitual arrangement by which a member of an organization employs unauthorized means, or obtains unauthorized ends, or both, thus getting around the organization's assumptions as to what he should do and get and hence what he should be. Secondary adjustments represent ways in which the individual stands apart from the role and the self that were taken for granted for him by the institution" (189). That is a first-legal-order understanding of Goffman's insight. He notes, though, that there are difficulties in using the concept as he defines it, which difficulties demonstrate a second-order way for understanding secondary adjustment. For example: "There are some secondary adjustments, such as a worker's practice of supplying his family's needs for the product he helps produce, that become so much an accepted part of the workings of an organization that they take on the character of 'perquisites,' combining the qualities of being neither openly demanded nor openly questioned. And some of these activities . . . must remain unofficial if they are to be effective" (191). He cites and quotes Melville Dalton: "Although informal reward ideally is given for effort and contribution beyond what is expected . . . it is also granted for many other purposes, often . . . formally taboo yet important for maintaining the organization and winning its ends. For example, it may be given . . . for understanding and aid in the operation, and the defense, of the unofficial incentive system. . . . There are, of course, more subtle supports which may not be articulated but are intuitively recognized and rewarded where possible. These include . . . habitual tacit understanding of what superiors and colleagues expect but would not in some cases want to phrase, even unofficially; and expertness in saving the face of superiors and maintaining the dignity of the organization under adverse conditions."

2. A desire for order is compatible with secondary adjustment and may even be a necessary condition, as Lawrence Sanders's unconventional, moderately lawless business detective, Timothy Cone, says when his associate Joe Washington asks him if he believes in the rules: "Sure, I believe in the rules. If you don't, then you've got no game at all. It's just a mess. I spent three years of my life with no rules [in Viet Nam], and I didn't like it."

3. I learned from my teacher Robert E. Rodes, Jr., that the anthropology in a business enterprise—and therefore of corporate law—is what the jurisprude Otto von Gierke called *gesamtwille*, togetherness. That, I think, is what Mr. Highmark, in his business practice, sought to discern as moral order, and then to serve. Professor Rodes, as his later scholarship demonstrates, did not understand this communal an-

thropology to be something lawyers merely serve; corporate lawyers also influence and persuade the business communities they (as we lawyers put it) "represent": "The burdens of poverty are fashioned in the Wall Street offices faster and more effectively than the legal services and public interest offices can lift them. If you spend the day on corporate takeovers and plant closings without thinking about the people you put out of work, you cannot make up for the harm you do by giving a woman free legal advice when her unemployed husband takes out his frustrations by beating her" (in our *Dayton Law Review* piece). What a corporate lawyer "represents" and what might justify reference to the prophets, is the memory and commitment that is also present in what Gierke sought to identify, more as collective will then as the morality I infer from it.

4. Aestheticism is another of the dangers of self-deception and arrogance, especially among lawyers presiding over this first legal order. An example is an often naive attraction to the style and high artistic taste of wealthy clients, especially, in Auchincloss's stories, of clients in New York who have "old money." His story "The Fabbri Tape" tells of the Faustian self-destruction of the son of Italian immigrants who became an Episcopalian, joined the country club, and practiced first-order corporate law. Oscar Fairfax, in another Auchincloss story, says toward the end of his life: "I have latterly come to the conclusion that I have placed too great an emphasis on the dramatic aspects of dramatically interesting people. It is all very well to prefer good art to bad, but people are people."

5. The lawyers who are not to know are, of course, the first-order lawyers. However, in that the second order *is* an order, and a legal order, in some sense it has its own lawyers, who (a) use the pressure put on sales managers as a legal defense or mitigation; (b) fashion political, legislative, and administrative arguments against maintaining and enforcing the antitrust laws, and (c) make common cause with regulators in removing or lessening the effects of competition.

6. My son, Professor Brian C. Shaffer, argues that this is a legitimate use of business influence in politics.

7. The transaction is the change in ownership of the business, rather than any specific proposal for arranging and financing the change. The drama in Burrough's and Helyar's story is built on the fact that the R.J.R.-Nabisco deal started as a leveraged buy-out (LBO), proceeded, through five or six competing proposals, and ended as an auction followed by a friendly takeover.

8. Example: Richard Beattie, lawyer for Henry Kravis's bidding team, wrote a letter to Peter Atkins, lawyer for the R.J.R.-Nabisco board of directors, complaining that the board had given Mr. Kravis inaccurate information. Mr. Atkins was offended, not at the accusation, but because Mr. Beattie wrote a letter when he should have made a telephone call. Mr. Atkins was afraid that "Beattie's protest would be a black mark on the auction's otherwise spotless record" (*Barbarians*, 411)—and, no doubt, that the letter would be available for first-order legal business.

9. Members of the Group are careful to promptly return one another's phone calls, understand and observe arcane standards of personal conduct, and hasten to apologize when the standards are violated.

10. I confess to some small personal experience. I was chairman of the special committee of the board of directors, and senior member of the board, in the Fort Howard Corporation LBO in 1988. Burrough and Helyar discuss the Fort Howard case briefly: Mr. Atkins was our lawyer; James Maher and his First Boston team (prominent in *Barbarians*) were our investment bankers.

11. I suppose I mean *male* ego. Linda Robinson, publicist for one of the contenders, speaks thus of "an intensely competitive clique of macho, Park Avenue bullies in pinstripes" (*Barbarians*, 311). Michael Lewis says, "Wall Street . . . corporate finance is still a jungle full of chest-pounding males" (*Liar's Poker*, 19).

12. This was in the Fort Howard case. Burrough and Helyar, and one judge in Delaware, believe that the CEO and principal figure in the buyout was the person who chose Mr. Atkins to be the board's lawyer, apparently because Mr. Atkins had done other legal work for the corporation (*Barbarians*, 181–82). This would have been improper and would even have suggested that Mr. Atkins then pursued the CEO's agenda as the lawyer for the board. But I was there, and I deny it. The storytellers report the Delaware judge's criticism of Mr. Atkins; the judge was, I think, performing a first-order judicial ritual. He is as aware as anybody of the way the Group works—that it is a repertory company—and of the fact that members of the Group change places every day. As an investment banker said to me, "It's not having a conflict of interest that's the [moral] problem; it's what you do with it." In any event, the judge (of course) ended up supporting the Deal.

13. I am grateful for the assistance and encouragement of the late Professor John W. Houck, an old and valued friend. I also had good help from Matthew J. Barrett, Linda Harrington, Dwight B. King, Jr., Carmela Kinslow, Kathleen Ley, Robert E. Rodes, Jr., Elizabeth R. Schiltz, Brian C. Shaffer, and Nancy J. Shaffer.

BIBLIOGRAPHY

Aron, Nan, Barbara Moulton, and Chris Owens. "Economics, Academia, and Corporate Money: Justice for Sale in America." *Antitrust Law and Economics Review* 1992–93, 17.

Auchincloss, Louis. *Diary of a Yuppie* (for Mr. Blakelock). New York: Garland, 1996.

———. *The Education of Oscar Fairfax*. New York: Houghton Mifflin, 1995.

———. *Fellow Passengers: A Novel in Portraits* (for Dan Ruggles, Clement Ludlow, and Abel Donner). Boston: Houghton Mifflin Company, 1989.

———. *Powers of Attorney* (for antitrust lawyer). (1963; New York: Avon, 1971).

———. *The Great World and Timothy Colt*. Boston: Houghton Mifflin, 1956.

Ben & Jerry's Annual Report. 1992.

Bondine, Larry. "Management: Going to Sidley's Corporate College." *Legal Times,* February 5, 1996, 28.

Brueggemann, Walter. "The Prophet as a Destabilizing Presence." In *A Social Reading of the Old Testament: Prophetic Approaches to Israel's Communal Life,* Patrick D. Miller, ed. Minneapolis: Fortress Press, 1994.

Burrough, Bryan, and John Helyar. *Barbarians at the Gate: The Fall of RJR-Nabisco.* New York: Harper & Row, 1990; Harper Perennial ed., 1991.

Dalton, Melville. *Men Who Manage.* New York: Wiley, 1959.

Demaree, Allan T. "How Judgment Came for the Plumbing Conspirators." *Fortune,* December 1969, 69.

Djilas, Milovan. *The New Class.* In Mendel, *Essential Works of Marxism.*

Elon, Menachem. *The Principles of Jewish Law* (from Encyclopedia Judaica). Brooklyn: Hemed Books, n.d.

"Ethics in America: Anatomy of a Hostile Takeover." WNET (television). October 31, 1987.

Fingarette, Herbert. *Self-Deception.* London: Routledge & Kegan Paul, 1969.

Fort Howard Corporation Shareholders Litigation, 1988 Delaware Chancery 3 (Lexis 110) (August 4, 1988) (Allen, Chancellor), affirmed 547 A.2d 633 (1988).

Goffman, Erving. *Asylums: Essays on the Social Situation of Mental Patients and Other Inmates.* Garden City: Anchor Books, 1961.

Hoffman, David. "Resolutions in Regard to Professional Deportment." In vol. II, David Hoffman, *Course of Legal Study,* 2d ed. Baltimore, 1836; reprinted in Thomas L. Shaffer, *American Legal Ethics,* New York: Matthew Bender, 1985.

"How the M&A Lawyer Is Handling New Dealmaking Challenges." *Mergers and Acquisitions,* March–April, 1992, 14.

Lager, Fred "Chico." *Ben and Jerry's: The Inside Scoop.* New York: Crown, 1994.

Lewis, Michael. *Liar's Poker: Rising Through the Wreckage on Wall Street.* New York: Viking Penguin, 1990.

Marx, Karl, and Friedrich Engels. *The Communist Manifesto,* in Mendel, *Essential Works of Marxism.*

Mendel, Arthur P., ed. *Essential Works of Marxism.* New York: Bantam, 1961.

Miller, Arthur. *A View from the Bridge.* New York: Bantam, 1961.

O'Connor, Ellen S. "Discourse at Our Disposal: Stories in and around the Garbage Can." Manuscript, 1996.

Osgoode, M. Letter to the editor, *Fortune,* April 1961, 28.

Powledge, F. "Something for a Lawyer to Do" (on Charles Morgan). *The New Yorker,* October 25, 1969, 63.

"Price Fixing and Bid Rigging in the Electrical Manufacturing Industry." Hearings of the Subcommittee on Antitrust and Monopoly of the Committee on the Judiciary of the United States Senate, May–June 1961.

"The Price-Fixing Case" (editorial). *Fortune,* March 1961, 102.

Rodes, Jr., Robert E. *Law and Liberation.* Notre Dame: University of Notre Dame Press, 1986.

Sanders, Lawrence. *The Timothy Files.* New York: Berkley Books, 1988.

Shaffer, Brian C. "Firm-Level Responses to Government Regulation." *Journal of Management* 21 (1995), 495.

Shaffer, Thomas L., and Robert E. Rodes, Jr. "A Christian Theology for Roman Catholic Law Schools." *University of Dayton Law Review* 14 (1988), 5.

Smith, Richard Austin. "The Incredible Electrical Conspiracy." *Fortune,* April 1961, 132; May 1961, 161.

Stevens, Amy. "In Media Deals, Lawyers Came Before Bankers." *Wall Street Journal,* August 21, 1995, B-1: 1.

Teitelman, Robert. "Flom's Way." *Institutional Investor,* February 1994, 30.

Trillin, Calvin. "American Chronicles: Competitors" (on Ben and Jerry's Homemade). *The New Yorker,* July 8, 1985, 31.

von Gierke, Otto Friedrich. *Political Theories of the Middle Age,* Cambridge: Cambridge University Press, 1900.

Weimer, George. "Who *Really* Runs U.S. Industry?" *Industry Week,* July 6, 1992.

West, Robin. "Economic Man and Literary Woman: One Contrast." In Leonora Ledwon, ed., *Law and Literature: Text and Theory,* 127. New York: Garland, 1996.

8

MEDIUMS, MESSAGES, AND THE ECONOMIC ORDER

The Legacy of
Marshall McLuhan Reconsidered

— ⊙ —

BERNARD MURCHLAND

When I first met Marshall McLuhan in the early sixties, his star had not yet risen as far as it would rise but it was already casting a considerable light. He has been a cult figure since the publication of *The Mechanical Bride* in 1954 and was gaining a certain reputation as a media guru and social critic. But our first conversation turned neither on the mechanical bride nor on the media. I was interested in a short essay McLuhan had written as a preface to a book by Hugh Kenner on Chesterton. In it he talked about paradox, analogical perception, the connaturality of being, and the power of the artist to shape our aesthetic and moral judgments.

I was particularly interested in what he had to say about art. He told me on that occasion he has been reading a book by Herbert Read, called *Icon and Idea,* in which Read put forth the thesis that art is the essential instrument in the development of human consciousness. The image always precedes the idea; all human action derives from some imaginative source; empirical reality reflects some formative ideal. As the poet Holderin said, "Art is the inaugural meaning we give to being." Because human consciousness is aesthetically shaped in certain ways, certain cultural forms are determined.

I later realized that what McLuhan said on that occasion about paradox and the aesthetic sensibility is the key to his work, the source, for example, of the axiom that the medium is the message. McLuhan had a rare and profound analogical mind that saw things in their interrelationships. This explains why so highly trained an academic mind could glide almost effortlessly into the worlds of popular culture, technology, and commerce. I would say he is unique among modern thinkers in making connections between the aesthetic sensibility and commerce, between art and business.

The intellectual roots of McLuhan's thought are to be found in the Greek Sophists, Renaissance humanists, contemporary art, and modernist writers like Joyce, Pound, Hopkins, and Eliot. It was as a graduate student at Cambridge University from 1934 to 1936 that the foundations of his later status as a communications theorist were laid. At Cambridge, such pioneers of modern literary criticism (which came to be known as The New Criticism) as I. A. Richards, William Empson, and F. R. Leavis, taught that literature was primarily a form of communication and should be studied in terms of how voice, words, and structure combined to achieve certain effects. Words, I. A. Richards taught, had multiple meanings, various contexts, and were highly ambiguous.

These are precisely the insights McLuhan would use later in his study of the media. If poetry could be studied in terms of its effects, why not other human creations—the wheel, money, films, etc.? Why could not the study of literature, mutatis mutandis, be applied to the social environment as a whole, to the analysis of advertising, journalism, or science fiction? McLuhan was particularly intrigued by advertising, which he called the highest of modern art forms. One of McLuhan's former students summarized the Cambridge experience in these words:

> If poetry was the sum of its effects on the reader, would not the same be true of any human artifact? No longer did one have to examine a poem in terms of what it had to say, or to examine a machine in terms of what it did. Better to examine a poem as a far-reaching arrangement and clarification of impulses in the reader's head. Similarly, one could examine a machine as a far-reaching arrangement produced in the lives of its users. One did not understand a photocopier by grasping that it reproduced documents. One began to understand it when one grasped the sum of its effects, which included the destruction of government secrecy (by making it easier to leak documents) and the conversion of writers into publishers.[1]

When he returned from Cambridge, McLuhan pursued a conventional academic career, first at the University of Wisconsin then at the University of St. Louis and, finally, at the University of Toronto, where he would spend the rest of his life. But he was hardly a conventional academic. Already in his first section of freshman English at Wisconsin he broadened the syllabus to include contemporary culture as it was reflected in advertising, newspapers, and comic strips. One of his first published articles in 1944 was entitled "Dagwood's America," in which he argued that Dagwood was a generalized symbol of the emasculation of men in American society. A short time later he wrote an article on American advertising, contending that advertisers were as skilled as artists in their success at producing certain effects in the human mind. The techniques they used were similar to those of Greek rhetoricians and symbolist poets because, in both cases, a medium of communication imposed its own assumptions on reality and created its own world.

When McLuhan moved to Toronto in 1946 he came under the influence of the economic historian Harold Innis, who had written books on the Canadian fur trade, cod fisheries, and the pulp and paper industry. At this point the link between art and economics was finally forged. Innis taught McLuhan that commercial staples were technologies that were modes of communication which altered the social environment, altered the ratio among the senses and, therefore, had a significance beyond their immediate context or use. An automobile is not merely a mode of transportation; it is an extension of the human sensorium. The content of newspapers is news but its greatest impact is how it refocuses our sense of time to a concern with the immediate and fragmentary over continuity. The French symbolist poet Mallarmé, for example, noted that the way in which newspapers juxtapose news items creates a unique symbolic world.

In his later works, *Empire and Communications* and *The Bias of Communication,* Innis made a distinction between those modes of communication that were space-oriented and those that emphasized a sense of time. Cultures are shaped by the types of media that predominate in them. Thus, stone and clay tablets, by reason of their durability, imparted a sense of timelessness. Papyrus and paper, on the other hand, could disseminate knowledge over large areas but emphasized the transient and immediate rather than the durable. Time-based cultures tended to be spatially limited, oral, and preoccupied with religious and moral beliefs. Space-based cultures, like the Roman Empire, extended over vast areas, emphasized the visual rather than the oral, relied heavily on writing, and tended to be preoccupied with political and military matters.

McLUHAN'S NOBLE MYTH

We find here the immediate source of the noble myth that controls McLuhan's thought with the force of an article of faith. Once upon a time we lived in a seamless culture of auditory space, an ear-culture of participation, community, and continuity; it was the natural state of humankind, the original global village. With the invention of the phonetic alphabet, the human sensorium was altered to give primacy to the visual over the auditory and our mental processes adapted to a more abstract, fragmentary, and objective mode of understanding. McLuhan tracks this lineage through Aristotelian logic, Euclidean geometry, and medieval scholasticism to a culmination point with the invention of printing and Renaissance three-dimensional painting. Here is the way McLuhan contrasts the two cultures:

> The man of the tribal world led a complex, kaleidoscopic life precisely be-cause the ear, unlike the eye cannot be focused and is synaesthetic rather than analytic and linear. . . . Audile-tactile tribal man partook of the collective un-conscious, lived in a magical integral world patterned by myth and ritual, its values divine and unchallenged, whereas literate or visual man creates an environment that is strongly fragmented, individualistic, explicit, logical, specialized and detached. The alphabet shattered the charmed circle and reso-nating magic of the tribal world, exploding man into an agglomeration of specialized and psychically impoverished individuals or units, functioning in a world of linear time and Euclidean space.[2]

In *The Gutenberg Galaxy*, published in 1962, McLuhan attempted to show how the invention of printing influenced the emergence of nationalism, mathematical physics, narrative chronology in literature, introspection in psychology, capitalism, and a money economy—all cultural forms of modes of communication that lock us into a sequential, linear, and highly individu-alized relationship to reality. The hallmarks of these modes of perception are specialization, repeatability and uniformity, detachment, and abstraction, precisely the characteristics that account for the technological dominance of Western civilization.

Only alphabetic cultures, says McLuhan, are capable of mastering con-nected linear sequences as a means of social and psychic organization—the separation of all experience into uniform units to generate the kind of control that is the condition of technological success. But, of course, such cultures pay a high price in schizophrenia and alienation. "The print-made split between head and heart is the trauma which affects Europe from Machiavelli till the present," McLuhan wrote in *The Gutenberg Galaxy*. It was the achievement of Renaissance perspectival painting, said McLuhan, to have framed the world from the "fixed point of view"—Newton's single vision and what W. B. Yeats called the Lockean swoon—to the "hypnotic trance" brought about by emphasizing the visual component of experience until it eclipsed all others. We find a good summary statement in *Under-standing Media* (1964):

Printing from moveable types became the archetype of all subsequent mechanization. From Rabelais and More and Mill and Morris, the typographical explosion extended the minds and voices of men to reconstitute the human dialogue on a world scale. . . . For print presented an image of repeatable precision that inspired totally new forms of extending social energies. Print released great psychic and social energies by breaking the individual out of the traditional group while providing a model of how to add individual to individual in massive agglomeration of power. The same spirit of private enterprise that emboldened authors and artists to cultivate self-expression led other men to create giant corporations, both military and commercial. . . . The fragmenting and analytic power of the printed word in our psychic lives gave us that dissociation of sensibility which in the arts and literature since Cézanne and Baudelaire has been a top priority for elimination in every program of reform in taste and knowledge.[3]

ART AND TECHNOLOGY

The Gutenberg Galaxy is an exhaustive analysis of the interrelationships between art and the new technologies that came into being in the post-Gutenberg era. McLuhan especially considered Shakespeare a masterful analyst of this transition period between two modes of apprehending the world. He appropriately begins *The Gutenberg Galaxy* with an analysis of *King Lear,* which, according to McLuhan, "offers a complete demonstration of how it felt to live through the change from medieval to Renaissance time and space, from an inclusive to an exclusive sense of the world." Thus the opening words: "Meanwhile we shall express our darker purpose. Give me the map there. Know we have divided in three our kingdom."

We note three things about this passage. The "darker purpose" referred to would have been recognizable to an Elizabethan audience as an echo of Machiavelli, who argued an individualist and quantitative idea of power, thus challenging the more corporate political theories of the feudal Middle Ages, a concept that, as McLuhan believed "abstracted personal power from the social matrix. Second, the reference to the map is important. "Give me the map there." Cartography was a new science in the sixteenth century, reflecting Renaissance ideas of the space-time continuum and the privileging of the visual. One reads a book. It may be that Lear's blindness is meant to symbolize the hypertrophy of the visual sense as a kind of blindness. The third thing we note is that Lear divides his kingdom in accord with the shift of power from the center to the margins of society (thus favoring the development of nationalism) and with the general methodology introduced by modern science of dividing problems into their simplest parts. This, notes McLuhan, is the image of a society as segmented into a homogeneous mass of quantified appetites, of society as an association of competitive individuals.

When Lear says, "Tell me daughters . . . which of you shall we say doth love us most that we our largest bounty may extend," he sets them against one another in a typically modern mode of competition. Thus, Goneril proclaims, "I love you more that words can wield the matter, dearer than eyesight, space, and liberty." It is worth remarking that the visual, the spatial, and individual freedom were typical Renaissance values. Regan tries to outbid Goneril and says, "I profess myself an enemy to all other joys which the most precious square of sense professes." Only Cordelia remains fixed in the medieval values of her conscience, her sensibility, and her sense of role. But roles are precisely what are being sacrificed in the new calculus of human relationships. Henceforward, one looks to the competitive advantage, the fragmentation of the senses, and the motive of exact calculation. McLuhan comments:

> King Lear is a kind of elaborate case history of people translating themselves out of a world of roles into the new world of jobs (i.e., specialized skills). This is a process of stripping and denudation which does not occur instantly except in artistic vision. . . . It is a kind of medieval sermon-exemplum to display the madness and misery of the modern life of action. Shakespeare explains minutely that the very principle of action is the splitting up of social operations and of the private sense life into specialized fragments.[4]

Lear serves McLuhan's purposes well. To bring out the specific influence of the new commercial culture on character and society I would probably opt for a play like the *Merchant of Venice,* which shows even more clearly the commodification of personality. Nonetheless, McLuhan illustrates well the relationship between art and other cultural media including the commercial. He was fond of quoting Ezra Pound to the effect that artists are the antennae of the race, and believed that the function of the artist was to both anticipate changes in technology and to educate the human sensibility to the new environments created by those technologies.

Through the Vanishing Point: Space in Poetry and Painting (1968) explores this function at some length and provides us with McLuhan's clearest statement on the social role of the artist. He develops Pound's insight and argues that art is a "teaching machine" to train perception and judgment. Most of us live in a homeostatic present, fear change, and cling to the securities of custom and routine. Artists, on the other hand, are at home with novelty and crises, and use their art to compensate for the distortions of our sensorium brought about by technological changes. Artists are like "navigators" who chart our bearings through the turbulence caused by innovation. Thus, they are indispensable to our survival.

OUR ELECTRONIC CULTURE

McLuhan's noble myth concludes with the invention of the electronic media in the nineteenth century which created environments that challenged the primacy of the mechanical technologies. It is an axiom of McLuhan's thought that while mechanical technologies are extensions of one or another of our senses, electronic technologies are extensions of our entire nervous system. In this sense, electronic culture recapitulates significant features of tribal culture: a greater emphasis on involvement and community; the restoration of the auditory and tactile senses; and, above all, the organic character of tribal culture.

The mechanical age, McLuhan thought, could be viewed as an interlude between two great organic eras of culture. The telegraph, the first of the electronic media, he compared to a social hormone because it created an organic interdependence among all the institutions of society, the way hormones regulate the functions of all the organs. Television has become the central nervous system of society as a whole. "In television, images are projected at you. You are the screen. The images wrap around you. You are the vanishing point. This creates a sort of inwardness and demands participation and involvement in depth of the whole being, a sort of reverse perspective which has much in common with Oriental art."[5] In *Understanding Media* he says, "We live today in an age of information and communication because electric media instantly and constantly create a total field of interacting events in which all participate. Now the world of public interaction has the same inclusive scope of interplay that has hitherto characterized only our private nervous systems. The simultaneity of electric communication makes each of us present and accessible to every other person in the world."[6]

As was his wont, McLuhan turned to writers and artists for a greater understanding of electronic culture: to the Romantic poets for their influence in creating that culture; to James Joyce for analogies between the stream of consciousness technique which translated the effects on the human psyche of electronic technologies (technologies, McLuhan shrewdly pointed out, that are like the stream of consciousness insofar as they overwhelm the human psyche with huge amounts of undigested and unconnected information); to

T. S. Eliot for clarification on the auditory imagination; to modern painters to learn from their efforts to unify the random scraps of information that bombard the human sensorium. Thus, impressionism and the play of light in the worlds of Monet and Renoir; thus, the pointillism of Seurat. About Seurat, McLuhan says, "The stipple of points in his paintings is close to the technique of sending pictures by telegraph, and close to the form of the TV image or mosaic made by the scanning finger. All of these anticipate later electronic forms because, like the digital computer with its multiple yes-no dots and dashes, they caress the contours of every kind of being by the multiple touches of these points. Electricity offers a means of getting in touch with every facet of being at once."[7]

A similar point can be found in *The Medium Is the Massage:* "Electric circuity profoundly involves us with one another. Information pours upon us, instantaneously and continuously. As soon as information is acquired, it is very rapidly replaced by still newer information. Our electrically configured world has forced us to move from the habit of data classification to the mode of pattern recognition. We can no longer build serially, block-by-block, step-by-step, because instant communication insures that all factors of the environment and of experience co-exist in a state of active interplay."[8] Only McLuhan could point out a parallel between the invention of the telegraph and the publication of Kierkegaard's *The Concept of Dread* in 1944. "The age of anxiety had begun," he said. "For with the telegraph man had initiated that outering or extension of his central nervous system that is now approaching an extension of consciousness with satellite broadcasting. To put one's nerves outside and one's physical organs inside the nervous system, or the brain, is to initiate a situation of dread."[9]

RETHINKING BUSINESS ETHICS

I have found McLuhan's insights helpful in understanding our present economic system and particularly helpful for the teaching of business ethics. For McLuhan, the first ethical imperative was to understand what was happening. In the beginning of his career he was a moralizer with a portable podium. His first book, *The Mechanical Bride,* was an impassioned yelp of protest against modern culture. Eventually, he came to see that this was an ineffective approach. To adopt the posture of protest and lamentation with understanding was merely sentimentality and, as he said, "sentimentality, like pornography, is fragmented emotion; a natural consequence of the high visual gradient in any culture."[10]

McLuhan's controlling ethical perspective is drawn from Poe's story "A Descent into the Maelstrom." The effects of technology are comparable to the descent into the maelstrom; they make us somewhat delirious, induce a sense of helplessness but, paradoxically, sharpen our intellectual curiosity and resources. In Poe's story, an old sailor recounts to some companions how he had been once caught in a fierce storm off the coast of Norway. The storm created a powerful whirlpool that began to pull him under. After initial panic, Poe's sailor takes up a speculative attitude toward his predicament. He becomes reflective, indeed calculating about the storm around him, the dangers and risks it creates but as well the hope it offers. He observed, for example, that large bodies were sucked into the vortex more quickly than small ones, that spherical bodies sank sooner than others, and that cylindrical bodies stood the best chance of survival. The sailor therefore lashed himself to a water cask and threw himself into the ocean. Thus, he was saved while all others perished.

In McLuhan's analogy, technology has plunged us into the vortex but we can think in the eye of the storm. We can study its slope and strength, its force and direction, to determine the conditions of our survival. Thought becomes our lifeline. McLuhan always retained a pronounced distaste for the culture he was analyzing. He was by temperament a cultural conservative, premodern in his basic philosophical outlook, a devout Catholic and daily communicant who was visibly dismayed when his students and his own children went with the flow of the electronic culture. But he never wavered in his conviction that ethics were primarily a matter of understanding the kind of world in which we live.

McLuhan always paid special attention to the business world and was a long-time consultant to companies such as General Electric and IBM. He famously told IBM that they were not in the business of making business machines but were really in the business of information dispersal and effecting wide-reaching changes in the social environment. He saw commercial organizations as extensions of the human mind, like any other technology, which release their own unique fields of energies, organize human behavior in specific ways, and produce certain effects. Business activities are analogous, he said in the *Global Village*, "to the interdependent relationship of the left and right hemispheres of the brain. The line functions of a company are like the left hemisphere, concerned with verbal speech-frames of thought which produce quantitative closed-system measurements of the internal and external relationships of the corporate entity. The right hemisphere is concerned with social intelligence which cannot be logically formulated, e.g., the spatial, the mystical, the artistic, and the symbolic."[11]

The global economy we live with today was clearly seen by McLuhan in the 1950s. The downsizing of large corporations is very much in line with his thinking about smaller, more participatory, and indeed more creative commercial units. No one any longer has a guaranteed place in a fixed organizational chart. The large corporation is a dinosaur of the mechanical age, and the extravagant salaries of CEOs represent the lump in the throat of the electronic serpent that has swallowed an antiquated business culture. The large corporation was based on efficiency. But the trouble with efficiency is that it gets us too far too fast. We reach our goal and find out we are in the wrong place. The corporation in the aural-tactile space of the electronic age will not so much be efficient as creative, surf-boarding along the electric waves of multiple possibilities.

This might be one of the meanings of the present merger mania—more is less, big is small. McLuhan's erstwhile colleague, Peter Drucker, seems to be of the same opinion. In a recent interview in *Wired* magazine he said, "The big companies have no future. By and large there is no more advantage to big business—only disadvantages. Young, educated people do not want to work in the big institutions."[12] Drucker went on to note that, while almost all business graduates start with big companies, it used to be the case some eight or ten years ago that only two out of five changed from a big company to a small- or medium-sized one. Now more than half do. Furthermore, Drucker pointed out, there has been practically no growth in big companies in the last fifteen years. On the other hand, medium-sized companies are growing very fast.

As a consequence, the nature of work is changing. The news on this front is somewhat scary and anxiety-provoking, certainly for my students, but it is not entirely bad news. What is scary is that the conventional notion of what constitutes a job is changing quite drastically before our eyes. As McLuhan put it, in an electronic society people do not have jobs, they have roles. Jobs, as we have understood them, are a relatively recent adaptation to the industrial age. But what worked in the industrial age, says McLuhan, "cannot serve for survival or sanity in this new time. Under conditions of electric circuity, all the fragmented job patterns tend to blend once more into involving and demanding roles or forms of work that more and more resemble teaching, learning and human service, in the older sense of dedicated loyalty."[13]

McLuhan's prose often took a visionary and pentecostal edge. He sometimes talked as if electronic technology would bring about a kind of collective consciousness that would be the realization of the mystical body of Christ.

The visionary note sometimes creeps into what he says about work and jobs, as for instance in this passage from *Understanding Media:* "In an age of instant information man ends his job of fragmented specializing and assumes the role of information-gathering. Today information-gathering resumes the inclusive concept of culture, exactly as the primitive food gatherer worked in complete equilibrium with his entire environment. Our quarry now, in this new nomadic and workless world, is knowledge and insight into the creative processes of life and society."[14] This is a little too poetic to be of much practical guidance.

Let us consider for a moment the role of money and its relationship to work and society. In preliterate cultures, money was a commodity. It was a moderate technology of extending human power from immediate staples to more distant ones. Money in the form of coinage extended human power still further as trading became the cement of more complex, more civilized societies. Paper money based on print technology created the uniform currency needed for marketable and portable goods, the basic building blocks of a market economy. Thus, money can be seen as the analogue of literacy. The letters of the alphabet are comparable to the numbers on bills and constitute, McLuhan said, an extremely aggressive extension of the body.

Today, of course, money in the form of coinage or paper is rapidly becoming obsolete. We are entering the era of virtual money or digital cash as it is sometimes called. Money still performs its ancient function as a social metaphor that both transmits information and regulates social relationships. As Derrick de Kerckhove, a former colleague of McLuhan's and now director of the McLuhan Center for Technology and Communication at the University of Toronto, writes in *The Skin of Culture:* "Money has always functioned as human intelligence's parsing mechanism: it allowed us to keep track of and differentiate between portions of space, stretches of time and outputs of human energy." The problem now, he goes on, "is that money in its present form is simply not fast or complex enough to act as a proper evaluation mechanism. Indeed, as it migrates to digital convergence in purely electronic financial transactions, the nature of money is changing. When money reaches the speed of light it becomes pure energy. In the future the function of money will be confined to parsing the myriad digitized operations of our single global computer."[15]

The evolving nature of money runs parallel with the evolving nature of work. We can envisage three scenarios on the relationship between the two. It may be that, in the not too distant future, each newborn child will be encoded with a cash-chip that will guarantee financial security for life. We can balance this somewhat utopian possibility with two more realistic scenarios. We might imagine the modern corporation adapting to something resembling a feudal arrangement in which everyone has a role and lifetime security. That, as I understand it, is the tendency in Japanese corporations. We could evolve in that direction in this country. After all, that was the idea behind tenure in universities and many organizations such as labor unions that have de facto tenure, and the idea could catch on more universally.

This suggests a third scenario which is perhaps more appealing. Let us accept for the sake of argument that the three traditional engines of the economy—agriculture, manufacturing, and services—are in decline. Let us accept, too, that work as it was invented in the modern age is becoming obsolete. Let us even accept the gloomy conclusions of Jeremy Rifkin's recent *The End of Work*. It still does not follow that we have reached some kind of dead end. By the way, Rifkin's book would have been better titled *The End of Jobs*. Jobs, not work, are the issue. There will always be lots of work to do. What we are struggling with today is some new, more socially functional equation between money and work. Here is a suggestive idea from de Kerckhove's book. If, he says, "information is truly the staple of today's economy, it might be useful to keep in mind that information is the only substance that actually grows with use, rather than depleting like our natural resources. We are looking at an economy of abundance."[16]

These considerations, it seems to me, are relevant to the teaching of business ethics. For years I taught such a course. I taught it as I had been taught, which might best be described as the tool-kit approach. On the one hand we have some business practices; on the other some ethical prescriptions like utilitarianism, pragmatism, materialism, determinism, and other isms. The idea was to get the right "ism" attached to the appropriate business practice, very much like pinning the tail on the donkey. In this children's game the tail most often got pinned to the wrong part of the donkey's anatomy. So, too, in business ethics using the tool-kit approach. I came to find it a highly unsatisfactory pedagogy. So I gave myself a sabbatical for the purpose of rethinking how business ethics might be taught better. When I teach the course again these would be some of the ingredients:

- Plenty of literature and art.
- More exposure to popular culture—MTV, for example, and *Wired* magazine would be required reading. Much of what I now do in a course called "Technology and Environmental Ethics" would be incorporated into the business ethics course to get at the point that business is a technology with far-reaching effects for the social and ecological environment.

- I would have many more field trips and have students report directly on their own work experiences.
- I would incorporate insights from postmodern thought about power—how it is generated and distributed in society—to make the theological point that power is the secular equivalent of grace.
- Above all, I would teach business ethics through a range of narrative ethics.

The principal shortcoming of the tool-kit approach was that it was excessively theoretical. Think of ethics not as a theory but as a story. Thus, Richard Rorty recommends storytelling which edifies, promotes solidarity, and reduces the sum total of cruelty in the world. He would substitute conversation for epistemology. Conversation with our fellow human beings, he says, is our only source of guidance because it captures the contingent character of the human situation better than theory. Narrative cannot grasp life as a whole given contingency, but it can grasp life as a unity, fitting the parts together, establishing coherent phases of past, present, and future, relating individual lives to larger social patterns.

Thus viewed, narrative has two advantages over theory: it overcomes the fragmentation of social life and provides an alternative to the abstract nature of much traditional morality. Talking about rights, equality, and happiness at a high level of abstraction is one thing; talking about the same values in a narrative context, is quite another. Alisdair MacIntyre writes an exceptionally compelling account of narrative in his *After Virtue*. It is natural, he says, to think of the self in the narrative mode. All human action is "enacted narrative." This is because human action necessarily has a historical character, unfolding in time in alternate modes of contingency and remembrance. Historically, the principal means of moral and political education was through the telling of stories. Communities were formed, sustained, and remembered through the telling of stories.

Without narrative we would not only not know who we are but our social roles would lack coherence. The world, Sartre said, comes to us in the shape of a story. According to his latter-day disciple J. F. Lyotard, narrative education provides a threefold competence: knowing how, knowing how to speak, and knowing how to listen—three competencies that define the fundamental dynamics of a community. Business is the great story of our time, the closest thing we have to a metanarrative. Not to see it as such, tell it as such, and teach it as such would be to fundamentally misunderstand its function; and to not understand, as McLuhan so forcefully reminds us, is to be unethical.

NOTES

1. Philip Marchand, *Marshall McLuhan: The Medium and the Messenger* (New York: Ticknor & Fields, 1989), 36–37.

2. "Playboy Interview: Marshall McLuhan," *Playboy*, March 1969, 59.

3. Marshall McLuhan, *Understanding Media: The Extensions of Man* (New York: McGraw-Hill, 1964), 170–72.

4. Marshall McLuhan, *Gutenberg Galaxy: The Making of Typographic Man* (Toronto: University of Toronto Press, 1962), 17.

5. Marshall McLuhan, *The Medium Is the Massage: An Inventory of Effects* (New York: Bantam, 1967), 125.

6. McLuhan, *Understanding Media*, 248.

7. Ibid., 249.

8. McLuhan, *The Medium Is the Massage*, 63.

9. McLuhan, *Understanding Media*, 252.

10. Marshall McLuhan, *Through the Vanishing Point: Space in Poetry and Painting.* (New York: Harper & Row, 1968), 131.

11. Marshall McLuhan, *War and Peace in the Global Village* (New York: Bantam, 1968), 121.

12. *Wired*, August 1996, 118.

13. McLuhan, *The Medium Is the Massage*, 20.

14. McLuhan, *Understanding Media*, 138.

15. Derrick de Kerckhove, *The Skin of Culture: Investigating the New Electronic Reality* (Toronto: Somerville House, 1995), 198.

16. Ibid., 180.

9

"IF LIFE HANDS YOU A LEMMON..."

Business Ethics from The Apartment
to Glengarry Glen Ross

— ☉ —

DENNIS P. McCANN

The Lemmonade I am hoping to make here is a profile of the businessman who emerges from three memorable films in which Jack Lemmon has
starred, *The Apartment* (1960), *Save the Tiger* (1973), and *Glengarry Glen
Ross* (1992).[1] Although the films have little in common, save Jack Lemmon
and a business setting, I want to view them as if they were three scenes from
the life of a single individual who struggles not very successfully with the central issue of personal integrity throughout his business career. What results
from this retrospective is not likely to be of much comfort to business ethicists, for these films do not model the ideal of doing well while doing good
that business ethics holds out to our students. Nevertheless, I think exploring
this perspective is useful because it may help raise questions, not only about
the way standard business practice is usually portrayed in feature films, but
also about certain deeper issues we all must face that are simply beyond
morality.

BUSINESS ETHICS, HOLLYWOOD STYLE

A review of what is available for viewing may suggest that business is
not readily portrayed on film.[2] The last ten years, however, may have wit-
nessed the release of more films in which business has been a prominent
theme than in the entire previous history of the motion picture industry.
Although many of these films remain negative in their attitude toward busi-

ness, particularly toward finance, and skeptical about the prospects for business ethics, there is some evidence of a shift in perspective. Let me cite two very different examples—*The Hudsucker Proxy* (1994) and *Disclosure* (1994)—and then contrast them with what I take to be Hollywood's usual view of business and business ethics, as depicted in *The Firm* (1993). Taken together, these three contemporary films help define conventional expectations, against which we will try to measure the excellence of our Lemmonade.

In *The Hudsucker Proxy,* Tim Robbins plays Norville Barnes, a recently hired mailroom clerk who is elevated overnight to chief executive officer, as part of a plot by Hudsucker's board of directors. The idea is to drive share prices down so the firm can be sold to an investor group dominated by its board chairman, a wily old villain played by Paul Newman. The plot backfires when Norville makes the firm wildly successful, thanks to his recent invention of the hula hoop. Although *The Hudsucker Proxy* is visually reminiscent of earlier comic depictions of business—notably the first few scenes in Charlie Chaplin's *Modern Times*—it is very up-to-date in its essentially benign view of business. The board of directors may not be on the level, but their evil plan is defeated by a kid who possesses the one thing necessary for business success, namely, incredibly good luck.

Luck also plays a role in *Disclosure,* insofar as it allows the hero, Tom Sanders (Michael Douglas), to document Meredith Johnson's (Demi Moore) gross malfeasance in supervising Seattle-based DigiCom's overseas production of a vitally necessary microchip. Ostensibly, *Disclosure* is about sexual harassment, a very prominent topic among business ethicists today. But that is only a foreground issue in a larger morality play about personal integrity and corporate loyalty. The point is not that Tom is able to prove Meredith has falsely accused him of sexual harassment, but that competence coupled with personal integrity—as well as good luck—still have a fighting chance in the corporate world today. The film's final scene, in which Tom and his colleagues welcome their new boss, Meredith's successor, shows Tom at peace with himself and the firm that still employs him. Despite the way in which CEO Bob Garvin (Donald Sutherland) and his staff have failed to support Tom in his crisis, the audience is not invited to question whether Tom's loyalty to the firm has been misplaced. *Disclosure* does not deny that radical evil can surface in the modern business corporation, but it does suggest that justice may yet triumph, provided the protagonists are smart and tough enough to persevere in pursuing it.

In contrast to these two films is *The Firm* (1993), Sidney Pollack's rendition of the popular novel of that name by John Grisham. Here, the moral contrast between a basically decent individual and an evil organization is played out in the conflict between Mitch McDeere (Tom Cruise), an ambitious yet only normally avaricious young man, and a prestigious Memphis law firm that hires him fresh out of Harvard Law School. Mitch soon awakens to the fact that the firm is mired in the full spectrum of corporate corruption, and he finds himself caught between the proverbial rock and a hard place. Both the FBI and the firm's senior partners are pressuring him to go along with their plans, either by turning state's evidence against the firm or simply by cooperating with the firm's criminal activity. As a review in the *CineBooks' Motion Picture Guide* observed, "More often than not, *The Firm* seems a half-hearted moral lesson about the greedy decade just past."[3] Compared to *The Hudsucker Proxy* and *Disclosure,* business ethics here seems nonexistent. The moral individual must fight alone against the forces of evil whose strength, inevitably, is compounded by the power of efficient organization.

Although hardly as interesting as the other two, *The Firm* is typical of Hollywood morality plays concerning business. Hollywood usually sees business as just another institutional venue in which to act out the grand mythology of American individualism and the protean conflict theologian Reinhold Niebuhr memorably captured in one of his titles, *Moral Man and Immoral Society.* All decent moral impulses, however dormant or deformed, reside in the individual, while organizations—whether for-profit or not-for-profit—remain either indifferent or hostile to these impulses. Power, particularly organizational power of any kind, is evil. It corrupts; it alienates the individual from his or her own decent dispositions, making it increasingly difficult for the individual to understand or act ethically.

Overcoming such power requires heroic resistance, based on personal charisma, which may take the form of superior insight, superior determination, superior virtue, or some combination of all three, mixed well, of course, with a superior streak of luck. The heroic individual learns nothing about morality from organizations, save possibly the cunning with which an organization can mask evil as good. If, against all odds, the individual succeeds in vanquishing evil, his or her success results not from the mobilization of organizational power but from the willingness to go it alone when the chips are down, trusting only in him or herself, close friends, and family. Sex is essential to this success, for it creates a personal bond that is outside and, hence, beyond the control of the organization. The heroic individual apparently knows no bounds other than those based, one way or another, on sexual or familial relationships.

The intellectual pedigree of Hollywood's version of the great American myth should be obvious. It is the rather banal mixture of Freud, Marx, and

Nietzsche that defines conventional modernity as an arena of moral struggle.[4] Although modernity is under siege today by both feminists and fundamentalists of various persuasions, what should interest us is the fact that the bias is directed less against business corporations than against organizations as such. Even when business is a major theme in a film, Hollywood seems less interested in the business activities than in their wider, as it were, existential implications. If this is true, it should no longer surprise us that business provides merely a stage setting for reenacting the epic of the heroic individual. This myth seems capable of generating a moral and social imagination in which business itself is less interesting than the personal dramas that occur within business.

MAKING LEMMONADE

Jack Lemmon has appeared in over fifty feature films, many of them memorable and several of them in a business setting. I have restricted my focus to three films in which being in business is crucial for defining the characters Lemmon portrays: C. C. Baxter, the young insurance clerk seeking the fast track to corporate success in *The Apartment* (1960); Harry Stoner, the desperate CEO of Capri Classics, Inc., in *Save the Tiger* (1973); and Shelly "The Machine" Levene, a shady salesman working for Mitch and Murray in *Glengarry Glen Ross* (1992). Other memorable Lemmon films could have been included, such as *Days of Wine and Roses* (1962) and *The China Syndrome* (1979), but business, in my view, is peripheral in these stories, in a way that it is not in the ones I have chosen. If, for the sake of this experiment, we combine the three characters from the films in which business is a central theme, we have a composite picture of the beleaguered American businessman. Let us christen him C. C. "Harry" Levene.

The Apartment catches a glimpse of Harry still early in his career. He is the typical young man on the make, with a not very original strategy for corporate success. He easily yields to pressure from his superiors who commandeer his in-town apartment for their adulterous trysts. Despite the inconveniences, Harry is eager to please, and soon he is promoted to a position where he comes to the attention of higher-ups, the chief of whom is the supercad, J. D. Sheldrake, convincingly, if uncharacteristically, portrayed by Fred MacMurray. Sheldrake, too, wants the key to Harry's apartment; but this time Harry runs into trouble, because Sheldrake needs the apartment to carry on an affair with an elevator attendant, Fran Kubelik (Shirley MacLaine), to whom Harry also is attracted. Not surprisingly, Harry goes along with Sheldrake, but he also uses the situation to demonstrate a special concern for Ms. Kubelik. When Fran, faced with the fact that Sheldrake is incorrigibly married, attempts suicide in Harry's apartment, Harry nurses her back to health. Eventually, he has a showdown with Sheldrake, in which he quits his job. Later—fittingly on New Years' Eve—Harry and Fran begin a new life together.

Here is the scene toward the end of *The Apartment*, where Harry, known in the film as "Baxter," finally refuses to cooperate with Sheldrake:

Sheldrake (over the intercom at his desk): Baxter, would you mind stopping in here for a moment?

Baxter (voice over the intercom): Yes, Mr. Sheldrake. (Baxter enters Sheldrake's office.)

Baxter: Here's the breakdown of figures on personnel turnover; 37 percent of our female employees leave to get married and 22 percent . . .

Sheldrake: Baxter, you're working too hard. It's New Year's Eve. Relax.

Baxter: Yes, sir.

Sheldrake: I suppose you'll be out on the town tonight celebrating.

Baxter: Naturally.

Sheldrake: Me, too. I'll be taking Miss Kubelik out. I finally talked her into it.

Baxter: I see.

Sheldrake: Only thing is, Baxter, I'm staying at the Athletic Club and it's strictly stag. So if you don't mind . . .

Baxter (pause): Don't mind what?

Sheldrake: You know. The other key to your apartment. (Pause.) Well, when we had that little scare about Miss Kubelik, I thought I'd better get rid of it quick. So I threw it out the window of the commuter train.

Baxter: Very clever.

Sheldrake: So now I'll have to borrow your key.

Baxter: Sorry, Mr. Sheldrake.

Sheldrake: What do you mean, "Sorry"?

Baxter: You're not bringing anybody to my apartment.

Sheldrake: I'm not bringing just anybody; I'm bringing Miss Kubelik.

Baxter: Especially not Miss Kubelik.

Sheldrake: How's that again?

Baxter (firmly): No key. (Pause.)

Sheldrake: Baxter, I picked you for my team because I thought you were a very bright young man. Do you realize what you're doing, not to me but to yourself? Normally, it takes years to work your way up to the twenty-seventh floor, but it only takes thirty seconds to be out on the street again. You dig?

Baxter: I dig.

Sheldrake: So what's it gonna be?

(Baxter fishes a key out of his pocket and tosses it on Sheldrake's desk.)

Sheldrake: Now you're being bright.

Baxter: Thank you, sir.

(Baxter exits to his own office, and begins to put things in order, as if to leave.)

(Sheldrake enters Baxter's office.)

Sheldrake: Say, Baxter, you gave me the wrong key.

Baxter: No, I didn't.

Sheldrake: But this is the key to the executive washroom!

Baxter: That's right, Mr. Sheldrake. I won't be needing it because I'm all washed up around here.

Sheldrake: What's gotten into you, Baxter?

Baxter: Just following "Doctor's Orders." (Pause.) I've decided to become a Mensch. You know what that means? A human being.

Sheldrake: Now, hold on, Baxter!

Baxter: Save it. The old payola won't work anymore. Goodbye, Mr. Sheldrake.

(Baxter heads triumphally for the elevators to exit the twenty-seventh floor.)

Although *The Apartment* conveys a dim view of business ethics, it does not fit smoothly into the typical Hollywood perspective on business. To be sure, the insurance company that employs Harry and Fran is reminiscent of Robert Jackall's "patrimonial bureaucracy," in which it is "not what you know, but who you know" that counts.[5] Being smart as well as ambitious, Harry has already figured that one out and is more than willing to meet the company's unwritten code for success. The villainous Sheldrake, who personifies the code, seems to regard preying upon young women like Fran as just another business perk. Fran, however, is not simply an innocent victim. She, too, buys into the code as it applies to women, seeing no other way to fulfill her own aspirations than by inviting a big shot like Sheldrake to seduce her and, she hopes, to marry her. Nor is Harry a knight in shining armor. Eventually, he and Fran redeem each other by falling in love, but they are also willing accomplices in each other's accommodation to the sleazy ways of corporate success. Having severed their ties with the wicked Sheldrake—like the Little Tramp and his beloved Gamine in *Modern Times*—they face a future defined by nothing but their touching desire for each other.

Despite its deep skepticism about business ethics, *The Apartment* remains optimistic about the moral dispositions of individuals. In this sense, it is closer to the standard Hollywood perspective on business and the American individual. The sexual bond between Fran and Harry creates a private space where their basic decency and genuine concern for one another can emerge, without impinging on their public personae. Their relationship, however, may also embolden them to pull up stakes and try something new. Although the film itself offers no encouragement for this speculation, I cannot help imagining a denouement in which, having left their jobs at the insurance company, they move to Los Angeles. This, I am arguing, is where we catch up with them when, some thirteen years later, in the opening scenes of *Save the Tiger* (1973), they are alas, very married and encumbered with a successful business that is increasingly worrisome, especially for Harry. Not all Harry's problems have to do with the business—manufacturering women's apparel. He and "Fran"—now disguised as a wife named Janet (Patricia Smith)—are no longer lovers. She is indifferent to his business problems, save as they spill over into their home life. Harry is going through some kind of midlife crisis and this time Fran is not there for him because, early in the film, she exits for New York and her uncle's funeral. Phil Green (Jack Gilford), Harry's business partner, is now his alter ego. He serves as Harry's conscience, without holding out much hope that, like the tiger, either Harry or the business can be saved.

Because *Save the Tiger* presents a full-blown moral dilemma, it is one film that is frequently shown in courses on business ethics. Harry and Phil need capital to finance the latest line of fashions that they are marketing, but their options seem narrowed either to making a deal with mafia loan sharks or torching one of their factories to collect the insurance on it. Here is the scene, early in the film, where Harry and Phil wrestle with the moral dilemma.

Phil (sitting at his desk, talking on the telephone as Harry walks into his office): You wanna foreclose? O.K. I'll see you in court in five years. Yes. Right. (Listens, then, in a softer tone . . .) Alright, Sam. (Phil hangs up the phone and turns to Harry) Good afternoon. Where the hell have you been?

Harry: What happened at the bank?

Phil: What the hell do you think happened? Just like I told ya. The best is 50 cents on every dollar.

Harry (as he turns from Phil and goes toward his own office): Not enough.

Phil: What?

Harry: Not enough!

Phil: It's a g–d– shame! We've got a helluva line. Rico did a brilliant job. I went over all the patterns with the old man. Everything figures: materials, labor, fittings, accessories, packaging, shipping, sales commissions. Everything. It's all there! (Pause.) If the country doesn't go in the crapper, we'll have a great season. We'll make some money for a change.

Harry (coming into Phil's office, pacing the floor, hovering over Phil's desk): How many dollars do we need?

Phil: Dollars? . . . Oh! . . . If . . . if you can write $300,000 this afternoon . . .

Harry: Christ, I can't . . .

Phil: Alright, if you can write $300,000 this afternoon, discount it at the bank, we'll get $150,000. . . .

Harry: And . . .

Phil: We'll need another $142,000 in less than sixty days. The mills are on our back. We owe 'em a bundle from last year.

Harry: Alright. What about the Long Beach factory?

Phil: What about it?

Harry: What are we using that for?

Phil: I dunno. We're turning out three numbers down there. Pant suits . . .

Harry: Policies all paid up?

Phil: Of course, they are.

Harry: O.K. (Takes a piece of paper from his pocket with a telephone number on it and flips it onto Phil's desk.)

Phil: What the hell is that?

Harry: Charlie Robbins. What's the policy worth? (Pause, then, raising his voice . . .) What's the policy worth?

Phil: Forget it, Harry. We can ask the unions, the mills, to carry us. After all . . .

Harry: We tried that last year and they told us to take a walk. How much is the floater worth?

Phil (raising his voice, defensively): I will not get involved with Robbins. There's a line I will not cross . . .

Harry: G–d– it! (Pause.) One simple question (pause): How much is the floater worth?

Phil: Forget the f–ing floater.

Harry: Phil, do I have to ask Marvin? How much is the floater worth? Huh? Phil?

Phil: A hundred thousand.

Harry: That's enough to squeeze through . . .

Phil: We've cut a lot of sharp corners together, but this is insanity.

Harry: Oh, Christ! If we were flat on our ass and we made missiles, Congress would send us a certified check. We happen to make dresses . . .

Phil: That's b–s–! You can't rationalize a thing like this! Admit it. . . .

Harry: Charlie Robbins is the best. There's never going to be any questions.

Phil: Will you wake up? There are always questions.

Harry: How do you think Beckman pulled out? Do you think his fire was spontaneous combustion?

Phil: I don't give a good g–d– . . .

Harry: Well, I give a good g–d–. We almost went on our ass last year, and this is our only chance to bail out.

Phil (pause): Then, we'll file for bankruptcy.

Harry: Yeah, we file for bankruptcy and we get audited. Would you like Linda to visit you in Chino? Huh?

Phil: Arson, Harry, Arson! This is a major felony! You're talking about twenty years . . .

Harry: Arson or fraud. It's the same accommodations.

Phil (pause): It's out of the question. I won't do it. I'm not gonna get involved with Robbins, and that's it.

(Pause: Harry takes back the paper with Robbins' number, and goes to dial Robbins on his own phone. Phil watches the phone light up, indicating that Harry is on the phone. He goes into Harry's office and glares at Harry.)

Harry: Son of a bitch! (Pause.) Do you think I enjoy doing this, Phil? What the hell else am I gonna do? Just tell me. We invented a new kind of arithmetic last year.

Phil: But we survived. We kept our people working—seventy-one girls, fourteen salesmen. Secretaries. All making a living. . . .

Harry: Phil. (Pause.) The government has another word for survival and it's called fraud. You. Me. Fraud. (Pause.) You haven't been out on the street for thirty-eight years. You wanna start looking for a job now? (Pause.) Well, neither do I . . .

(Harry takes up the telephone and begins to ring up Robbins, as Phil looks on.)

Save the Tiger does not allow the filmgoer to see how this dilemma is resolved, but it does a masterful job of conveying the sleazy situation in which Harry and Phil must act. The whole world seems stacked against them. This is southern California in the early 1970s, complete with gargantuan traffic jams and several pointed references to smog-related illnesses. Nothing seems to work. The war in Viet-Nam is not over yet. Television truly is a wasteland. In this paradise, slowly choking to death on its own excesses, Harry and Phil have already compromised their integrity to keep Capri Classics going. Now they confront a bail-out strategy that is riskier than any of their previous schemes. Phil can overlook a lot of things but he feels he must draw the line at arson. Harry, on the other hand, is still willing do whatever it takes; but, increasingly, he withdraws to an imagined past where his own lost innocence may still be preserved.

Harry is more than just a nostalgia buff. His favorite audio tape for the commute into work features Bunny Berrigan's rendition of "I Can't Get Started," a haunting piece that seems to epitomize his unhappy situation. He complains about baseball, because nobody plays like Cookie Lavagetto anymore, or Johnny Van der Meer, or a host of other names that Harry obsessively reviews in his spare moments. Harry is in a bad way, and it gets worse as the film continues. A one-night stand with a generous hippie woman—with whom Harry insists on playing the name game, to her visible discomfort—is as close as he can get to the way he wishes things were. Come next morning, the unforgiving sun rises once more on a Los Angeles that is just the same as it was the previous day, and Harry must put on his game face and renew his impossible struggle to save the tiger. But even the arsonist cannot get started, for his inspection of the factory yields enough code violations to make it unlikely that Harry and Phil will ever collect on the insurance, were he to light the match.

Like Marley's ghost in Dickens's *Christmas Carol,* I must fast-forward you now to the future where a visibly older Harry has hit rock bottom. *Glengarry Glen Ross* (1992) features a claustrophobic little sweatshop, in which a desperate group of salesmen are confronted with the Sisyphean task of conning ordinary people into fraudulent real-estate investments. It is not hard to imagine how Harry got into this mess. Either he did or he did not have the factory torched. Either the company went into bankruptcy and Harry lost everything, including Fran, when their creative accounting was discovered, or the factory did burn but Harry got caught, with the same result. Nearly twenty years later, Harry resurfaces in Chicago, where he, along with an office full of other losers—brilliantly portrayed by Alan Arkin, Ed Harris, and Al Pacino—must either reach their sales goals or lose their jobs. Harry is particularly desperate, because he has had a streak of bad luck and needs some commissions to pay his daughter's hospital bills.

Glengarry Glen Ross is an object lesson in business ethics from Hell. Its author, David Mamet, depicts a situation in which the logic of selling is played out in an end game worthy of Samuel Beckett. It is selling, totally severed from marketing, relentlessly pursued, unencumbered by any connection with a product of real value. "Always Be Closing" is the mantra this sales force must live by, as they challenge each other with textbook tales about how they got a foot in the door, exploited customers' weaknesses, and actually persuaded some to give up their precious nest eggs in exchange for title to mostly worthless property in Florida and Arizona. Harry, known in the film as "Shelly" Levene, has done well enough to earn the respect of his peers, especially Ricky Roma (Al Pacino), who has given him his nickname, "The Machine." Harry has been very good at this game, although that does not win him any favors now. Having just endured a breathtakingly abusive pep talk from one of the successful salesmen from downtown (Alec Baldwin), Harry and his colleagues are given forty-eight hours to close a deal, any deal, or they are out the door. The reward for those who survive is the Glengarry leads, a more promising list of unsuspecting marks who have responded to an advertisement in a magazine.

The only relief to be found in this diabolical scenario is of the "misery loves company" variety. The salesmen are frequently at each other's throats but they are united in their deep loathing for the office manager, John Williamson (Kevin Spacey), who, because of his family connections, has been given the thankless task of enforcing company policy, however sadistic it may be. One of the salesmen, Moss (Ed Harris), retaliates by plotting to steal the Glengarry leads and sell them to a competitor. The filmgoer sees him trying to recruit the hapless George Aaronow (Alan Arkin) but, after the police have stepped in to investigate the burglary, it is Harry who inadvertently gives himself away as the culprit.

Here is the scene, toward the end of *Glengarry Glen Ross* where Harry, after hectoring Williamson for inadvertently messing up a deal that Ricky Roma was trying to close, has been caught in a slip-up. Having admitted to Williamson that he was the one who took the Glengarry leads, Harry tries to talk his way out of getting fired and going to jail:

Levene: Okay. I . . . Hey. Hey, John, listen. Last night. I'm going to tell you, I was ready to Do the Dutch. Moss gets me, "Do this, and we'll get well . . ." Why not. Big f–in' deal. I'm halfway hoping to get caught. Hey. To put me out of my misery. (Pause.) But it taught me something. What it taught me . . . you've got to get out there. (Pause.) I wasn't cut out to be a thief. I was cut out to be a salesman. And now I'm back, . . . and you know, John, you have the advantage on me now. Whatever it takes to make it right, we'll make it right. We're going to make it right.

Williamson: I want to tell you something, Shelly. You have a big mouth. (Pause.)

Levene: What?

Williamson: You've got a big mouth, and now I'm going to show you an even bigger one. (Starts toward the Detective's door.)

Levene: Where are you going? Hey, you can't do that, you don't want to do that. . . . Wait. Wait. Wait. (Pulls money out of his pockets.) Wait. . . . Uh, hold on. . . . (Starts splitting money.) Look, twelve, twenty, two, twen . . . twenty-five hundred. It's . . . Take it. (Pause.) Take it all. . . . (Pause.) Takè it!

Williamson: No, I don't think so, Shel.

Levene: I . . .

Williamson: No, I think I don't want your money. I think you f–ed up my office. And I think you're going away.

Levene: I . . . what? Are you nuts? I'm . . . I'm going to close for you, I'm going to . . . (thrusting money at him). Here, here, I'm going to make this office . . . I'm going to be back there Number One. . . . Hey! . . . Listen. Just one moment. Here's what . . . Here's what we're going to do. Twenty percent. I'm going to give you twenty percent of my sales. . . . (Pause.) Twenty percent. (Pause.) For as long as I am with the firm. (Pause.) Fifty percent. (Pause.) You're going to be my partner. (Pause.) Fifty percent. Of all my sales.

Williamson: What sales?

Levene: What sales? I just closed eighty-two grand. . . . Are you out of your f–in' mind? I'm back. . . . I'm back, it's just the beginning.

Williamson: Just the beginning. . . .

Levene: Abso . . .

Williamson: Where have you been, Shelly? Bruce and Harriet Nyborg. Do you want to see the memos? They're nuts. . . . They used to call in every week. When I was with Webb. And we were selling Arizona. . . . They're nuts. . . . Did you see how they were living? How can you delude yourself?

Levene: I've got the check. . . .

Williamson: Forget it. Frame it. It's worthless. (Pause.)

Levene: The check's no good?

Williamson: You stick around I'll pull the memo for you. (Starts for the door.) I'm busy now. . . .

Levene: Wait a minute. . . . their check's no good? They're nuts? . . .

Williamson: Call up the bank. I called them.

Levene: You did?

Williamson: I called them when we had the lead . . . four months ago. (Pause.) The people are insane. They just like talking to salesmen. (Williamson starts for the door.)
Levene: Don't.
Williamson: I'm sorry.
Levene: Why?
Williamson: Because I don't like you. (Pause.)
Levene: My daughter. . . .
Williamson: F– you.

So Harry is washed up, isolated, and about to be given over to the tender mercies of the criminal justice system. It is hard to imagine that the system would tolerate an operation as sleazy as this one, but such civic scruples count for nothing next to the fact that Harry has been caught red-handed. He cannot talk or buy his way out of this one because even the sale he had worked so hard to get the night before is worthless, based as it was on a lead that Williamson knew was no good. Williamson's act of malevolence is as pure as any to be found on film. What life yet holds in store for Harry seems grim, indeed. If he survives almost certain incarceration, what next?

The cumulative impact of these three scenes from Harry's dismal career in business suggests a futility that is cosmic in its dimensions. Harry is a twentieth-century Everyman. He is a victim of circumstances but hardly "innocent." Success has eluded him to the point where the very idea of it seems illusory. Love has not been strong enough to redeem him. Harry can still remember love and still believes in it enough to want it, as he did while trying to save the tiger, but by the time he is doing the real-estate scam for Mitch and Murray, only love's encumbrances in the form of his daughter's medical bills are left. Harry's suffering summons our compassion, but his is not the stuff of tragedy. It is just what happens in a world that is as screwed up as ours is. You will not find any Nutrasweet here, not in this Lemmonade.

FLAVORING BUSINESS ETHICS

Jack Lemmon is a major talent who, presumably, has his pick of the parts he decides to play. This is especially true of Harry in *Save the Tiger*, a film which could not have been released without Lemmon's willingness to forgo his fee when the project went over budget. Lemmon, obviously, believed in *Save the Tiger*, and although he won an Oscar for his part in it, his belief seems to be more than a measure of the film's artistic merit. Is it simply a coincidence that Lemmon has chosen to do so many films in which a business setting is prominent? Business may be a handy metaphor for what Everyman is likely to encounter in the modern world, but Lemmon's insight into it seems more deeply, more personally rooted. The meager biographical notes on him seem to yield a clue here. His father was a successful executive in the doughnut industry; and by every indication Lemmon looked up to his dad, who sent him to Harvard, from where eventually he launched his acting career. So why the increasingly grim view of business? I suspect that like many successful executives, Lemmon's father brought home with him only the horror stories. He may have wanted to impress his son with how formidable the challenges were that he faced daily, how hard it was to maintain one's integrity when everyone else was cheating. But such table talk, however self-serving, is bound to make an impression on the young, coming as it does from such an unimpeachable source.

Lemmon's significance for business ethics, however, is not that he dramatized the essentially Manichaean struggle between the heroic individual and the evil organization his father may have dramatized each evening. Instead, he has created a memorable set of characters whose predicament transcends the confines of any Manichaean perspective on business. Those of you who still find theology illuminating may suspect an Augustinian move at this point. Is there a truth in Lemmon's business films that transcends Manichaeanism?

Augustine's path toward Christian faith, you may recall, took a decisive turn when he adopted the Manichaean perspective, and then abandoned it because of its failure to account fully for the human condition as he knew it.[6] It slowly dawned on him that Manichaeism is a moral and metaphysical form of dualism, in which good and evil are polarized, and deceptively so. Spirit is good; matter is evil; the human spirit is trapped in an evil body, embedded in an evil social world from which it must find release to achieve an ultimate reunion with God, who is, of course, absolutely good and infinitely pure in spirit. To the casual observer, this may sound like an apt description of classical Christianity. But, as Augustine discovered, it is not.

On Manichaean premises it is impossible to understand the central truth of Christianity, namely, its insistence that "The Word became Flesh," that is, a metaphysically realistic confession of faith in the divine humanity of God's only Son. If the human body and the world is evil by definition, how, then, as Christians confess, could God become human? Why was it necessary for Jesus the Christ to become one of us, to suffer like us and die like us, to accomplish our salvation? If a wholly innocent spirit is trapped in matter, it ought to take no more than a clear and simple revelation of this truth to set spirit on the path of its own liberation. What Augustine knew from experience, and Christian faith helped him understand, is that spirit is as much part of the problem as it is part of the solution, as is the human body, as is the social world, all of which are dimensions of the cosmic tiger that Jesus Christ has saved. There is no innocence here, and salvation cannot be equated with the illusory pursuit of innocence. This is the logic of the incarnational faith that Augustine, at least, discerned through his struggle to overcome Manichaeanism.

The Lemmonade I have distilled from these three films is meant to highlight certain aspects of that struggle as they continue to manifest themselves in the modern business world. Harry may be searching for his lost innocence but he never claims to have found it. His desires are understandable but they are never presented as pure. The world in which he must act may be fallen but it is not totally depraved either. Some of the people he must deal with—like Sheldrake, Williamson, and Charlie Robbins (Thayer David), the arsonist—may seem diabolical, but there are others—like Fran and Phil, and even Ricky Roma—whose loves suggest that virtue can, and often does, coexist with vice, and hope with despair. The businesses within which Harry tries to earn his daily bread are never given as an easy excuse for evildoing. There is, as Augustine pointedly observed, honor even among thieves. Harry lectures Williamson on the loyalty that a salesman should feel instinctively for his partner, after having betrayed the firm by selling the Glengarry leads. Working for shady real-estate agents like Mitch and Murray may be as close to a season in Hell as any salesman would care to get but, even in Hell, as Augustine taught, the presence of God can be apprehended in His very absence. Grace sometimes is revealed only in the abscesses formed by our misdirected longings for salvation.

When a younger and not yet wiser Harry gives Sheldrake his comeuppance, he self-righteously announces, "I have decided to become a Mensch. You know what that means? A human being." But in God's own mercy, such a moral makeover usually takes a lifetime to accomplish. So it is with Harry, who seems to know himself better the less he succeeds in business. Stealing the Glengarry leads is not simply an act of financial desperation; at his age, it may be all he can do to get back at Mitch and Murray for the way they have degraded his humanity, his and that of the salesmen he regards as his partners. Perhaps. But he also needed the money for his daughter. Perhaps not.

Thus, Harry is a portrait of the businessman, struggling not always successfully to be a Mensch. This Lemmonade may seem rather bitter but only until we compare its taste with what is on offer from the competition. Harry is hardly an ethical role model. He does not claim to be virtuous in any exemplary way. But he does embody, beyond virtue and vice, Everyman's struggle for a salvation that, seemingly, the world cannot give. Harry shows us that being a businessman exempts no one from that struggle. People in business, like all other human beings, will ultimately be judged, as Augustine taught, by who and what they love, no more and no less.

Business ethics, as it is usually practiced in U.S. academic circles, could well use a dose of this Lemmonade. The idea is not to quench our thirst for success, as if there were something wrong with the hope of doing well while doing good, but, just as business ethics has moved more deeply—beyond the application of moral theories to difficult quandaries—into subtle questions concerning personal and corporate integrity, so it must not turn away from these questions without confronting the religious assumptions that, one way or another, define integrity for us. Business ethics can pursue no higher goal than the one Harry sets out for himself, enabling ourselves and others to become fully human, not in spite of, but precisely in and through our routine business practices. Savoring this Lemmonade, however, may put us on notice that there is more to becoming a Mensch than simply wishing it were so. Becoming fully human is always a struggle, not least of all with our expectations of what it means to be saved.

NOTES

1. The films are still available for rental through commercial distributors like Blockbuster Video. The transcripts of scenes quoted in this paper were taken directly from the films. The dialogue in the film version of *Glengarry Glen Ross* was checked against the text of the original stage play by David Mamet (New York: Grove Press, 1982).

2. In one database I used to search for movie themes, only 315 of some 90,000 films were listed as having anything to do with business.

3. The review from *Cinebooks' Motion Picture Guide* is available in Microsoft's CD-Rom, *Cinemania95*.

4. Still useful as an indication of the pervasive hold of individualism on popular culture in the U.S.A. is Robert Bellah et al., *Habits of the Heart: Individualism and Commitment in American Life* (Berkeley: University of California Press, 1985).

5. Robert Jackall, *Moral Mazes: The World of the Corporate Managers* (New York: Oxford University Press, 1988).

6. An interpretation of Augustine's life and theology that supports this sketch is Eugene TeSelle's *Augustine: The Theologian* (London: Burns and Oates, 1970).

PART III

— ✦ —

The Business World

Shaping Our Vision of the Good Life

10

DOES HOLLYWOOD BASH BIG BUSINESS?

— ◉ —

MICHAEL MEDVED

I want to speak to you about not only what Hollywood, what the entertainment industry *can* do to promote ethics in business but to demonstrate what the entertainment industry is doing, and has been doing for several decades, to discourage ethical reflection and to discourage ethical behavior in the business world. This discouragement really takes two forms and has two thrusts.

Number 1 is through message and number 2 is through example. I want to take these in turn and then come back to talk about the way the entertainment industry might be able to change, and to alter and revise its currently destructive impact.

When it comes to message, anyone who has been paying attention, even in the slightest manner, to motion pictures, television, and popular music over the last twenty years has to have noticed the profound and seemingly irrational hostility to business that inflicts virtually every television show, virtually every motion picture in which business people appear. One need only look this week at the list of film releases that are performing at the box office and you will see no shortage of examples: *First Wives Club,* the no. 1 film in the country, hardly creates an image of sensitive, morally accountable, ethical and decent business people. The business people who appear in the film are caricatures, and negative caricatures. The no. 2 film this week is called *Extreme Measures* which deals with precisely those extreme measures people in the medical business will take, sacrificing health and even the lives of patients to maximize profits. Perhaps most shockingly and surprisingly, the no. 6 film is a rather charming little production called *Fly Away Home.* Based on a true story, this is a film about an experiment in which, through the use of gliders, Canada geese are taught new migration patterns. The film, however, has a very peculiar subtext added to it that has absolutely no correlation to the real incident that inspired it and that goes very much to the point of Hollywood's underlying hostility to business. The subtext is this: greedy developers in North Carolina are trying to rape a natural area, so the geese must be led to this area of natural beauty to stop the evil exploiters who are waiting there with their contracts, their lawyers, and their bulldozers.

The world of television, which is monitored, by and large, by souls more courageous than I, falls into the same pattern. Professor Stanley Rothman of Smith College and his colleague, Bob Lichter, did a survey for their book, *Watching America,* in which they looked at all the major television series (they did not watch every series made but took a random sampling) and correlated all the series between 1955 and 1965, and then between 1965 and 1985. What they saw was absolutely extraordinary. Between 1955 and 1965, there was a somewhat better than a two-to-one chance that a businessman would be portrayed positively. In the following two decades, from 1965 to 1985, the ratio was more than reversed, and there was almost a three-to-one propensity to portray businessmen in a negative light. In, fact, subsequent studies by the Media Research Center in Alexandria, Virginia (which does an amazing job monitoring *every* television series), indicated that of all identifiable occupational groups, businessmen are most likely to commit crimes on prime-time television, second only to gangsters. According to the Media Research Center, some 44 percent of all murders in prime-time television in the first five years of the 1990s were committed by businessmen. What is going on here? There is something incredibly bizarre about all this.

Films based on Michael Crichton's novels are just a few examples from the world of motion pictures about this kind of stereotyping. There is *Rising Sun,* which has a good cast, with Sean Connery and Denzel Washington, and is a dreadful film. What is it about? It is about an evil, massive conspiracy aimed at American businesses, which are being bought and sold by evil Japanese conglomerates. It is all about how these evil Japanese interests are murdering innocent Americans and doing do so with the connivance, of course, of big American corporate bosses. Then, of course, there was *Disclosure,* with Demi Moore and Michael Douglas, one of the few films to portray the rather glamorous world of Silicon Valley, the high-tech world of big computer businesses. Is it shown as a world of tremendous inventiveness, of creativity, of imagination and drive and productivity, which I believe it is in reality? After all, this is one business area where the United States has done very well, where people, using very few natural resources (unless you count grains of sand), are remaking our world through the power of the human mind, an accomplishment very little treated in motion pictures or on television. In any event, the world of Silicon Valley depicted in *Disclosures* is a dark, conspiratorial world, where Demi Moore uses charges of sexual harassment (false charges because she has actually been pursuing Michael Douglas) to mask a much deeper conspiracy at the very heart and soul of this company, which is utterly corrupt and utterly evil.

Then, most striking of all, there is the most popular film ever made, *Jurassic Park.* Who are the bad guys? Businessmen and lawyers, of course (the lawyers are negligible; one sitting on a toilet is devoured by a dinosaur, which, of course, is a very satisfying and gleeful film moment to all of us who dropped out of law school). In *Jurassic Park* the view of American business is very much in line with what I have been talking about here, where businessmen will do absolutely anything to maximize profits: exposing the visitors of *Jurassic Park* to danger, exploiting these dinosaurs, exploiting this wonderful technology for the sake of business and greed, going back again to the old stereotype from some years ago in *Jaws,* where the local businessmen want to hide the danger of shark attack.

This notion of greedy business has been driven home so insistently and so unvaryingly that to say "greedy businessmen" is almost unnecessary; you do not need the adjective. Whenever you say "businessmen" in the media, you can assume greed. It is extraordinary. Take a look at films that purport to show the inner workings of business, for instance, *The Hudsucker Proxy.* An absolutely dreadful film by the Cone brothers; they had to subpoena people to go to see it. Starring Paul Newman, the film shows that business success is never based, in Hollywood's version, upon brilliance, hard work, heroism, creativity, or sacrifice. It is always based on dumb luck, inherited wealth, or crookedness. In *Other People's Money,* starring Danny De Vito; in *Head Office,* starring Jane Seymour; in *Secret of My Success* (aptly titled), starring Michael J. Fox, people rise in the business world either through comical circumstance, sheer charm, or very often trickery.

Oliver Stone's films in this one regard almost fit into the pattern. They are not the kind of paranoid, marginal entertainments they are on political subjects. When it comes to portrayals of the business world, and only in that regard, Oliver Stone is mainstream. An appalling thought, by the way. Oliver Stone made *Wall Street,* starring Michael Douglas and Charlie Sheen; Michael Douglas won the Oscar for saying, "Greed is good!" Once again, everyone on Wall Street is shallow and greedy and horrible. Who is the hero in *Wall Street?* Who is the voice of conscience who tells Charlie Sheen, the up-and-coming young businessman, "Get out of Wall Street, get out of that corrupt den of thieves and horrible people"? It is his father, played by his real-life father, Martin Sheen, a committed Catholic, one of the very few in Hollywood. Martin Sheen plays a union officeholder, and, of course, the organized labor point of view is also the point of view of conscience, as opposed to the surrogate father played by Michael Douglas, who represents the point of view of corruption and evil and business.

Then look at all the other Oliver Stone films. In *JFK* the caricatures of businessmen include Clay Shaw, played by Tommy Lee Jones, and they are directly involved in the conspiracy. I thought it was an absolutely brilliant marketing strategy that Stone used in *JFK*. The entire approach was that he assumed if everyone he implicated in the Kennedy assassination came to see the film he would be guaranteed a box-office hit because absolutely every American institution and organization, including the Camp Fire Girls, seems to have been involved in trying to kill John Kennedy, according to the feverish swamp of Oliver Stone's paranoid imagination. But, then, in *Nixon* (no one saw *Nixon*, and a good thing too—it is three hours and fifteen minutes of excruciating tedium) there are several scenes, again invented out of whole cloth, showing the president of the United States paying obeisance to evil businessmen located—where else—in Dallas. These evil businessmen are, by implication, the same evil businessmen who have murdered John Kennedy. They are telling Richard Nixon what to do, and eventually bring him into their business-oriented conspiracy called Watergate.

This kind of thing is so bizarre that one would be worried about it in any event. But what I think particularly worrisome is that it is never balanced by more affirmative views of business institutions or business individuals. Think of a recent film, and by recent I mean in the last twenty years, that portrays a businessman in anything like a favorable light. I can think of two, and they are remarkable exceptions. One of them is *Tucker,* a Francis F. Coppola film. It is a wonderful film in my opinion, loosely based on a true story about the would-be automaker in the post-World-War II era, who created, out of his vision, a magnificent car. *Tucker* shows some of the romance of business, and it shows an entrepreneur in an admiring way (beautifully played by Jeff Bridges, one of those consistently underrated American actors), but the entrepreneur has his golden dreams crushed at the end by Ford, Chrysler, and GM and by a totally fictional senator played by Jeff Bridges' real-life father, Lloyd Bridges. So even though this one film shows an entrepreneur as an admirable person, ultimately the business system, the industrial system in the United States, is still indicted and still seen as corrupt and evil and destructive of any kind of goodness or heroism.

The other film (actually two films because there is a sequel) that portrays a businessman in a somewhat more affectionate light is *Father of the Bride*. Steve Martin plays a factory owner, running a business that seems to make women and children's clothing. One of the reasons he is portrayed in an affectionate light is because it is a remake of an old film from 1950, in which Spencer Tracy played the businessman role. That is why *Father of the Bride* (1990) and *Father of the Bride II* (1995) both seem to have some lingering affection for this George Banks character, played by Steve Martin. But it is also interesting to note that the same people who made the 1995 film (Charles Shyer and Nancy Meyers, the director and writer, as well as the co-producer team), as if to demonstrate they do not have any personal affection for the business world, have also made several other films, including two that are very dire indictments of business. For instance, their film *Baby Boom* is one in which Diane Keaton is a driven tiger-lady in business. Is it not obnoxious and antifeminine stereotyping when virtually every strong female in a business position in films is portrayed as a cartoon, as an evil, sexually manipulative, cold, frigid, emasculating word that rhymes with witch?

This is true of Jayne Seymour's character in *Head Office*, of Sigourney Weaver in *Working Girl*, and of several characters in *Secret of My Success*. It is also true of the Diane Keaton character in *Baby Boom*, except that she has an awakening, as people often do in films about business, and learns that business is evil and horrible. She leaves her high-pressure corporate career and retires to a small town in Vermont and gets enlightenment.

Another film Charles Shyer and Nancy Meyers made more recently (if you blinked you missed it), was called *Looking for Trouble*, starring Nick Nolte and Julia Roberts. A dreadful film all about bovine growth hormones. Roberts and Nolte play intrepid reporters, exposing yet another massive business conspiracy where businessmen not only hide evidence about bovine growth hormones, which are poisoning all Americans, ruining our milk, and killing our kids, but actually murder people, including reporters and, potentially, the heroes.

Another example of a stereotypical businessman who gets enlightenment through unconventional means is in *Regarding Henry*. I think one could characterize it as a film in which Harrison Ford is a 1980s, greed-is-good, Reagan Republican who gets shot in the head, loses three-quarters of his brain capacity, and becomes a liberal Democrat. That is a good summary of the film. He does get shot in the head and then adopts a little dog. It is almost a pathetic caricature, it seems to me, of the kind of film that we are talking about.

In any event, it does not have to be this way, and the evidence for that is the old Hollywood, the Hollywood of the "golden age." You would have no problem at all in finding business people who are portrayed very affectionately and very heroically if you were looking at films of the 1930s and 1940s.

For instance, one wonderful film that comes to mind is *Dinner at Eight*. The central character is Lionel Barrymore. He is the head of a shipping company and is rather heroically trying to keep his company afloat, and I do not mean that just as a metaphor; he is literally trying to keep the company going and that is seen as good thing, not an evil thing. It is a recognition that people are depending on him for their jobs; his wife is depending on him, the whole family and the whole dinner party is depending on him, and he is trying and struggling to keep his business going. Perhaps most striking of all is a 1940s film called *Union Pacific*, in which railroad builders are portrayed in an extraordinarily positive way. It is almost unidimentionally heroic.

Perhaps most famously, the most beloved American film of all time is *It's a Wonderful Life*. You see it every year. George Bailey, the Jimmy Stewart character, what does he do for a living? He is a banker! The film shows that some of the people he is associated with are not as compassionate as he is, but try to imagine any film about a compassionate *banker* today. It is not because compassionate bankers do not exist in the real world—they do. They do not exist in the world of imagination as cycled back to us by Hollywood.

So let me ask two more questions about this message before I move on to the second part of the destructive impact of this ethical bias in Hollywood films. First of all, What difference does it make? Second, Why is it there?

I would submit that it makes a good deal of difference because, unfortunately, the impact of Hollywood, the impact of what we consume through television and motion pictures is their power to define and redefine morals. We all spend more time with popular culture than we do with any other aspect of our lives. The average American will spend in his lifetime more time watching television than he will spend at work. Why? Because, you usually begin your work life when you are between sixteen and eighteen, or between twenty-five and twenty-seven, depending on who you are, but you begin your television watching life when you are one or two. You take vacations from work, sometimes long vacations, but very few people take vacations from television. You retire from work but few people ever retire from television; in fact, retirement years are years of maximal television watching. By the age of eighteen the average American will have spent more time watching television than that person will have spent in classrooms, for the same reason. People take vacations from school; they do not take vacations from television.

The impact of this material is indicated by the twenty-six hours a week, on average, that Americans watch television. The devastating power of the entertainment medium is to define "normal," and, by defining corruption and greed and callousness and crookedness as normal in the business world,

Hollywood does two things: (1) It discourages idealistic people from going into business because the images of heroic, idealistic, committed, thoughtful, compassionate business people do not exist. There are very few images in the popular culture to encourage you to do good in the world by going into business. (2) It regularizes and normalizes corruption so that people who do go into business feel that if they are cutting corners, if they are cheating, if they are betraying, they are simply following the normal course of affairs for anyone in the business community. These images matter a great deal.

The second question I would pose is, Why is this bias there? Why is Hollywood so unremittingly negative about the business community? It does not seem to make any sense because, after all, Hollywood itself is business. It is the entertainment *business*, it is show *business*. Why does Hollywood turn against the very principles, ideas, and profit motives that clearly are alive and well in most corporate board rooms in the entertainment industry? There is a rather evocative answer suggested by Ben Stein, a sometime actor who played Ferris Beuler's groaning high-school teacher. Ben Stein has also written a book called *Sunset Boulevard* in which he suggests that the people who write this material, who after all are the source of the images you see on screen—the screenwriters—tend to have very limited experiences of business. What is the only business model they ever see? Hollywood, and its producers. I worked as a screenwriter too for three years, and it is a very ugly back side of the business world. Every negative stereotype that is applied by Hollywood screenwriters to business generally is usually true about the people in Hollywood. They are dumb, they are crooked, they are ugly, they are selfish, they are mean—all of these things. These are the business experiences every screenwriter has had. I have had these experiences. Screen writers are very low down on the food chain, on the level of paramecium.

The truth is that screenwriters have this miserable experience with business and they believe it is representative of America at large. But there is a deeper reason. This is my own analysis, to supplement Ben Stein's. Anyone who knows Hollywood knows the tremendous truth of a famous dictum by a screenwriter named William Goldman, who said that the first truth about Hollywood is that nobody knows anything and that, basically, things are unpredictable. You can make a wonderful film and release it and no one will see it, and then you can turn around and make a piece of really charmless garbage and it will become a major or substantial hit. This happens all the time. People in Hollywood know there are people who are earning $9 million and $12 million a film, who have less talent than most *waiters* in southern California. That is true because virtually every waiter in southern California has an agent and is looking for an acting career.

You have a model in the film business of rewards being handed out irrationally, a random system, a system that has very little to do with creativity or honor or productivity or reward for excellence. It really is a roulette wheel, and that model is the only model of business that most people who create motion pictures know personally. So that model ends up as applying to all business and to the larger world of business.

The second thrust is the role of example. Mike Frankovich, who was a famous producer of the fifties, once said that everybody in America has two businesses: their own and the film business. This has never been more true than it is today. A very big change has happened over the last four or five years. Every Monday they release the figures on the films that perform at the box office. They make a big deal of it. It is like a horse race, like presidential polls or football standings. They release the films that are leading at the box office. They release the top-rated television shows—they never used to do that. But people use the entertainment industry as the model for business generally, not just in Hollywood but in America at large.

That is why the force of example is so powerful here and so destructive, because, when it comes to demonstrating the whole free enterprise system, people are more conscious of the example of Hollywood than of any other example in the country. This is a business that clearly gets more attention in the media than computers, than cars, than home building, than producing widgets, than anything else. People care about winners and losers, ups and downs, and investments that get returned. It is amazing to me. You find people very far removed from Hollywood who will tell you, "Oh, yea, well they seem to do a lot of business on *Waterworld*. After all, it made $90 million but I do not think they will earn back their investment." This is something people talk about in America, and it is a very destructive example. Why do I say that? Because it is so clear to America at large that Hollywood is not run on ethical principles.

Most people in the country believe the entertainment industry is harming our society. There have been countless polls and surveys. I know of at least thirty that are fairly authoritative and they show that upward of 75 percent of Americans of every political stripe think the net impact of the entertainment industry is destructive—bad for kids, bad for adults, bad for America. It is a tremendously destructive example when the most visible business in the country is seen to be undermining values about which we all care. What makes it even more destructive is the excuse Hollywood uses, a specious and fallacious excuse. What does Hollywood say when people attack the entertainment industry for destroying the values of kids, appealing to violence, glorifying promiscuous sexuality, and showing vulgar behavior and crude language? What do people in the entertainment industry say? "It is what people want to see. We are in business. We have to give the public what it wants." Leave aside for a moment that they display the same morality as cocaine dealers. "We just give the public what it wants. People want to use our products so we give it to them." The fact is that this argument makes Hollywood worse than cocaine dealers and tobacco companies because, in the case of Hollywood, it is not true that it gives the public what it wants.

However, the entertainment industry, which everyone assumes does horrible things because of the profit motive, is actually remarkably insensitive to the profit motive and ignores its own self-interest regularly. This, by the way, has made my work particularly controversial in the entertainment industry. It is not the fact that I call these folks bad citizens. Everybody calls them bad citizens, they are used to that. I call them something much worse. They are bad businessmen. They are lousy businessmen. They are profoundly and, seemingly, incurably stupid.

In 1995, according to the Motion Picture Association of America, 62 percent of all films released in the United States were rated R. Of the box office top ten, 20 percent were rated R? The number 1 film in the country was a PG13 film, a bad film called *Batman Forever;* it was the softest of the three Batman films. Number 2 was a PG film called *Apollo 13,* a wonderful film. Number 3 was *Pocohantas.* Number 4 was another dark, cutting-edge, blood-soaked shocker called *Toy Story.* Number 5 was another PG13 film, a not particularly good picture but one that glorified other bodily functions other than violence, a film called *Ace Ventura: When Nature Calls.* Number 6 was *Casper,* another PG-rated film.

In other words, the entire top ten, except for two, were rated PG or PG13. The only two to make it to the top ten that were rated R were *Die Hard with a Vengeance* (no. 7), a very bloody Bruce Willis film, and *Crimson Tide,* one that had no violence in it at all; it was rated R because of language. But you really could not object to the language because it is a film about a nuclear submarine at a time of world crisis and I, for one, am willing to believe that, at such moments, perhaps even members of the United States Navy resort to impolite language.

The point is that, in 1995, where is the evidence that America is motivated by some kind of atavistic blood lust, or the evidence that people are demanding dismemberment and horror and cruelty? It does not exist. You can look at 1994 and the evidence is even more striking. In 1994, the two films that dominated the box office and became among the top five money-making films of all time were the *Lion King* (no. 1, rated G), and *Forrest Gump.*

You can look for twenty years, and I am sure you can look before that as well, but I have only done the study for twenty years. Plug into the computer for every film released in America. Then, classify the films by their MPAA ratings, NC17, R, or PG13, PG, G, and look at the box office returns reported by *Variety*. It is absolutely consistent; there is not a single year where PG- and G-rated films do not out-perform R. In fact, over the stretch of twenty years, they beat R by an average of nearly three to one, which indicates that the industry is profoundly dysfunctional because, during that same time period, the percentage of R-rated films, which have a much bigger chance of going bust and a much lower chance of making big money, have become more and more common.

If you figure in video sales it is even more disproportional because the video market is even more dominated by PG- and G-rated titles. The list of the fifty top-selling videos of all time is utterly dominated by Disney releases. *Lion King* is no. 1 and *E.T.* is no. 2. I believe *Snow White* is no. 3. When you add on foreign sales it closes the gap somewhat. R-rated films do a little better abroad, but they still do not perform as well abroad as PG and G.

Let me give you two indications of just how bizarre it is. Most films are rated R not because of violence, not because of sex, but because of language. What sort of stupidity is it to think that the American people are craving foul language in films? Have you ever heard of anybody who leaves a motion picture theater saying, You know, I like that film but I just feel cheated because the language in it was too clean? There is no reason in the world that PG as a rating should stand for Profanity Guaranteed.

Let me give another example. I have written elsewhere very extensively about Hollywood's propensity to attack religious beliefs. How stupid is this? This is a religious country. According to a *Newsweek* poll, 70 percent of us pray every day, 60 percent of us say grace over meals regularly, and 40–45 percent of us go to church or synagogue every week. Why, then, attack religious believers? In Holy Week of 1995, the Disney Company released a film called *Priest*, perhaps the most anti-Catholic film ever made, and a film that shows five different members of the priesthood all of whom are tormented by the preachings of the church and its teachings. Then, in Holy Week the next year, Paramount Pictures released *Primal Fear*, about an archbishop in Chicago who is murdered and everybody is in mourning because he is such a saintly, wonderful man. It turns out that he has been secretly forcing altar boys to do pornographic films for him. What sense does this make?

It is unbearably bizarre. It would be appropriate for a lecture in the psychology department, because we are really talking about psychopathology.

We are talking about people who harm their own business interests consistently—in pursuit of what?

They are in pursuit of peer respect, and this relates to something that Rabbi Goldberg says in his chapter in this book. The problem with people coming out of film schools as opposed to people coming out of law or business schools, is that they are not greedy enough. People coming out of film schools do not have any healthy sense of greed or profit. Why? Because they all want to be Martin Scorsese. What is wrong with being Martin Scorsese? I will tell you what is wrong. He has made thirty-eight films but only one of them has made a profit—his worst film, *Cape Fear*. His films lose money. He is not a commercially successful director. Who else do film school graduates want to be? They want to be Woody Allen. A characteristic of Woody Allen's work is that it loses money. Only two films, *Annie Hall* and *Hannah and Her Sisters*, out of Woody Allen's entire canon of more than thirty films, have made a dime. It is utterly absurd.

Do film school students come out wanting to be Steven Herrick? They have not even heard of Steven Herrick. He made a wonderful film last year called *Mr. Holland's Opus* that made $80 million. He also made *The Mighty Ducks*, which made even more than that. He tends to make family-oriented films and that is not respected in Hollywood.

Everybody here knows the name Quentin Tarantino. He is a director on the cutting edge and critically acclaimed, but Quentin Tarantino has only one commercially successful film—*Pulp Fiction*. He has had several ventures since then, all which have gone right down the toilet, made no money at all. But Tarantino is the inspiration for a whole generation of young directors. No one wants to imitate Elliot Minkoff. He directed a film called *Lion King* which, worldwide, has done ten times the business of *Pulp Fiction*.

This is the essence of the problem. At the same time that people lose faith in business because of Hollywood's messages, they also lose faith in business because of Hollywood's example.

It is not fair, because people think that what they are seeing in Hollywood is an example of greed gone wild; they are not. If Hollywood would display more enlightened greed, they would make a lot more films like *Father of the Bride,* which made a great deal of money; like *Mr. Holland's Opus*; like *Apollo 13*; like *Forrest Gump*. They would make films that appeal to broader audiences. People use Hollywood as an example of corrupt business, but Hollywood does not even follow normal business principles in its choices of product. So what is to be done?

On the first half of the equation—changing the message—there is a profound need for the entertainment industry to begin reconnecting with

America. This is an industry that is almost hermetically sealed, and when people arrive from elsewhere they are almost instantly co-opted into a dysfunctional culture, a culture hostile to families, to religion, and shockingly hostile to an enlightened pursuit of profit.

Here is one example from the newspaper this morning. There is a new film, a comedy about abortion, called *Citizen Ruth,* and it stars Laura Dern. It just won an award at the Montreal Film Festival. Here is the description: "Laura Dern plays Ruth Stoops, a pregnant, vapor-inhaling drifter. 'She is a very challenging person to like. She is a mess, a hero you would not necessarily want to even be on the same bus with.'" Good idea! This will pack them into the seats, right? Then she goes on, "'Audiences know from the first two minutes that this is a funny film,' Dern says. Ruth is seen having sex right off." (That shows it is a funny film!) "Soon she is pregnant for the fifth time and facing felony charges for her inhaling."

It is this kind of attitude—that you know it is a funny film because you see her having sex right off—that characterizes people who work in this business. I wish people in Hollywood would listen to my one-hour radio talk shows. Listen to the calls. Listen to the people. Reconnect.

On the second issue of pursuing enlightened greed, what is desperately needed in Hollywood is changing our standard of what deserves praise. Right now in the entertainment industry we tend to praise and reward shock value, films that "challenge us." What "challenge us" usually means is "offends us." *Pulp Fiction* could be the most critically overpraised film of our time—it won every major critic's award—but there are many films like *Pulp Fiction* that similarly seem to be singled out as deserving of all kinds of magnificent critical attention but really have very little to recommend them. They are emperor's-new-clothes kinds of films that only exist for shock value and tend not to be very popular with the general public.

What we need to do is change the standard of what constitutes great work, to change the standard of these bald, gold statuettes called Oscars because people in the entertainment industry, even more than most, are profoundly insecure. It is a terribly vulnerable position to make your living by getting up in front of millions of people and pretending to be someone you are not. You are subject to the kind of reviews you get, the way your peers react, and, of course, you crave praise and acceptance.

One of the ways to change this equation is for more people of conscience, in particular for more people of religious faith, to get involved in the entertainment industry. Edmund Burke said a long time ago that all that is necessary for evil to triumph is for good men to do nothing. For too long, the religious communities, Catholic, Protestant, and Jewish, have shunned the entertainment industry, viewed it as Babylon, as something corrupt, something not to engage in because it is of the devil. That has to change.

I will end with an example of how to change the whole equation of the entertainment industry's impact on the culture: The best way to change what is on screen is to change the people behind the camera. Steven Spielberg made *Schindler's List,* which I consider to be a great film. He made it partially because of a personal spiritual journey. Because of his wife's conversion to Judaism, he began taking classes in Judaism for the first time. He was not raised in a religious home. His mother became religious long after Steven was an adult and away from home. He had always derided anything Jewish or religious, and you can see this in his early films. Something changed. What changed was him. *Schindler's List* was one of the results. His wife went through conversion, by the way, under Orthodox auspices, which is a rather challenging process; certainly for someone in a high-visibility Hollywood position it would indeed be a challenge to go through that process.

As you know, Spielberg has launched a new business enterprise worth billions of dollars. Dreamworks SKG is the new studio. Their first major motion picture release is called *Prince of Egypt,* and it is the story of Moses. I have spoken to some people in the company and part of the thinking behind it appears to have been that, with this new venture, it would be a good thing to start it off with a blessing. It is also very good business, as biblical films almost always make money. What is great about this decision is that it shows the fusion of business self-interest and true enlightenment because, in making *Prince of Egypt,* Dreamworks SKG is adapting the best-selling book of all time and they do not even have to pay for the rights.

11

GENERAL JOHNSON SAID . . .

— ◉ —

DAVID E. COLLINS

My topic is corporate social responsibility—the myth and the reality. Using the example of Johnson & Johnson, a company for which I worked twenty-six years, I will describe how its leader—General Robert Wood Johnson—and the businessmen trained by him created a business climate that stimulated not only ethical reflection but ethical actions as well.

In 1971, a few years after the General's death, Philip B. Hofmann, then chairman of the board and chief executive officer of Johnson & Johnson, published and distributed to his associates a book entitled, *General Johnson Said* . . . . The book, 125 pages in length, was a collection of some of the written messages the General was so fond of sending to those who worked with and for him. Through such writings, through the early and innovative use of film to communicate to his "boys," and through the extensive use of video technology by his successors, the "new industrial philosophy," as the General originally called it—of responsibility to consumers, employees, and the community as well as to shareholders—was taught to the J&J family. I will explore how these initiatives led to concrete results, but first let me return to the subject of myth.

In the recent book, *Is the Good Corporation Dead?* edited by John Houck and Oliver Williams, Professor Richard T. De George writes about the myth of corporate social responsibility. He takes note of the two meanings of the term "myth." The first refers to something that is completely a figment of one's imagination. The second meaning refers to a story woven with threads of fact and fiction, designed to explain and often promote a belief or practice. It is this second meaning that De George uses in his discussion of social responsibility of corporations.

I suggest that much of what modern popular literature and film present on the topic of business behavior today suggests that corporate social responsibility is a myth of the first kind—a figment of one's imagination. This is illustrated in a recent Steven Segal film, *On Deadly Ground*, about oil exploration in Alaska. The last minutes of this film feature a speech by Segal, accusing big business and big government of polluting the environment and endangering life in the interest of profit.

This image of business, particularly big business, as socially irresponsible is reflected also in the novels of such popular authors as Robert Ludlum and John Grisham. The phenomenon is so widespread that the Public Broadcasting System (PBS) made it the subject of an hour-long report several years ago, entitled "Hollywood's Favorite Heavy Businessmen on Prime Time TV." During the spring of 1996, when public concern with corporate downsizing was the subject of daily press reports, *Newsweek* magazine (February 26, 1996) chose to characterize the executives involved in the decisions as "killers."

Lest you think that I am pinning responsibility exclusively on those outside the business community, let me point out that there are some in business who seem to cherish a reputation of the cold-hearted capitalist! For example, Albert J. Dunlap, the current chief executive officer of the troubled Sunbeam Corporation, allowed himself to be portrayed as "Rambo" in the August 30, 1996, issue of *USA Today*.

The famous British takeover artist, Sir James Goldsmith, was proud to proclaim in a PBS special on "Ethics in America" that:

> I'm in business for money. That's the best reason for anybody to be in business. The demagogue will tell you that he's in business for all these constituencies—suppliers, communities, employees and everything else. That's not true. And if it is true, it's a mistake. . . . It's pure demagoguery.

These popularized images of business have had a predictable and, I believe, unfortunate effect, that of destroying the reputation of business and people in business in the minds of the American people. Let me illustrate. A recent Yankelovitch survey probed the attitude of the public on matters of interest to those of us at this conference. The survey did not read well for the credibility or reputation of business. Only 7 percent of respondents had a great deal of confidence in statements made by major corporations explaining their points of view on major issues. Business barely edged out auto salesmen in the battle for last place. Even worse, perhaps, 67 percent agreed with the statement that "even well-known, long-established companies cannot be trusted to make safe, durable products without the government setting industry standards." Further, 55 percent agreed with the statement that "if the opportunity arises, most businesses will take advantage of the public if they feel they are not likely to be found out." Worst of all, 83 percent agreed with the statement that "American business is too concerned about making a profit and not concerned enough about its responsibilities to workers, consumers, and the environment."

Admittedly, I do not approach this subject as a learned academician, nor a researcher steeped in the results of studying many businesses. My viewpoint was formed "in the trenches" as a result of meeting, working with, and reading about many businesses, large and small, and business people over the course of thirty-five-plus years. But with this caveat, it is my opinion that corporate social responsibility is *not* a myth of the first kind. It is not a figment of one's imagination. To the extent that it has aspects of the second kind of myth, in practice it contains more fact than fiction in the mix.

I want to take this second kind of myth of corporate social responsibility and convert it to reality in the history of one company. In the process I will link that reality to a set of beliefs or a corporate culture strongly supported by actions and by the written and spoken word. Before closing, I will raise some questions about the negative impact of today's literature and films on the goal of promoting socially responsible behavior on the part of the business community.

The *real* events I want share with you are the Tylenol poisoning episodes of 1982 and 1986. As I will try to show, the handling of these terrible events by Johnson & Johnson, while singular in their total dimensions and in the publicity they attracted, were part of a pattern of socially responsible behavior by this company and its executives, stretching back almost forty years.

There were two Tylenol poisoning episodes, but the more famous was the first. You may recall the events which took place just over fourteen years ago on the west side of Chicago. Seven people died as a result of taking Tylenol capsules containing cyanide. The initial reports came in on September 30, 1982, and at first it was not clear whether the cyanide was introduced in the manufacturing plant or after the bottles reached the local store shelves. Johnson & Johnson, working with the local authorities, immediately advised consumers to stop taking Tylenol capsules until the facts could be determined. They also withdrew from sale all remaining bottles from the same manufacturing lots as the implicated Tylenol capsule containers. Although it soon became clear that the tampering took place at the local level, Johnson & Johnson decided to withdraw all Tylenol capsule products from the U.S. market and from all markets around the world where the product was sold. It did this to protect the consumer from the danger of copycat crimes. This step, which cost the company over $100 million in out-of-pocket costs alone, was taken despite the fact that the product was not at fault and there was no legal obligation to withdraw the product.

The company withdrew and destroyed thirty-one million bottles of capsules in total, testing eight million of them in the process. We found two additional contaminated bottles; thus, at least two lives were probably saved by the action.

The events attracted extensive news coverage and generated widespread fear among consumers about the safety of their food and drug products. Johnson & Johnson's response to this was to adopt a policy of openness to the public and the press. Through devices such as 800-number consumer call lines, mailings to and personal calls on medical and trade professionals throughout the country, visits to professional associations and hospitals, and easy availability to the press, the company did what it could to keep the public advised of developments. It also made its senior executives available for television interviews, starting with my appearance on the *Nightline* show on Tuesday, October 5, 1982, the day we announced the nationwide withdrawal. This openness culminated in the *60 Minutes* episode which aired in November 1982.

In further recognition of the existence of fear on the part of the consumer, the company canceled all advertising for the Tylenol brand immediately, and did not resume advertising until early in 1983. The company began consumer surveys within days of the poisonings and hence was able to track consumer sentiments as the days and weeks passed. Its chairman, James E. Burke, was especially concerned not to exacerbate the consumers' fears by challenging them through advertising. The company did go on television in October to announce to the public that it was going to bring the brand back in a tamper-resistant container, and to offer free replacement of Tylenol tablets to anyone who threw away their capsules.

The company did return the capsule product to the market in November, with a new triple-tamper-resistant package. Once again, it offered to give a bottle of the reintroduced product to any consumer calling a designated 800 number.

While it was involved in the withdrawal and reintroduction, the company was cooperating with both law enforcement officers and the Food and Drug Administration (FDA). It offered a reward of $100,000 for the capture of the poisoner, and worked with the over-the-counter industry and the FDA to devise and implement new voluntary regulations governing the use of tamper-evident packaging.

Within one year of the original poisoning, the Tylenol brand had regained its leading market share. Unfortunately, a second poisoning occurred in February 1986, and the Company then withdrew the consumer capsule product from the world market for good, at an additional out-of-pocket cost of $150 million.

While the actions of Johnson & Johnson in the two Tylenol poisoning episodes have been widely recognized and praised as models for socially responsible action by a large corporation, they are relevant for my purposes because they were part of a pattern of responsible behavior, preceding and succeeding the poisoning events, most of which received no favorable public recognition or publicity. It is this pattern that I submit gives reality to the myth of corporate social responsibility. Included in this pattern were the following:

- In the early 1970s, in need of new worldwide headquarters to house its growing staff, the Company elected to stay in its home city of New Brunswick, then a decaying town suffering from urban flight and decaying infrastructure. Rejecting the option of moving to attractive New Jersey suburbs where it would be closer to its employee population, the company began and led a community revitalization process that has today transformed New Brunswick and reversed its slide into decay.
- In the mid-1960s, the company canceled an advertising program of great promise for its Johnson's Baby Oil—one that promoted its use as a tanning enhancer—when its medical director warned about the danger of sun burning, particularly to young skin, due to the magnifying effect of the oil on the sun's rays.
- In the early 1960s, the company canceled a popular-line extension of its famous Band-Aid brand of bandages—the so-called "battle Band-Aids"— when it received complaints from mothers that kids were using the product for play rather than for its intended use.
- Throughout the years, the company was a leader in advancing employee safety. Thus, in the decade of the 1980s, it was the first to recognize the risk to employees from a widely used gas sterilization process and to take steps worldwide to eliminate that risk.
- It mandated the installation of sprinklers in all of its facilities worldwide, owned or rented; adopted a sophisticated worldwide program of machine guarding to reduce on-the-job injuries, and made the audit of compliance with this program a part of the responsibility of its financial auditing teams; and introduced a worldwide program of driving safety and training for its traveling employees.

In these cases, as in the cases of the Tylenol poisonings, I have deliberately noted the worldwide nature of the actions that the company took, to emphasize that the demands of social responsibility do not stop at the U.S. shores for Johnson & Johnson.

How is one to explain these actions, particularly in light of the popular regard for big business as evidenced by the Yankelovitch surveys? To understand, one has to go back to the early 1940s when General Johnson, newly released from the Army Supply Corps, published a book entitled *Or Forfeit Freedom,* in which he set forth in some detail the "new industrial philosophy" to which I referred earlier. This was the earliest public statement of the famous Johnson & Johnson Credo (see fig. 1).

In introducing the Credo in his book, the General used this reasoning:

> We may be sure . . . that both alarm and bitter anger will arise if huge corporations either abuse their power or fail to render the service required by society. The evidence on this point is clear. American institutions, both public and private, exist because the people want them, believe in them, or at least are willing to tolerate them. The day has passed when business was a private matter—if it ever really was. In a business society, every act of business has social consequences and may arouse public interest. Every time business hires, builds, sells, or buys, it is acting for the American people as well as for itself, and it must be prepared to accept full responsibility for its acts. This is a proper situation, and a good one for America.

This proposition and the Credo—its language modernized but its principles unchanged—represent the standard by which Johnson & Johnson and its successive generations of managers have judged their conduct for the last fifty years. It is, I submit, a clear affirmation that the responsibility of business goes beyond the bottom line.

To ensure that the company and its people keep the Credo imperatives in mind, it appears on the walls of all Company facilities, is part of all employee orientations, is the subject of biannual employee surveys and annual employee performance reviews, and is a frequent subject of presentations carried on the company's worldwide employee video network.

An incident in the mid-1970s illustrates the vitality of the Credo culture and relates directly to the later handling of the Tylenol poisoning episodes.

In 1975, an incident involving commercial bribery in Latin America led the senior management of J&J to question whether the commitment to the Credo principles was as widespread as they thought. This led to the initiation of a series of Credo challenge meetings involving the top managements of all 150-plus J&J companies from around the world. At these meetings, which spanned three years, these managements were asked to challenge the continued vitality of the Credo's principles and priorities. Were they still realistic and well founded in the industrial world of the late twentieth century?

Our Credo

We believe our first responsibility is to the doctors, nurses and patients,
to mothers and fathers and all others who use our products and services.
In meeting their needs everything we do must be of high quality.
We must constantly strive to reduce our costs
in order to maintain reasonable prices.
Customers' orders must be serviced promptly and accurately.
Our suppliers and distributors must have an opportunity
to make a fair profit.

We are responsible to our employees,
the men and women who work with us throughout the world.
Everyone must be considered as an individual.
We must respect their dignity and recognize their merit.
They must have a sense of security in their jobs.
Compensation must be fair and adequate,
and working conditions clean, orderly and safe.
We must be mindful of ways to help our employees fulfill
their family responsibilities.
Employees must feel free to make suggestions and complaints.
There must be equal opportunity for employment, development
and advancement for those qualified.
We must provide competent management,
and their actions must be just and ethical.

We are responsible to the communities in which we live and work
and to the world community as well.
We must be good citizens — support good works and charities
and bear our fair share of taxes.
We must encourage civic improvements and better health and education.
We must maintain in good order
the property we are privileged to use,
protecting the environment and natural resources.

Our final responsibility is to our stockholders.
Business must make a sound profit.
We must experiment with new ideas.
Research must be carried on, innovative programs developed
and mistakes paid for.
New equipment must be purchased, new facilities provided
and new products launched.
Reserves must be created to provide for adverse times.
When we operate according to these principles,
the stockholders should realize a fair return.

Johnson & Johnson

Should the language change to reflect the modern realities of the marketplace and the changed relationship of business and government which had come to characterize the post-1960s America?

The conclusion of these series of meetings was a reaffirmation of the Credo's principles, and a renewed awareness of their applicability to the business of Johnson & Johnson. To ensure recommitment to the Credo principles by *all* employees, not only those attending the meetings, the company produced a video, narrated by Edwin Newman, showing a discussion by senior executives of the meaning and challenges of the company's Credo. The video was distributed throughout the worldwide family of companies.

This recommitment found its most visible expression in the company's handling of the 1982 Tylenol poisoning. As you can imagine, that incident required thousands upon thousands of individual decisions made in a crisis environment, with little or no time for the customary "checking up the line" which is characteristic of the traditional command/control organizational structure of business. Yet, most of these, and certainly the important ones, incredibly proved to be the right ones. Let me give you a few examples of decisions made on the spot and without benefit of input from higher-ups:

- The pattern of openness to the public and the press was set on the first day by the medical director of McNeil Consumer Products, the maker of Tylenol, a man with no training or experience in dealing with the press. Responding to the presence of the media at the doors of McNeil in Fort Washington, Pennsylvania, he went outside and told them we knew little or nothing about the reports of poisonings, but that we would tell them what we knew and would keep them informed as we learned more.
- In a local television interview, the president of McNeil stated that no one would lose their job because of the poisonings, despite the fact that almost 40 percent of McNeil's production had been halted as a result of the withdrawal.
- Later, this same executive, in answer to an unanticipated question from a television interviewer, stated that the company would not pass on the added costs of the improved packaging to the consumer.

It is my belief that the reason these executives felt comfortable in making these decisions was because of the Credo and the tradition of living up to it, a tradition built and reinforced over the years by actions, and by communications, including the Credo challenge meetings to which I just referred.

I have gone into great detail about the principles on which J&J does business, but let me assure you that this company is not unique in this regard.

For example, in the last few years these names come to mind: Procter & Gamble; Malden Mills; Levi Strauss; Guardsmark; Servicemaster; and Tom's of Maine—businesses large and small.

This brings me back to the positioning of corporate social responsibility as a fable or myth. It is both untrue and unfair as a characterization of business behavior in this country. It is true, of course, that there are business people who skirt the edges of the law, and some who violate the law. There are those who do not live up to the standards of societal expectations above and beyond the law. However, at times even the best of companies slip, and a mistake is made. These incidents make interesting reading, perhaps more interesting than the stories of responsible behavior. But to use these examples as a basis for characterizing business in general, as it is commonly done in today's media, is like condemning all journalists because of the lies of one anonymous author.

In a curious way, I admit, this characterization has a beneficial effect on behavior. Business people are citizens, have families, and belong to a community; they do not like nor do they want to be cast as villains. Therefore, this distortion of business behavior does tend to limit that behavior in a positive way. I remember that, during the 1970s foreign bribery scandals when business was searching for a process its people could self-administer to check on the propriety of their behavior, one international oil company president told his people to avoid any action they would be reluctant to disclose on national television.

But I am more concerned with the possible existence of a feedback mechanism here. Most would agree that socially responsible actions on the part of business people is in the best interest of all of us. However, if you tell a person repeatedly how they are expected to behave, particularly with the new entrants to the marketplace, generally they will behave that way. As evidence of this, a survey of recent MBA graduates reported in a 1995 edition of the *Wall Street Journal* indicated that a substantial percentage of them would cheat and lie if that is what it took to save their business or advance their career. Is this because these folks are inherently dishonest, or is it because that is what they have been taught by the influences of our popular culture?

As I am a citizen and businessman, I see a further and more troubling risk in this myth. The aforementioned Yankelovitch survey data indicate that these characterizations of business help to form public opinion in support of increased government control of business activity; when the public does not trust business to act responsibly, it will turn to government to take appropriate steps. This will virtually always result in further restrictions on the ability of the business sector to do the job only it can do in our society, to

create wealth and to enhance the standard and quality of life. These caricatures of business behavior to which I have referred serve then to tip the
balance away from the workings of the free market in many situations in
which decisions need to balance the values provided by freedom of action
with those provided by a communitarian or egalitarian approach.

Is there a solution to the problem of myth to which I have referred? Perhaps this conference is a step in that direction. The efforts of the Center for
Ethics and Religious Values in Business, and similar initiatives, are important
contributions. Certainly, the answer does not lie in any advertising or public-
relations approach undertaken by the business community. The Yankelovitch
surveys show how little the American public trusts the word of big business.
These efforts are seen as self-interested and are discounted accordingly.

Better for business to turn its resources—meaning actions, words, and
films—to its employees, to educate and perpetuate the commitment to socially responsible behavior because, without question, business must live up
to these public expectations. But today, it cannot expect applause. We are no
longer in the era of Jimmy Stewart and *It's a Wonderful Life*. Rather, we are
in the era when AT&T's precedent-setting program to secure jobs for its ter-
minated employees was lost in the noise of criticism of its chief executive
officer and his compensation. General Johnson had a thought on challenges
like this:

> Our people must be realistic and face the situation objectively. We have no
> room for false enthusiasm and wishful thinking.

Right on the money, I think, just like a lot of what . . . *General Johnson Said.*

12

THE MORAL CHALLENGE
TO BUSINESS TODAY

— ⊕ —

CHARLES VAN DOREN

Businessmen and women tire of being told they have moral responsibilities other people do not have. This is understandable. Why should businessmen and women be required to be more virtuous than other people? They have to make a living too. Besides, they owe allegiance of one kind or another to many institutions ordinary people can usually ignore. The market. The government. The bottom line. To say nothing of family and the demands of leisure and learning. Is there time and strength to deal with any other pressures?

These things are true. Yet there is one great moral challenge to business today that business cannot ignore. The challenge is, in a way, very simple. Yet I believe that if the challenge is not met there will be dreadful consequences.

UT PICTURA POESIS

This famous phrase comes from the Roman poet Horace who lived two thousand years ago. A very free modern translation would be: One picture is worth a thousand words. Let me begin, therefore, by drawing a picture, an image I hope you will keep before you as I proceed. We are standing on the bank of a river. The river is almost at flood stage, and the current is fierce. A large number of other persons are standing near us on the bank, observing the power of the stream with various emotions, ranging from excitement to terror. They are speaking to one another in loud voices so as to be heard over the roar of the water.

Suddenly we become aware of something remarkable and unexpected that is being carried by the roiling waves. What is it? At first it is hard to tell.

Then we realize it is a young woman, perhaps a girl. As she approaches, it becomes apparent that she is in great distress. Barely able to keep her head above the rushing water, she is waving her arms and crying out to us and the others for help.

We cannot fail to notice the diversity of reactions of the persons standing near us. Some are running, shouting instructions and encouragement, but to no avail. Others are exclaiming that someone ought to do something, for example, plunge into the water to help the struggling girl—although they are quick to add that they cannot do this themselves because they do not know how to swim. A few have fallen on their knees and are imploring their god or gods. But the majority seem little moved. They assure one another that the girl is really not in any danger. After all, she has been swimming for a long time and is used to such exertion; there is no reason why she cannot swim a while longer. Besides, they say, there is a Ranger headquarters around the bend where there are surely experienced and knowledgeable experts with the appropriate equipment and machines to save her—if in fact she really does need saving.

We, however, realize the Ranger headquarters is upstream, not downstream. The girl has already passed it. We also seem to be the only onlookers who know there is a waterfall around the bend, over which the water must be crashing down. We realize the girl is being swept to her death.

We try to convey these concerns to our companions on the bank. But they do not hear us and the few who do, repeat that there is nothing they can do. Many shrug their shoulders and turn away. It is not their problem; besides, it would be foolhardy to enter the rushing waters. To our horror we realize the girl is very close to us now. There is very little time. To our greater horror we realize that we, who are strong swimmers, are the only ones who can save her.

She approaches—she sees us—her eyes are filled with dread. She calls out to us, but her words are lost in the roar of the water. We must decide quickly what to do. There is only a moment. . . .

Forgive me for breaking off at this point. I must leave this young woman suspended in her peril. I will return to her and her plight soon enough.

UNDERSTANDING THE UNIVERSE

In his ingenious book, *Ten Faces of the Universe*,[1] Sir Fred Hoyle makes this remarkable declaration of faith:

There will never be any long-term purpose for our species other than understanding of the universe. If this purpose does not prove sufficient for us, if
we are impelled to invent all manner of nonsensical substitutes, then very
likely we shall not survive as the dominant animal on Earth for very much
longer.

Perhaps the name Fred Hoyle is not as well known as it was half a century ago. Hoyle was a great cosmologist; he also wrote very good science-
fiction novels. He was known in the 1950s, when I was a student of his at the
University of Cambridge, for his opposition to the Big Bang theory of the
origin of the universe. Instead, he proposed a so-called Steady State theory, a
concept of continuous coming to be of matter at a very slow but steady rate.
According to the theory, a single atom of hydrogen simply appears in each
cubic meter of space (empty or not) every day, or year, or century. I do not remember the exact details, but the idea seemed thrilling to me, a very young
cosmologist, at the time. It also explained, as the Big Bang theory does, why
this universe is expanding. But, in addition, Hoyle was saying that matter is
inherently fruitful, that somehow, mysteriously, it constantly creates itself.

His daring hypothesis was opposed by almost everybody, and Hoyle
himself abandoned it in later years, to my regret. But what of his claim that
there is no long-term purpose for our species other than understanding of the
universe? Is this correct?

It may be so. A long time ago, as we ourselves view the past of our
own species, we humans placed our bet on progress in knowledge. We put all
our eggs in that one basket, and we have been living with the consequences
of that choice—made by us alone of all the living beings in the world—ever
since.

For the last three thousand years, and perhaps ten or even fifty times
longer, we have attempted to understand the universe in two different ways:
one is the way of science, the other is the way of art.

To make a long and complicated story much too short, the way of science is to declare war on the universe—on "nature," that omnibus word.
Science tries to control, to dominate nature. Explicitly, its aim is to change the
world to make it more accommodating to and comfortable for us. Implicitly,
its aim is to destroy nature, the universe, and replace it with something made
by human beings. The scientist, typically—qua scientist—both denies the
Creator and desires to be divine.

The way of art attempts to see nature as it is. Art depicts, expresses, or
reveals the universe as it appears to us to be, or it tries to do so, without ever
succeeding perfectly. Art seeks to understand the universe—nature—not to

control or dominate it, but for the sake of understanding itself. The artist—qua artist—accepts nature as it is and attempts—again unsuccessfully, of course—to perceive nature as if there were no human beings to perceive it, including the artist himself. The artist praises the world as the greatest of all works of art, the supreme achievement of the Creator. The painter, painting, is praying. The storyteller is offering homage. The musician composes a joyous dance in honor of that which is not man and is greater than man.

Through the centuries, these two ways of attempted understanding, although fundamentally in conflict, have lived together in an uneasy peace. In our time the conflict has become more heated. Today the way of science has defeated the way of art.

SCIENCE TRIUMPHANT

Science, triumphant, declares its intention of *defining* the understanding of nature, the universe, the real world, and it will do so for good and all. The definition is well known to us, but it is not often described accurately. Basically, there are ten principles that underlie the attempt at definition, the attempt to preempt our way of knowing the world. The most important for our present purposes are these:

1. Nothing exists that is not material.
2. Nature is rational.
3. Mathematics is the key for understanding nature.
4. The universe is a machine.
5. Science is rational, and everything else is quackery.

The radical materialism expressed in the first principle—nothing exists that is not material—is denied vociferously by many persons, among them not a few scientists. But if anything exists that is not material, what is it?

Minds? No; neurologists, as well as most philosophers, hold that the mind is merely a function of the brain. If we can construct a man-made brain that is sufficiently complex, it too will have a mind. Of course, anything man-made is material.

The life principle? No; this antique concept is nothing but DNA, the "selfish gene," as the noted evolutionist Richard Dawkins calls it. He writes: "All the organs and limbs of animals; the roots, leaves, and flowers of plants; all eyes and brains and minds, and even fears and hopes, are the tools by which successful DNA sequences lever themselves into the future."[2]

This is materialism, and anything else, for Dawkins and thousands of other eminent thinkers, is a "nonsensical substitute."

Angels? No again. Although angels are amusing to speculate about, they are either material (can be photographed, for example, or detected on a fluoroscope, or ring a bell on a Christmas tree), or they do not exist.

God? If he is a he, or even a she, then, of course, he or she is material.

The axiomatic assumption that nature is rational is also at the heart of this preemption of the meaning of meaning. Nature is rational, the scientist declares; if it were not, we could not understand it. The circularity of the reasoning is obvious.

Nature is rational and mathematics is its prophet, science further proclaims. Mathematics is the tool with which mankind unlocks the world, measures it, controls it. The universe is fundamentally mathematical; the proof is that mathematics *works*. This reasoning, too, is circular.

More important, mathematics reveals how science substitutes its own creation for that of nature's creation of itself. Mathematics is not found in nature; it is wholly a creation of our minds, which, being material, are machines, like the universe itself. Thus, we become indistinguishable from computers which, within a few short years, will begin to be mistaken for men, women, or children, and vice versa.

Finally, there is the Socratic bifurcation between science and quackery. A quack is a charlatan who knows naught of what he claims to understand. Poets, artists, philosophers, and human beings may be nice fellows, good guys, but if they are not scientists they are quacks.

I am aware that, in the foregoing, I have left a great deal unsaid. I am especially aware that many persons, including some distinguished scientists, deny that these principles underlie modern knowledge. They might have claimed this a century ago, perhaps, but not in our more enlightened, quantum-mechanical age. I realize they are as uncomfortable as I am with the situation that exists today in the knowledge industries. Nevertheless, it remains true that genuine, respectable, "scientific" knowledge is always based, more or less, on these principles. If the principles do not underlie any "serious" statement about the way things are, about the universe, nature, even about the human animal, it is ordinarily dismissed as quackery.

I am also aware of the deep discomfort felt by physicists, especially, concerning the so-called principle of uncertainty, to say nothing of the new science of chaos. These two important twentieth-century discoveries (or inventions) seem to challenge the faith we once had in the so-called scientific paradigm. But do they really? True, understanding the universe may be more difficult than we thought it would be; but we were arrogant if we thought it would be easy. The rationality of nature, if there is any such thing, is probably more complex than we thought; the mathematics we believe nature "exhibits" in its workings is more difficult than we expected. There are some who even begin to suspect—or fear—we may not be smart enough to attain our goal. Alas for humanity if it turns out to be impossible to realize Hoyle's dream! What a tragedy if we are forced to accept some nonsensical substitute!

ART WITHDRAWN AND RECLUSIVE

The way of art has its problems, too. The artist, now more than ever, is ringed round with critics and censors. In his or her effort to depict the world as it really is (or really seems to be) he or she is constantly confronted by the master illusionists who control, dominate, and direct so much of our imaging. Artists find it easier—and safer—to depict the world as *they* would like it to be rather than as it is. Jesus was not the last great artist to suffer condemnation for his depiction of the way things really are.

The artist must also be aware of the corrosive effect even the best works of art have on our attempt to understand the universe. It is appropriate to take a poem by Wallace Stevens as an example, because Stevens was a successful businessman. An insurance executive who wrote poetry in his spare time, he was also one of the best American poets of this century.

The poem is titled "Anecdote of the Jar."

> I placed a jar in Tennessee,
> And round it was, upon a hill.
> It made the slovenly wilderness
> Surround that hill.
>
> The wilderness rose up to it,
> And sprawled around, no longer wild.
> The jar was round upon the ground
> And tall and of a port in air.
>
> It took dominion everywhere.
> The jar was gray and bare.
> It did not give of bird or bush,
> Like nothing else in Tennessee.[3]

What is the jar? It may not be a fine one, expensive, a work of "art." It is only something made by *us*. It does not belong there on the hill in Tennessee, as everything else in that slovenly, sprawling, surrounding wilderness does. Yet its presence, apparently innocent, mocks the wilderness, makes it sprawling and slovenly. We might not have noticed if not for the jar.

Art can have that effect. It can help us indulge our human hubris. If it was up to us we could make a better universe than the one we have.

Art also reminds us how little the world needs our effort to understand it. Here are two more poems, one by Mark Van Doren ("If They Spoke"), the other by Edwin Muir ("The Animals").

> The animals will never know;
> Could not find out; would scarcely care
> That all their names are in our books,
> And all their images drawn bare.
>
> What names? They have not heard the sound,
> Nor in their silence thought the thing.
> They are not notified they live;
> Nor ask who set them wandering.
>
> Simply they are. And so with us;
> And they would say it if they spoke;
> And we might listen; and the world
> Be uncreated at one stroke.[4]

Why did my father say "the world would be uncreated at one stroke"? He did not mean *the* world, of course, the one that was here before we were, and will, if it is fortunate, survive our attempts to understand it. He meant *our* world, the one we have made by naming it. The world we have made with words.

> *En arche ein ho logos. Kai ho logos ein pros ton theon. Kai theos ein ho logos.* "In the beginning was the word, and the word was with God, and God was the word."

How richly do we value our words and our wordiness! How profoundly do we disdain the animals, who have no words!

We humans are certain that our distinctive ability to speak not only serves to distinguish us from all other animals, but also confirms our position at the apex of life, as the goal of creation and evolution, as the masters of the Earth, with the God-given right to consign all other species to death or life, as it pleases us or serves our interest.

Our creation myth confirms this. It tells us we are right to believe ourselves the reason for history. But what kind of history would a virus tell?

Would it not view us as a convenient source of nutriment, but finally of no greater purport than we assign to pigs or lettuce?

Humanity's hubris is expressed in the phrase "dumb beasts," where "dumb" also connotes its other meaning of stupid and slow. Indeed, it is true that no other animal speaks as we do: out loud, in booming voices, in sentences in a pattern we call grammar. The animals are (mostly) silent. We are very noisy.

But is it possible to talk noiselessly?

It seems so. Not only dogs and cats but also snakes and elephants, even bacteria, talk to one another in ways we have forgotten to understand, even to hear.

But they do not talk to us.

Apparently it was not always so. Until quite recently—perhaps two centuries ago, or ten, or fifty—human beings could talk to animals, and animals could talk to them. A few persons continue to be able to do this. We call them "primitive," and we try to convert them or (the same thing) kill them.

Those primitive men and women and children learned a lesson from the animals that we, in our new "dumbness," have forgotten: All living things have a right to live if any have. No species has the right to kill, except for need, and no species has been awarded dominion over all the others.

Think of what that concept of "dominion" has entailed. From it has flowed the continuance of the two great wars we struggle with today: the war of mankind against nature, and the war of man against man. Think, and realize that we will never cease to struggle as long as these wars continue, for neither can be won.

Edwin Muir's great subject was time.

> They do not live in the world,
> Are not in time and space.
> From birth to death hurled
> No word do they have, not one
> To plant a foot upon,
> Were never in any place.

> For with names the world was called
> Out of the empty air,
> With names was built and walled,
> Line and circle and square,
> Dust and emerald;
> Snatched from deceiving death
> By the articulate breath.

But these have never trod
Twice the familiar track,
Never never turned back
Into the memoried day.
All is new and near
In the unchanging Here
Of the fifth great day of God,
That shall remain the same,
Never shall pass away.

On the sixth day we came.[5]

Time is our creation; the real world, before us, had no need of time. The animals, Muir says, have no past, no future, only the present. "All is new and near / In the unchanging Here / Of the fifth great day of God." And then, naked, shivering, awestruck by our own omnipotence: "On the sixth day we came."

The other name for time is change. The artist, knowing time, recognizes how we have changed our world. John Berger, in his essay "Why Look At Animals," tells us that

the 19th century, in western Europe and North America, saw the beginning of a process, today being completed, . . . by which every tradition which has previously mediated between man and nature was broken. Before this rupture, animals constituted the first circle of what surrounded man. Perhaps that already suggests too great a distance. They were with man at the center of his world.[6]

Why look at animals? To remind ourselves of what we have lost in our effort to make a world that is seemingly, although perhaps not truly, more comfortable for us. The most important loss is our newfound inability to talk to animals. We, living in time as they do not, and as tragically silent as they are, can only remember how things used to be.

Since animals can no longer speak to us, or rather we can no longer hear and understand them, we have decided it is acceptable to treat them as raw materials. Animals required for food are processed like any manufactured commodity. We permit a dwindling few to roam in small, isolated, semiwild places of the Earth so we can hunt them. Others are pets; we love them and like to believe they are happier with us than they once were in the vast original common of the world. Then there are zoos.

Zoos all began at the time when animals were starting to be withdrawn—exiled—from daily life. John Berger writes:

Everywhere animals disappear. In zoos they constitute the living monument to their own disappearance. . . .

All sites of enforced marginalization—ghettos, shanty towns, madhouses, concentrations camps—have something in common with zoos. . . .

The zoo cannot but disappoint. The public purpose of zoos is to offer visitors the opportunity of looking at animals. Yet nowhere in a zoo can a visitor encounter the look of an animal. . . .

That look between animal and man, which may have played a crucial role in the development of human society, and with which, in any case, all men had always lived until less than a century ago, has been extinguished. Looking at each animal, the unaccompanied visitor is alone.[7]

Let us not fail to see the point of this. It is we, in the last analysis, who have been marginalized. We have been isolated, confined to the sterile, mechanical world we have made, exiled from the world we once knew, the one we inherited, the one we less and less clearly remember. Time, our greatest invention, imprisons us.

THE BEAUTY OF THE WORLD

Moss Hart once remarked, as he was being shown around the gorgeous landscaping of his host: "It just goes to show what God could do if he had the money!"

Comic writers teach us, as do tragic authors, with irony. Hart's irony here is bitter, cold. Doubtless there are many who do not recognize the irony at all. They genuinely believe the world we have made is not only more comfortable, more predictable, and more safe, but also more beautiful than the one it replaced. Should we not ask whether that is true?

Admittedly, there are arguments for both sides. As I write, I read in today's newspaper about lethally toxic genes that can "jump" from one kind of bacteria to another, making it a desperate act to consume any hamburger that is not burned to a crisp; about new types of grain that, it is fervently hoped, might alleviate the growing and by now pandemic hunger of the entire continent of Africa; about a threatened famine in China, as the population soars and the amount of agricultural land dwindles; about the approaching drought in the American Middle West that will require new kinds of crops that can survive entirely on rainwater; about forests in my own

Northeast that simply do not grow any more because of the acid in the soil. I will not take the risk of boring you with more stories of this sort.

At the same time, for every pessimist there is an optimist who sincerely believes that all the above and many other perils are only apparent, or if real can be averted. Since we do not know—perhaps no one knows—I am willing to entertain the notion that Clever Man, as the tragic poet Sophocles called him, will be able to survive as a species, whatever his numbers and whatever the chaos he produces in his furious, frenetic, and feverish need to understand the universe and bend it to his will.

After all, we are a lot smarter than the dinosaurs, are we not?

Or perhaps it will not be we who are smart but instead that Great Being that is called, by James Lovelock, Gaia. Gaia, Lovelock tells us in his book of that title,[8] is a single living organism constituted of all living things, which, according to his theory, form a complex system that has the capacity of keeping the Earth a place fit for life.

Life on Earth, Lovelock points out, is no new arrival. It has been here in one or another of its thousands of millions of manifestations for more than four billion years. Life has survived more severe depredations and "pollutions" in the past than humanity is inflicting upon it today. Gaia will probably survive whatever we may do.

However, that may not be the point. Consider this bit of dialogue from Michael Crichton's novel, *Jurassic Park:*

"What advances?" Malcolm said irritably. "The number of hours women devoted to housework has not changed since 1930, despite all the advances. All the vacuum cleaners, washer-dryers, trash compactors, garbage disposals, wash-and-wear fabrics . . . Why does it still take as long to clean a house as it did in 1930?"

Ellie said nothing.

"Because there haven't been any advances," Malcolm said. "Not really. Thirty thousand years ago, when men were doing cave paintings at Lascaux, they worked twenty hours a week to provide themselves with food and shelter. The rest of the time, they could play, or sleep, or do whatever they wanted. And they lived in a natural world, with clean air, clean water, beautiful trees and sunsets. Think about it. Twenty hours a week. Thirty thousand years ago."

Ellie said, "You want to turn back the clock?"

"No," Malcolm said. "I want people to wake up. We've had four hundred years of modern science, and we ought to know by now what it's good for, and what it's not good for. It's time for a change."

"Before we destroy the planet?" she said.

He sighed, and closed his eyes. "Oh dear," he said. "That's the last thing I would worry about."[9]

Crichton is treated with disdain by literary and scientific critics alike. Who is he, they ask indignantly, to proclaim what is good or bad for humanity? Indeed, he is only a teller of popular tales; and his character, Malcolm, is a disgruntled skeptic. Yet, are we certain he is wrong to suggest that humanity, as distinguished from Gaia, may be able to look forward only to a very limited future?

On the other hand, is it not more likely that resourceful humanity will discover a way to construct a new and totally impregnable home for itself on this beleaguered planet? A successful Jurassic Park? But if our descendants manage to do that, will their world be as beautiful as the one we more and more faintly remember? Will there be forests and prairies, clean rivers and oceans, great weathers, vast and silent skies? Or will there be no room for these things in that brilliantly conceived and executed nightmare?

Aquinas declared, following Aristotle, that the beautiful is that which pleases upon being beheld. This famous definition, admittedly old-fashioned, suggests that beauty is in the eye, and only in the eye, of the beholder. This may be so, although I would be loathe to concede that there is no such thing as beauty itself, that beauty is entirely subjective.

Objectively, it seems that many parts of Earth are no less beautiful than they once were. We, who are destroying the old world as quickly as we can in order to replace it with a better one, are also preserving some of it when we can.

Any war—especially modern wars, in which, typically, as many as 90 percent of the casualties are innocent bystanders—produces not only dead, dying, and mutilated victims, but also casualties that survive. They are usually driven from their homes and forced to gather together in small and isolated places that they believe, because the combatants tell them so, are safe. These persons are called refugees.

J. N. Darling was head, for two creative years during the 1930s, of the U.S. Land and Forest Service, in which capacity he established a dozen or more areas where birds, animals, or fish might gather for survival. Because these creatures were casualties in the oldest war of all, that of humanity against nature, Darling called these "safe" places refuges. Refuges are places where refugees go when they can no longer live in their homes.

One of the refuges, named after Darling, is on Sanibel Island, off the west coast of Florida. It is a lovely, magical, surprising place, the temporary abode of many migrating fowl and the permanent home of many others. As you move through the refuge, in a long line of creeping automobiles, you cannot but be impressed by what the world would look like if we only had the money to leave it as we found it.

We try. Some of us do. But these efforts, viewed from afar—from the moon, say—are tiny and probably of little permanence. The "Ding" Darling Wildlife Refuge houses thousands of birds on its hundred or so acres. But there are entire Chinese provinces where birds no longer sing, not a single one.

From a satellite, it is apparent how much of the once blue-green Earth is changing to yellow-brown-gray desert. The process is rapid. Is it irreversible?

That is not my present concern, which is, rather, the beauty of the old world that is being consumed by the new. Thirty billion human beings might be able to live "well enough" on this small planet, producing, with wonderful machines, enough food, water, and air. But the Earth would be a desert, with no other living things beside ourselves and our food.

Except, of course, for some billions of trillions of bacteria and viruses that, if they had nothing else to eat, would have to eat us.

THE MORAL DILEMMA

Enough of this doomsday messianism. It is, as I have suggested, rather boring, and then there is the question whether or not a lot of it is true.

However, even if we are only half-convinced that the Earth is in peril, should we forget the terms of Pascal's wager? When there is everything to be gained by belief, he told us, and very little to lose if the belief is not well-founded, then it is folly not to believe.

Be that as it may, there is one question that ought to concern us, whether we believe or not. If it is true that the beautiful world we have known and loved is in danger, is there anything we can do to save it?

I think perhaps there is.

Let us return now to my fear-stricken girl being swept down the river, probably to her death. Remember the position in which I placed us. The other onlookers were either in total panic; or convinced there was nothing to worry about; or confident there was someone just around the bend who would do whatever had to be done (if anything); or unconcerned on the grounds that the girl was not their problem and besides they were busy. We knew there was no helpful person or institution around the bend. Most important, we were strong swimmers and had a chance to save her if we tried—if we tried *now*, and did not wait another moment.

This kind of situation has produced legal controversies. Is such a person legally obliged to help the girl in the water—or the victim of a mugging just outside the window? The law is not always clear; fortunately we are not lawyers or jurists.

It is easier to answer the question whether such a bystander has a *moral* obligation to do whatever he or she can. I believe we do have such an obligation. I cannot imagine reasonable arguments that would deny this.

Remember again what the situation is. We have good reason to believe the girl is in peril; we perceive that no else will or *can* save her; but we know we can. In that case, must we not try?

I am sure my cautionary tale is clear. The girl being swept to her death is Earth itself, or if not that then humanity itself, or if not that—last but not least—the beautiful world we are rapidly losing. I mean that, first, we have sufficient evidence to believe this to be so; second, we know, or suspect, no one else will be able to save it; third, and most important, we know we can. Given these three propositions, are we not morally obliged to try to save the world?

THE CRUX OF THE MATTER

I have spent time and effort trying to persuade you—perhaps vainly—of the peril. What of the other two propositions I have just stated?

It might seem that environmentalists would be the likely choice to undertake the enormous, and probably risky, task. Unfortunately, environmentalists, by and large, are often ineffectual advocates of their cause. They irritate as many as they persuade, and they bicker among themselves about what should be done, how much of it should be done, and what should be done first. Certainly they have accomplished good in the thirty or forty years the "Green Revolution" has been underway. But the fact is—or I think it is a fact—they will not, by themselves, get the job done, or done in time.

Politicians might seem other likely candidates. But the world's politicians—not just ours, in this or any other year—are an unenterprising lot. When they are instigating, conducting, or pretending to terminate the innumerable "absurd and truly tragic battles between tribal groups," as James Lovelock calls them, they speak eloquently about such high-sounding subjects as justice, liberation, and national self-determination.[10] At all other times they wait for the people to tell them what to do. If the people were to *demand* that they try to save the world, the politicians explain, they would try. But how can they be expected to do what the people do not want, or seem not to want? It is not their responsibility, they say, to tell the people what is good for them, whether or not they want it; the people must decide for themselves.

What *do* the people want? The answer is obvious: The people—all of us—desire the return of the Golden Age. We want to live good lives, to be happy. We want to pursue happiness in our own way. Other things being equal, we would prefer a beautiful world like the one we dream of, rather than the nightmare that is—or may be—just around the corner.

But other things are not equal. We people are not free. We have been taught, for centuries but more urgently in our time, to desire other things. Our desires have been shaped, and we cannot escape, because our masters will not let us.

The churches, too, although well-intentioned, and the schools, although they try hard, are also unable to undertake what is required to save the world. The schools foster in their pupils the belief that the goal of education is wealth.

Who, then, is left? Not the environmentalists; not the politicians or the people in general; not the pastors, rabbis, and priests; certainly not the disinterested scientific observers; not even the poets, who, Shelley proclaimed to a deaf world, are "the unacknowledged legislators of the world." Who or what remains with the ability to bring back the Golden Age?

All that remains is you, corporations and companies, manufacturers and financiers, businessmen and women of every nation of the Earth.

Say not that you cannot do it. You know how! You can make the rest of us—or lead us, rather, which is more gracious—to do and desire whatever you want us to do and desire. You employ the most creative artistic geniuses in the world to promote your message, your goods, your services. Employ them to accomplish this infinitely greater and more difficult task!

You have led us, down through the centuries unwittingly, to believe the good life is constituted by the production, purchase, and consumption of man-made things. This is and has been your universal message, in every country. I do not believe human beings have always thought this; I do not believe they must think it, that they do so "naturally." Can we turn back to find the better road? You have made us, down through the centuries—or helped us, perhaps—close our eyes to the beautiful world we once knew, in fact or myth or dream, and prefer the artificial, man-made world it has seemed to be in your interest to have us prefer. But this is no longer your real interest, if it ever was. For you too are people, in need of the good, the true, and the beautiful. You too desire the return of the Golden Age.

Businessmen and businesswomen of the world, unite to save us! Break all the antitrust laws, or change them to accord with the emergency we face!

Ignore the protests of your stockholders, who, after all, are people, too! Instead of profits, which will relentlessly become more and more meaningless, promise them a more beautiful world to live in! Act in our behalf, and in your own!

These injunctions may be nothing but noise. I can place before your minds the *end*, but I cannot describe the *means*. Either *you* know the means to the end we all seek, or no one does. The greatest moral obligation today, therefore, is the obligation that confronts you. No one else can save the world, and perhaps you can. Therefore you must try.

The alternative is prayer. I have my own small prayer, which I would like to share with you.

> Thank you, Lord, for this beautiful world, for this beautiful place, and for this beautiful day.
>
> Make our hearts glad and grateful for your innumerable precious gifts to us, and help us to treat them better than we do, and more in keeping with your glory, who are the creator of all things.
>
> We are so wasteful, so careless and destructive. We throw away what we can never replace, and we pollute the very air we breathe, the water we drink, and the soil on which we walk and in which we grow our food.
>
> Help us Lord! Save us from ourselves!

I admit that, although I believe in prayer, I am also a pragmatist. Praying together may not be enough. Let all of us begin to work together, too!

NOTES

1. In Richard Dawkins, *River Out of Eden* (New York: Basic Books, 1995), 150.

2. Ibid.

3. Wallace Stevens, "Anecdote of the Jar," *Collected Poems* (New York: Alfred A. Knopf, 1955), 76. "Anecdote of the Jar" by Wallace Stevens. From *Collected Poems* by Wallace Stevens. Copyright © 1923 and renewed 1951 by Wallace Stevens. Reprinted by permission of Alfred A. Knopf, Inc., and Faber & Faber, Ltd.

4. Mark Van Doren, "If They Spoke," *Collected and New Poems* (New York: Hill and Wang, 1963), 444. "If They Spoke" by Mark Van Doren. From *Collected and New Poems* by Mark Van Doren. Copyright © 1963. Reprinted by permission of the estate of Mark Van Doren.

5. Edwin Muir, "The Animals," *Collected Poems* (New York: Oxford University Press, 1965). "The Animals" by Edwin Muir. From *The Collected Poems* by

Edwin Muir. Copyright © 1960 by Willa Muir. Reprinted by permission of Oxford University Press and Faber & Faber, Ltd.

6. John Berger, "Why Look at Animals," *About Looking* (New York: Vintage Press, 1992), 3.

7. Ibid., 28.

8. James Lovelock, *Gaia: A New Look at Life on Earth* (New York: Oxford University Press, 1979, 1995).

9. Michael Crichton, *Jurassic Park* (New York: Ballantine Books, 1990), 285.

10. Lovelock, *Gaia*, 116–17.

13

COMPELLING STORIES

Narrative and the Production
of the Organizational Self

— ☉ —

ELLEN S. O'CONNOR

"The modern business of management is managing the insides—the hopes, fears and aspirations—of workers, rather than their behaviors."

Deetz (1993:37)

Organizations produce not only goods and services but also selves (Jacques, 1996), for they serve as sites of both personal and professional identity (Ashforth and Mael, 1989). Where we work and what we do become associated with who we are. Edgar Schein defines organizational culture as "the way we do things around here." In this chapter I explore a more profound meaning of the term, one particularly relevant in the Silicon Valley of California, the site of my research. In this context, culture is "who we are around here."

The word "identity" comes from the Latin, *idem*, meaning "the same." In this chapter, I consider how the narrative form in general, and certain narratives in particular, link individuals and organizations. My research suggests that, despite the fact of shorter tenures in shorter careers, organizations are increasingly exercising and refining their capacity to produce selves. Most of this activity occurs in conjunction with "deliberately designed corporate cultures" (Casey, 1995) which typically involve operations of change on employees' values, beliefs, and ideologies (Alvesson, 1987). These cultural changes may enact and provoke "a major paradigm shift" (Lawler, 1988: 49). They may be confrontational, threatening organizational members' "way of making sense of the world," and ultimately putting employees' "values and rationality (and thus in a sense . . . sanity) into question" (Ledford et al.,

1989: 15). In this way, these deliberately designed cultures call for self-transformation. "To manage change effectively, be prepared to change yourself" (Pugh, 1978: 30–31). Ironically, however, cultural change efforts are noted for resulting in layoffs (O'Connor, 1995). In a changing world, identity must be a temporary phenomenon; however, self-formation (and transformation) is not generally understood as such.

The project to form a human being is grounded in the discourses of ethics, i.e., questions which concern "who I am and who we are" (Habermas, 1993: xviii) and moral philosophy, by which I mean both MacIntyre's reference to moral philosophy as the definition of what it means to be human (MacIntyre, 1966: 139) and Murdoch's view of it as an inquiry into the good life (Murdoch, 1970: 78). Yet moral philosophers generally take relatively little interest in organizations, and management-organizational theorists take relatively little (moral-philosophical) interest in moral philosophy. However, the latter clearly practice moral philosophy, for they conceive of and enact the organization as a place and means to produce a certain self. Since there is much at stake in this philosophy and its practice, I offer this chapter as a contribution to greater collaboration across these domains.

To show how the narrative form in general, and certain narratives in particular, play a vital role in the production of individual identity, I draw heavily from both organization and literary theory. Organizational scholarship has recognized many remarkable features of narrative, such as its ability to aid in sensemaking (Weick, 1995: 127–31); information recall and dissemination (Martin et al., 1983); control (Wilkins, 1983; Mumby, 1987); and decision making (O'Connor, 1995). However, the most powerful function of narrative—identity production—has not been well recognized. This function of narrative dates back to the oldest traditions of the genre in aesthetic, religious, and cultural domains—and it prospers today in organizational contexts. Jacques Ellul (1990) saw modern life as imbued with "an unconscious and unsecularized religiosity" which projects a "sacred dimension" onto technique, science, progress, and the state. I suggest that we can add organizations to Ellul's list.

At the outset, I must clarify my use of the term "story." Consistent with contemporary narrative theory, I dissolve the conventional distinction between "fact" and "fiction." Recent narrative theorists (Herrnstein Smith, 1981; Prince, 1994; and White, 1978, 1980, 1981, 1987) posit that the narrative form, regardless of its genre or medium, inherently intermingles factual truth with "imaginative truth" (e.g., choice as to what to tell and how to tell it). If we take up the definition of narrative as "someone telling someone that something happened," as Herrnstein Smith suggests, we can readily apply a long tradition of literary and linguistic theory to narrative as it occurs in everyday organizational settings. More important, we can use this knowledge to understand organizational life better (O'Connor, 1995, 1996a).

ORGANIZATION THEORY'S NARRATIVE ABOUT PRODUCING THE SELF

Management and organizational theorists have long acknowledged their intent to produce a certain kind of self. Scientific management explicitly sought to improve the worker physically, intellectually, and morally. Frederick Taylor (1911) argued that once management had selected the "proper" worker, it had to make him still more proper through techniques of training, observation, evaluation, and compensation. In her classic work, *The Psychology of Management*, Lillian Gilbreth developed Taylor's concept of the work standard and applied it to the realm of worker subjectivity. She called for a "standardizing of the viewpoint," i.e., a "standard thought . . . present in all minds at one time" (1914: 179). In Gilbreth's view, scientific management replaced the individual's random play of "images" and "streams of consciousness" with recurring images of standard production methods. These new images would "recur often enough to drive down the old images and enable all men who desire, to settle down and concentrate on what they are doing" (1914: 236). However, Gilbreth did not address the problem of inculcating desire.

The Harvard "human relations" movement of the 1920s and 1930s filled in this lacuna in Gilbreth's theory. Drawing extensively from psychology (Freud and Janet), political philosophy (Machiavelli), and social theory (Pareto), this circle developed both theory and techniques which used worker emotions and subjectivity as means to organizational and social control (Hollway, 1991; O'Connor, 1996b; and Rose, 1975). These techniques—most notably Mayo's "counseling interview" or "confessional"—are practiced widely today (Townley, 1994), as is Barnard's notion (1938) of propaganda as a means to instill "moral codes" in employees. Indeed, contemporary human relations and culture theories may be viewed as an advanced state of these theories (O'Connor, 1996b).

However, it is in the theoretical-philosophical realm that the Harvard human relations views persist most clearly. The needs-based view of the individual, à la Maslow, dominate not only organizational but also popular culture (Polanyi, 1989). Douglas McGregor (1960, 1966) imported Maslow's theories to management (which Maslow did as well; see his 1965 *Eu-*

psychian Management). McGregor explained all human behavior as driven by the satisfaction of needs. "[W]hen we cease trying to satisfy our needs, we are dead" (McGregor, 1966: 40). The needs-based view was held as a means to "turn out a better kind of human being" and to "make a particular kind of people, of personality, of character, of soul" (Maslow, 1965: 79, 86, 102, 210). Maslow posited a "eupsychian" (utopian) work situation in which "the objective requirements of the situation, or the task, or of the problem, or of the group reign absolutely" and which was "totally introjected by everybody," meaning that "the task or duty was not any longer something separate from the self . . . but rather that [the individual] identified with this task so strongly that you couldn't define his real self without including that task" (Maslow, 1965: 122).

McGregor provided an explicit answer to the unknown in Gilbreth's theories. He stated that the individual applies himself to the organization to the extent that he is "committed" (McGregor, 1966: 265). McGregor counseled managers to achieve commitment by "creat[ing] conditions . . . such that members of the organization . . . can best achieve their goals by directing their efforts towards the goals of the organization" (1966: 212). Peters and Waterman, in their celebrated book *In Search of Excellence* (1982), spoke similarly in their endorsement of a "strong culture" with which organizational members would identify. Employees "sacrifice a great deal" to institutions that "provide meaning" for them (Peters and Waterman, 1982: 56). Indeed, this very term, "meaning," is found in early human-relations theory, where it is used synonymously with "sentiments" (Roethlisberger and Dickson, 1939: 561; the two were students of Mayo); thus, it belies an etymology and genealogy traceable to the earliest use of Freudian psychology in the workplace. Just as in the human-relations tradition, Peters and Waterman emphasized the potential that organizations could exploit by appealing to the "irrational side" of individuals and by getting them "to believe in what they are doing" (Peters and Waterman, 1982: 60).

Most recently, Collins and Porras (1994) continue this reasoning but intensify it. They endorse the "cult-like" environment of enduring organizations. Distinguishing features of such organizations include their use of (1) training programs with "ideological" content, e.g., teaching "values, norms, history, and tradition"; (2) incentive/advancement criteria "linked to fit with corporate ideology"; and (3) "tangible and visible penalties for those who break ideological boundaries," with severe violations being treated as "sins" (Collins and Porras, 1994: 138). Most important, Collins and Porras signal the role of narrative (e.g., narratives about organizational heroes) in instilling corporate ideology. For example, they say that cult-like organizations expose employees to "a pervasive mythology of 'heroic deeds' and corporate exemplars" and to "unique language and terminology . . . that reinforce a frame of reference and the sense of belonging to a special, elite group" (1994: 136). For Collins and Porras, narrative approximates what Chester Barnard, a member of the Harvard circle, called the executive's task of inculcation of values (1938: 142–60), functions he called "propaganda and persuasion," under the executive's responsibility to create morals for corporate employees (1938: 258–84).

To help account for this power of narrative, I turn to the narrative tradition in the humanities.

NARRATIVE IN THE LITERARY, ANTHROPOLOGICAL, AND PHILOSOPHICAL TRADITIONS

Narrative humanistic traditions view the self as engaged in a continual process of purposeful construction that takes linguistic, and particularly narrative, form (Harré and Second, 1972; Harré and Gillett, 1994; Linde, 1993; MacIntyre, 1981; Sarbin, 1986; Taylor, 1985a, b; Waele and Harré, 1979) and which has a moral nature (Johnson, 1993; MacIntyre, 1981). Narrative relates individual to other experience: "I can only answer the question 'What am I to do?' if I can answer the prior question, 'Of what story or stories do I find myself a part?'" (MacIntyre, 1981: 216). Here, narrative is both a social act—a placement in relationship of the self and the other—and an introspective act, for it presents the self to the self. By virtue of "the basic narrative quality of human experience," all stories are "about ourselves" (TeSeele, 1975: 159–60). In interpreting narratives, reader-auditors invoke their "own self-reflection against the background of the particular circumstances of [their] existence" (Unger, 1975: 109). As a result, they may "learn, understand, and receive something quite different from what was said" in narrative (Ellul, 1985: 176). At the same time, narrative produces "a symbiotic interpenetration of individual and society" (Turner, 1974: 56): an activity of self-knowledge, self-reflection, and self-construction (Sandel, 1982: 58–59, 152–53) and one of the individual "form[ing] himself in accordance with the communicative norms that match the cooperative ways of his society" (Burke, 1959: 563).

Following classical literary theory, this linkage is accomplished through identification (Aristotle, 1967). Burke (1959) theorized that the individual "acts upon himself persuasively" in the identification process (563). In this way, narrative is a process of self-modification, as described by Hauerwas

(1977: 73): "Some stories are not told to explain as a theory explains, but to involve the agent in a way of life. A theory is meant to help you know the world without changing the world; a story is to help you deal with the world through changing yourself." We may thus understand narrative as a "dialogical process by which self makes itself" (Asad, 1987: 174).

It is no accident that contemporary organizations, said to be surrounded by change, not only reproduce internally the change they face externally but also deepen change to touch the level of individual identity. It is also no accident that they do so through narrative.

The following case studies are taken from my recent and ongoing research on the use of narrative in Silicon Valley, California, where I am working with high-technology firms. Previous work (Saxenian, 1994) has noted the role of stories in the Silicon Valley culture. Due to the rapid pace of technological innovation and to the large size of collegial networks (e.g., linking industry, government, and academe), stories have overtaken the research paper as a key means of information dissemination. The role of stories in the identity of workers has not, to my knowledge, been researched. Given the importance of "founding myths" in Silicon Valley (e.g., Bill Hewlett and Dave Packard in their garage, Steve Jobs and Steve Wozniak in their garage, etc.) as well as the sheer structural propensity for organizational identification via stock purchase plans, Silicon Valley is a perfect site to study organizational narratives and how they help achieve employee identification. (Note: All proper names have been changed.)

Case 1: The Training Manual

In an interview with an employee of one of the largest high-technology companies in Silicon Valley, I had an opportunity to read his "Training Manual." Through no prompting on my part, this individual compared it to his ideological indoctrination in the kibbutz where he was reared. The manual provides a narrative about "who we are" in this particular organization, and the employee told me that he referred to it so he could "fit in" to the work culture.

The manual includes case studies of "heroic acts" of founders, executives, and managers of the organization—e.g., working extremely long hours to finish a project on or ahead of schedule and creatively solving a long-standing operational or technical problem by assembling cross-functional teams. Each chapter opens by defining a specific, desirable character trait. The body of the chapter presents the relevant narratives and some didactic conclusions, and the close poses a self-questionnaire. Here are some excerpts from the latter.

- Is customer feedback more important than your ego?
- How do you remove barriers to satisfaction created by the tendency to be defensive when faced with hostility or criticism?
- Is your personal pride inseparably linked to professional pride?
- Do you accept responsibility for the company's performance?
- Do you care?
- Do you encourage staff to be active in community affairs and to maintain healthy personal and family values?
- Do you use "we thinking" as opposed to "I thinking"?
- Are you really willing to stop being an individual contributor? [In the section on interpersonal and teamwork skills.]
- Have I been guilty of any of these sins of omission or commission? [In the same section.] If so, how will I rectify my mistake?

It is not much of a leap to see the relationship between these questions and the spiritual exercises of St. Ignatius Loyola or the confessions of St. Augustine (or those of any confessing Catholic).

An interesting didactic section makes a distinction between "contracts" and "covenants." The difference between the two is "intimacy." Managers "who interact superficially or who act with an orientation toward self rather than the good of the group, betray intimacy." One who covenants "experiences ownership," a key component of which is "passion." Hochschild (1983) would call this "emotional labor," meaning the kind of emotional display that is expected in association with work-related activity.

This brief example sketches the domain of "training" as subjectivity, per Maslow, one's "personality," "character," and "soul" (1965: 86). It is interesting to note the way in which the employee I interviewed approached the manual. He did not work with it on the literal level—e.g., as values he should "internalize" or assimilate; rather, he saw it—with some distance, and more than a little skepticism—as an artifact of the company's culture, a jargon to be invoked so he could get along better with the natives. I should add that he was of mature age, with grown children, and that he had only been with the company for a few weeks. As mentioned earlier, he drew a parallel between corporate and kibbutz ideological indoctrination. He also seemed somewhat amused by the text.

According to Collins and Porras (1994), the orientation of employees toward the acculturation process is precisely what distinguishes strong and enduring companies from weak and short-lived ones. I now turn to a more extensive case study, one which occurred in a company that Collins and Porras identify as "cult-like." In addition, this example illustrates the difference between a cynical and an appreciative stance toward the organizational "cult."

Case Study 2: Organizational Change at Macrotech, Inc.

The director of OD (organization development) at Macrotech has used narratives in large-scale change efforts beginning in the early 1990s. What I am calling "narratives" were for him lengthy "case studies" (twenty-five to thirty-five pages) of organizational change efforts at various sites of Macrotech (a worldwide company). These case studies not only document but also promote organizational change efforts (O'Connor, 1995). They are also the artifacts of an internal network which the OD director created to produce and reproduce "change agents." The use of narratives, change agents, and networks was part of an innovative strategy developed by the OD director to deal with an ambitious change agenda under severe financial constraints. Specifically, according to his employment agreement, the OD director's function was self-paying, meaning that as he won internal contracts, he was paid by billing the local site. However, at the same time, the senior executives who hired him expected him to change an 80,000-member organization.

How to enact change without being able to hire change agents? The OD director used case studies to recruit "change agents" from within Macrotech to temporarily work *with* (and, thus, in a way, *for*) him. He launched a change effort at a first site (which volunteered itself to him), to write up the "story" as a case study, and to disseminate this narrative to anyone at Macrotech who was interested in organizational change (a person the narratives call "a champion"). At the same time that he became involved at this first site, he created the OD Change Network (ODCN), which had the following function: The "champion" of any organizational change effort was asked to write up his case study and to present it at an OD Change Network (ODCN) meeting, two of which were held each year. The case study, as an artifact, was the price of admission to this network which was the sole means of obtaining access to the corporate OD director/function. It also served as a symbolic offering (Mauss, 1990) to the OD group and thus commenced the ongoing network of professional relations and mutual assistance. Without participation in the network, individuals were aware of the corporate mandate "to change" (through statements made internally by senior executives and even national conversations about global competition, e.g., Kennedy, 1987) but were not sure what to do about it. For example, some cases describe considerable confusion surrounding the nature and process of change until the pivotal encounter with the corporate OD function and director. The OD director called his general plan—cases, change agents, and network—a "pull strategy," by which he meant that because information about change was restricted to the ODCN which had entry barriers (most people in organizations do not like to write twenty-five-page documents), this paucity would in itself heighten and even create interest in change.

Today, the ODCN has 1,200 members and meets four times a year. Well over a hundred sites have been changed in ways similar to those described in the early narratives dating from 1991. The OD function now has a staff of six people, all of whom are on the corporate payroll and half of whom served as "champions" of local change efforts.

I have described previously how these narratives produced and reproduced important yet taken-for-granted "rules" about change (O'Connor, 1995) consistent with Perrow's (1986) notion of "unobtrusive controls." These rules included the type of change method employed (sociotechnical systems; Pasmore, 1988); the catalyst of that change effort (the corporate OD function—local "change agents" used corporate OD/its director as a vital resource and cited him as such); and normative issues such as what was meant by (1) "resistance" (ideological rejection) and how to manage it ("training"), and (2) "support" (agreement with and subordination to ideas of the "change team").

However, my earlier work did not address the question of identification, which, according to the OD director's statements, had to have served a pivotal function in convincing individuals (usually plant managers) at local sites to lead large-scale organizational change programs. Although the plant managers were traditionally responsible for plantwide operations, their decisions to initiate organizational change response posed considerable risk due to the scale of the change involved (encompassing social as well as technical issues) and uncertainty, both of which lie outside the typical preparation of engineers (most of Macrotech's plant managers were engineers). It is important to remember that at this point in the OD director's career at Macrotech, he lacked "success stories" (his expression), or a track record of experience within Macrotech, that would "give [potential internal clients] something to relate to."

The following analysis is based on a review of five of the early "case studies" (henceforth called narratives) and, specifically, the application of Burkean literary analysis to these texts. Burke developed a set of distinctions he called the "pentad" (1962). He used this construct to help account for social action. Since pentadic approaches have been used widely in the analysis of organizational narratives and action (Elmes and Costello, 1992; Mangham and Overington, 1983; Mangham, 1986; O'Connor, 1995), I will explain them only briefly here. Pentadic analysis concentrates on the role of narrative in directing attention to *five* pivotal narrative features: (1) act: what is done; (2) agent: who performs the action; (3) agency: the means or instrument used to perform the action; (4) scene: the place where the action occurs; and (5) purpose: the reasons for the action. I apply Burke's pentad to these early narratives of organizational change at Macrotech to illustrate how they serve, via identification processes, to change plant managers so they will become (transform themselves into) "change agents."

Agent

The narratives identify the central agent as the plant manager (PM). In formal terms, they follow the genre of the romance (Frye, 1957). This genre deals with identity, particularly the conversion of one form of identity (typically that of the adolescent, knight, or sinner) to another (adult, hero, saint). The designation "champion" (from the Latin *campus*, meaning, "a field of battle"), aligns these organizational narratives with medieval romances. Elsbree identifies this story form as an "archetypal" plot, or a "universal action sequence that is universally intelligible" through its enactment of rituals that "articulate basic phases of human growth" (1982: vii).

In addition, the narratives portray the PM as embarking on a journey. For example, the case study was described by the narrator as a "road map" for change efforts at Macrotech. One narrative concludes with a reference to the "many miles left to go" in the change project. The narrator asks that the plant be viewed as a "pioneer" in the organization. According to the OED, the word "journey" comes from the Latin *diurnus*, meaning a day's expanse of time, and particularly "the portion of a march or expedition actually done in one day . . . a day's performance in fighting, a battle, a fight." In this way, the connotations of journey and champion come together. In addition, the champion of the narrative encounters enemies—mainly allegorical and definitely unnamed figures (e.g., "resistance to change," especially by first-level supervisors and by temporary workers and those sympathetic to them). The champion's struggles with his enemies not only describe but also constitute his virtue. "Narrativizing" involves "moralizing" (White, 1981: 23). One case describes how the PM, with "vision and foresight," elected to pursue a complete redesign of the factory. This genre is perfectly in keeping with a text whose purpose is to change identity.

Agency

The agency, or means by which change is effected, is narrative itself, that is, in his exposure to narratives about the state (particularly the economic state) of his industry, his nation, and his firm, the PM decides to change himself. One narrative opens with the following story about its PM:

> Competition was increasing, distribution in certain areas of the world was particularly difficult, and areas of the organization were expressing dissatisfaction about the quality of work life in the area. This, coupled with increasing evidence of the decline of U.S. productivity versus the rest of the world began to create what became affectionately known as "sleepless nights."

It concludes, "the journey [our site] is undertaking can serve as a role model for Macrotech. We do not have to ship our manufacturing offshore. Our organizations, and our people, can be a competitive advantage that even the Japanese cannot duplicate!" The organizational change narratives are subplots of a much larger narrative—that of the threat to the "great powers" (Kennedy, 1987)—be they at the national, industrial, or technical level. Another narrative of agency is that of Pasmore (1988). The case studies cite this book as being a central source for the change efforts at Macrotech. In fact, one case study states that some "resisters" to change criticized the PM's ideas for "sounding like they were taken from a book." (They were—two narratives state that copies of Pasmore's book were given to all those involved in the organizational "redesign.")

Act

The act is change, change of an organization and change of self. One case opens with the following epigraph: "[A competitor] called Macrotech slow, arrogant, conservative, bureaucratic, and inflexible. That shows our history and baggage! We don't want to be that way anymore." A management consultant familiar with the company wrote, "Macrotech is an introverted company—the belief that the best ideas come from within. . . . Macrotech is trying to become an extrovert. Do you know how hard it is to change an introvert to an extrovert?" This quote well exemplifies the relationship between organizational and individual identity because the PMs, generally with technical and engineering backgrounds and similarly typecast as introverts, were the explicit focus of the OD director's strategy for change. To change the organization was to change the PMs. The narratives had to present compelling evidence of the need for both individual and organizational change.

An interesting variation on this theme occurs in one of the narratives. The PM is portrayed as having a "second chance," that is, a chance to write a new narrative about himself as a leader. The narrative describes an earlier experience he had with a change effort, one in which he took an "authoritarian" approach to change, in which the organizational redesign was done by "engineers and managers without the participation of those that actually did the work or supported the process." These excluded individuals were "unhappy" and "felt that the design had been done to them." The manager "resolved that his next design effort would be different." In addition, a formal evaluation had identified "joint decision making" and "consensus building behaviors" as "personal growth areas" for this particular manager. He "recognized that his new job provided an opportunity to redesign the factory in a more participatory way" and resolved to do so. The narrative describes his personal transformation into a more democratic leader and generously praises him for his success at this. Thus, PMs who may have had bad experiences with themselves (or with others) in their leadership activities are encouraged to "rewrite" themselves in this new change effort and with the help of co-authors (Pasmore and the OD director).

Scene

The scene is the workplace. The cases use vital workplace statistics such as headcount, production volume, and quality data to describe the "before" and "after" stages of the change process. However, the scene is also the private conversation the PM has with himself. Just as the narratives describe financial, quality, and productivity problems at the local manufacturing sites, they also portray the personal anxiety (e.g., "sleepless nights") experienced by the PM as he considers the change process, resolves to "embark" on it, and "pursues" it—all the while encountering various forms of resistance and sabotage but also "breakthrough" moments (and at times "peak" experiences). In this way, the individual organizational linkage is quite clear in the narratives. To embark on organizational change is not only an adventure but also a rewriting of one's life story.

Purpose

The narratives describe a business purpose for change, and the "results" sections clearly depict stunning success (all narratives include extensive statistics relating to productivity, quality, profit margins, etc.). At the same time, on the individual level, the narratives indicate a moral purpose for change. For example, several narratives describe the PM's care and concern not only about business but also about the "quality of work life." This expression evokes the organization as a side of life, and particularly a good life.

The rhetoric of this particular interest in change efforts appears in a number of terms frequently used in the narratives: "commitment," "trust," "satisfaction," "personal growth," "involvement," and "honesty." Feelings are emphasized: "Effective utilization of people is the heart of a successful manufacturing business"; "We are . . . not using the free resource of head and heart that comes with the two hands we hire"; "We are missing a great opportunity by viewing our people as just hands . . . and not enlisting the employees' creativity and caring"; "Our people are resources that need to be developed, not variable costs that need to be controlled." The romance has always appealed to the moral agency of the individual. The narratives have a number of "literal" morals: If you do not want to be moved offshore, embark on organizational change. If you want to keep your job, change yourself.

OBSERVATIONS AND REFLECTIONS

In identification processes, "Only those voices from without are effective which can speak in the language of a voice within" (Burke, 1962: 563). In sense-making processes, "the basic questions, 'who am I,' 'who are they,' and 'who are we' dominate" (Weick, 1995: 77). The PM, in an interview explained that he heard about the OD function at a very propitious time. He and his upper management had just decided upon a new strategy which would give them greater control and greater profits in relationship to a Japanese business partner. As the PM put it, this change in strategy "changed the definition of work" and "called for a higher degree of employee involvement." Without some accompanying organizational change, he said, "I thought to myself, 'This won't be a fun place to work or to manage. We have to do something different.'" As far as his knowledge about organizational change was concerned, he said, "We [the PM and his colleagues] knew only enough to be dangerous." He expressed great appreciation of the OD director's contribution to the change effort.

This example illustrates a coincidence and interweaving of narratives. To the narrative of competitive threat is joined the narrative of threat to one's livelihood, and to this narrative is joined the narrative of opportunity of change of oneself as well as change of one's organizational environment. "Man completes himself in expression" (Taylor, 1985a: 236), and this expression takes narrative form.

In early 1996, AT&T shed some 50,000 people, many of whom associated the company with their personal identity and family. In a 1996 article entitled, "For an AT&T Brat, the Anguish of Letting Go," J. G. Phelan wrote: "The corporation of my parents did . . . pay for my education and help me become a successful adult. At times, I wish I could stay in the secure arms of Ma Bell, but she no longer exists. So now it is time for me to make my own way in the world."

Collins and Porras (1994) did not classify AT&T as one of their "enduring" and "cult-like" organizations. But those who agree with their thesis will argue that AT&T, had it created more of a cult, may not have had to lay off 50,000 people. Management "gurus" and "bibles" generate a large industry that includes consultants, management trainers, management educators, and business schools. As occurred with another example of the genre, *In Search of Excellence* (Peters and Waterman, 1982), the next few years may well see a proliferation of techniques to build the "cult-like" organization. As Collins and Porras state (1994: 136), and as I have shown here, narratives contribute greatly to this process through the workings of identification in which narratees "act on themselves persuasively" (Burke, 1959: 563). "'[I]ndoctrination' exerts . . . pressure on [the narratee] from without; he completes this process from within" (Burke, 1959: 563). Narratives "involve the agent in a way of life" and "help you deal with the world through changing yourself" (Hauerwas, 1977: 73). This is a powerful process indeed. Organizations have tapped into it, and now serve as the site of "profound myths and rites of popular creativity" (Ellul, 1990: 141).

Yet, it is certain that most individuals (particularly the young who are perhaps most susceptible to organizational self-production—unlike my skeptical informant in Case 1)—will not spend their entire lives in these organizations. We also know that organizations do not, cannot, and I would argue should not, encompass the entire field of one's identity and selfhood. My biggest concern is the extent to which organizations and organizational theorists have developed and refined their theories with such little attention to the ethical dimensions of their project (for a few exceptions, see Scott and Hart, 1989, and Stephens et al., 1995). Although organizational theory is an interdisciplinary field, its linkages to philosophy are the least developed (Zald, 1996) and the most impoverished. Philosophers appear to take relatively little interest in organizations; organizational theorists, although they practice philosophy, neither appreciate the tradition in which they work nor recognize themselves as being part of it.

Organizations are important actors in the process of "secularized religiosity" (Ellul, 1990). On the one hand, I find in these organizational narratives the sense of quest, meaning-making, and life-making that I believe is constitutive of human nature. On the other hand, I also find in them a remarkable transferral of this process from traditional sites of identity production (e.g., the family, the church, and the cultural community) to the modern corporation. Deetz's work has linked organizational culture, ideology, and discipline (1993: 59). In ancient Hellenic and early Christian contexts, "discipline" referred to "the physical, intellectual, and moral cultivation of the person" (Asad, 1987: 168). In early monastic contexts, "discipline" followed from the concept of duty, a "programme of learning to lead a virtuous life under the authority of a Law" (Asad, 1987: 170). Narratives of organizational heroes not only follow the form (romance) but also the content (cultivation of self) of our earliest religious and cultural traditions.

With little ethical reflection on the ethical project and tradition that it is, this activity of "translation" (MacIntyre, 1988; Wolin, 1960) continues: from moral philosophy to "business ethics" and from personal life-narratives to organizational life-narratives. As with any activity of "translation," this brings to mind both a recognition, and loss, of tradition.

BIBLIOGRAPHY

Alvesson, M. 1987. *Organizational Theory and Technologic Consciousness: Rationality, Ideology, and Quality of Work*. New York: de Gruyter.

Aristotle. 1967. *The Poetics*. Ann Arbor: University of Michigan Press.

Aristotle. 1962. *Nicomachean Ethics,* trans. H. Rackham. London: Heinemann.

Asad, T. 1987. "On Ritual and Discipline in Medieval Christian Monasticism." *Economy and Society* 16, 2: 159–203.

Ashforth, B., and F. Mael. 1989. "Social Identity Theory and the Organization." *Academy of Management Review* 14: 20–39.

Barnard, C. I. 1938. *The Functions of the Executive*. Cambridge: Harvard University Press.

Burke, K. 1962. *A Grammar of Motives and a Rhetoric of Motives*. Cleveland: World.

Burke, K. 1959. *Attitudes toward History*. Los Altos, Calif.: Hermes Publications.

Casey, C. 1995. *Work, Self and Society after Industrialism*. London: Routledge.

Collins, J., and J. Porras. 1994. *Built to Last*. New York: HarperCollins.

Deetz, S. 1993. "The Negotiative Organization: Building Responsive and Responsible Workplaces." Working Paper, Center for Negotiation and Conflict Resolution, Rutgers University, Newark.

Ellul, J. 1990. *The Technological Bluff,* trans. G. W. Bromiley. Grand Rapids: Eerdmans.

Ellul, J. 1985. *Humiliation of the Word,* trans. J. M. Hanks. Grand Rapids: Eerdmans.

Elmes, M., and M. Costello. 1992. "Mystification and Social Drama: The Hidden Side of Communication Skills Training." *Human Relations* 45, 5: 427–45.

Elsbree, L. 1982. *Rituals of Life: Patterns in Narratives*. Port Washington, N.Y.: Kennikat Press.

Frye, N. 1957. *Anatomy of Criticism*. Princeton: Princeton University Press.

Gilbreth, L. 1914. *The Psychology of Management*. New York: Sturals and Walton.

Habermas, J. 1993. *Justification and Application: Remarks on Discourse Ethics*, trans. C. Cronin. Cambridge: MIT Press.

Harré, R., and G. Gillett. 1994. *The Discursive Mind*. Thousand Oaks, Calif.: Sage.

Harré, R., and P. Secord. 1972. *The Explanation of Social Behaviour*. Totowa, N.J.: Rowman and Littlefield.

Hauerwas, S. 1997. *Truthfulness and Tragedy*. Notre Dame: University of Notre Dame Press.

Herrnstein Smith, B. 1981. "Narrative Versions, Narrative Theories." In *American Criticism in the Poststructuralist Age*, I. Konigsberg, ed. Ann Arbor: University of Michigan Press, 162–86.

Hochschild, A. 1983. *The Managed Heart*. Berkeley: University of California Press.

Hollway, W. 1991. *Work Psychology and Organizational Behaviour*. London: Sage.

Jacques, R. 1996. *Manufacturing the Employee: Management Knowledge from the 19th to the 21st Centuries*. London: Sage.

Johnson, M. 1993. *The Moral Imagination*. Chicago: University of Chicago Press.

Kennedy, P. 1987. *The Rise and Fall of the Great Powers*. New York: Random House.

Lawler, E. E., III. 1988. "Transformation from Control to Involvement." In *Corporate Transformation: Revitalizing Organizations for a Competitive World*, R. H. Kilmann and T. J. Covin and Associates, eds. San Francisco: Jossey Bass, 46–65.

Ledford, G. E., S. A. Mohrman, A. M. Mohrman, and E. E. Lawler III. 1989. "The Phenomenon of Large-Scale Organizational Change." In *Large-Scale Organizational Change*, A. M. Mohrman, S. A. Mohrman, G. E. Ledford, T. G. Cummings, and E. E. Lawler III and Associates, eds. San Francisco: Jossey Bass, 1–32.

Linde, C. 1993. *Life Stories: The Creation of Coherence*. New York: Oxford University Press.

MacIntyre, A. 1988. *Whose Justice? Which Rationality?* Notre Dame: University of Notre Dame Press.

MacIntyre, A. 1981. *After Virtue*. Notre Dame: University of Notre Dame Press.

MacIntyre, A. 1966. *A Short History of Ethics*. New York: Macmillan.

Mangham, I. 1986. *Power and Performance in Organizations*. Oxford: Basil Blackwell.

Mangham, I., and M. A. Overington. 1983. "Dramatism and the Theatrical Metaphor." In *Beyond Method*, G. Morgan, ed. Beverly Hills: Sage, 219–33.

Martin, J., M. S. Feldman, M. J. Hatch, and S. B. Sitkin. 1983. "The Uniqueness Paradox in Organizational Stories." *Administrative Science Quarterly* 28: 438–52.

Maslow, A. 1965. *Eupsychian Management.* Homewood, Ill.: Irwin.

Mauss, M. 1990. *The Gift: The Form and Reason for Exchange in Archaic Societies*, trans. W. D. Halls. New York: W. W. Norton.

McGregor, D. 1966. *Leadership and Motivation*, W. G. Bennis and E. H. Schein, eds. Cambridge: MIT Press.

McGregor, D. 1960. *The Human Side of Enterprise.* New York: McGraw-Hill.

Mumby, D. 1987. *Narrative and Social Control: Critical Perspectives.* Newbury Park, Calif.: Sage.

Murdoch, I. 1970. *The Sovereignty of Good: Studies in Ethics and the Philosophy of Religion.* London: Routledge and Kegan Paul.

O'Connor, E. S. 1995. "Paradoxes of Participation: Textual Analysis and Organizational Change." *Organization Studies* 16/5: 769–803.

O'Connor, E. S. 1996a. "Telling Decisions: The Role of Narrative in Organizational Decision Making." In *Organizational Decision Making*, Z. Shapira, ed. New York: Cambridge University Press, 304–23.

O'Connor, E. S. 1996b. "Civilizing Work: Moral and Political Philosophy in Mayo and Barnard." Paper presented at the annual meetings of the Academy of Management, Cincinnati, Ohio.

Pasmore, W. A. 1988. *Designing Effective Organizations: The Sociotechnical Systems Perspective.* New York: Wiley.

Perrow, C. 1986. *Complex Organizations.* 3d ed. New York: McGraw-Hill.

Peters, T., and R. Waterman. 1982. *In Search of Excellence.* New York: Harper and Row.

Phelan, J. G. 1996. "For an AT&T Brat, the Anguish of Letting Go." *New York Times*, January 14, 12F.

Polanyi, L. 1989. *Telling the American Story.* Cambridge: MIT Press.

Prince, G. 1994. "Narratology," In *The Johns Hopkins Guide to Literary Theory and Criticism*, M. Groden and M. Kreiswirth, eds. Baltimore: Johns Hopkins University Press, 524–27.

Pugh, D. S. 1978. "Understanding, and Managing Organizational Change." *London Business School Journal* 3, 2: 29–31.

Roethlisberger, F. J., and W. Dickson. 1939. *Management and the Worker.* Cambridge: Harvard University Press.

Rose, M. 1975. *Industrial Behaviour: Theoretical Developments since Taylor.* London: Allen Lane.

Sandel, M. J. 1982. *Liberalism and the Limits of Justice.* Cambridge: Cambridge University Press.

Sarbin, T. 1986. *Narrative Psychology: The Storied Nature of Human Conduct.* New York: Praeger.

Saxenian, A. 1994. *Regional Advantage: Culture and Competition in Silicon Valley and Route 128.* Cambridge: Harvard University Press.

Scott, W. G., and D. K. Hart 1989. *Organizational Values in America.* New Brunswick: Transaction Books.

Stephens, C. U., R. S. D'Intino, and B. Victor. 1995. "The Moral Quandary of Transformational Leadership: Change for Whom?" In *Research in Organizational Change and Development,* 8. Greenwich, Conn.: JAI Press, 123–43.

Taylor, C. 1985a. *Human Agency and Language.* Cambridge: Cambridge University Press.

Taylor, C. 1985b. "The Person." In *The Category of the Person,* M. Carrithers, S. Collins, and S. Lukes, eds. Cambridge: Cambridge University Press, 257–81.

Taylor, F. 1911. *The Principles of Scientific Management.* New York: Harper and Row.

TeSeele, S. 1975. "The Experience of Coming to Belief." *Theology Today* 32, 2: 159–64.

Townley, B. 1994. *Reframing Human Resources Management: Power, Ethics, and the Subject at Work.* London: Sage.

Turner, V. 1974. *Dramas, Fields, and Metaphors.* Ithaca: Cornell University Press.

Unger, R. M. 1975. *Knowledge and Politics.* New York: The Free Press.

Waele, J. P., and R. Harré. 1979. "Autobiography as a Psychological Method." In *Emerging Strategies in Social Psychological Research,* G. Ginsburg, ed. New York: Wiley.

Weick, K. 1995. *Sensemaking in Organizations.* Thousand Oaks, Calif.: Sage.

White, H. 1987. *The Content of the Form: Narrative Discourse and Historical Representation.* Baltimore: Johns Hopkins University Press.

White, H. 1981. "The Narrativization of Real Events." In *On Narrative,* W. J. T. Mitchell, ed. Chicago: University of Chicago Press, 249–54.

White, H. 1980. *Metahistory.* Middletown, Conn.: Wesleyan University Press.

White, H. 1978. *Tropics of Discourse.* Baltimore: Johns Hopkins University Press.

Wilkins, A. L. 1983. "Organizational Stories as Symbols which Control the Organization." In *Organizational Symbolism,* L. Pondy, G. Morgan, P. Frost, and T. Dandridge, eds. Greenwich, Conn.: JAI Press, 81–92.

Wolin, S. S. 1960. *Politics and Vision.* Boston: Little, Brown.

Zald, M. N. 1966. "More Fragmentation? Unfinished Business in Linking the Social Sciences and the Humanities." *Administrative Science Quarterly* 41, 2: 251–61.

The Center for Ethics and Religious Values in Business

— ☉ —

The Notre Dame Center for Ethics and Religious Values in Business seeks to build bridges among business, business studies, and the humanities. Its programs are designed to strengthen the Judeo-Christian ethical foundations in business and public policy decisions by fostering dialogue between academic and corporate leaders, and by research and publications. The Center is under the codirection of Oliver F. Williams, C.S.C., associate professor of management, College of Business Administration. John W. Houck, who died in 1996 and who was a professor of management for forty years, founded the Center in 1978.

Publications by the Center include:

Full Value: Cases in Christian Business Ethics (1978)
"Quite successfully juxtaposes the power of the Christian story, in its biblical immediacy, to concrete problems Christians in the world of business are likely to meet."

— Michael Novak

"Religious traditions provide, as these writers observe, a story, for example the Christian story, which informs our moral outlook, creates our moral vision, sustains our moral loyalties, and nurtures our moral character."

— James M. Gustafson

The Judeo-Christian Vision and the Modern Corporation (1980)

In 1980 the Center hosted a national symposium bearing the same name, about which the *New York Times* reported, "there would be no facile resolution to the conflict between the values of a just society and the sharply opposing values of successful corporations." Further, the *Los Angeles Times* contrasted "the competitive success-oriented style necessary to corporate promotion with the traditional Christian view of the virtuous person."

Co-Creation and Capitalism: John Paul II's "Laborem Exercens" (1983)

The symposium "Co-creation: A Religious Vision of Corporate Power" was presented in 1982, focusing on Pope John Paul II's encyclical letter *Laborem Exercens*. *Newsweek* characterized the conference as a "free marketplace of ideas" exploring a religious vision of corporate power.

Catholic Social Teaching and the U.S. Economy (1984)

In December 1983, the Center assisted the U.S. Bishops' Committee charged to write a pastoral letter on the economy by convening a three-day symposium, "Catholic Social Teaching and the American Economy." The *Los Angeles Times* observed: "About one-third of the major speakers represented conservative viewpoints, the remainder voiced moderate-to-liberal positions." The *New York Times* reported that "contentiousness is commonplace here at Notre Dame. . . . And when dozens of business leaders, theologians and academics lined up against each other at the university this week, the debate over the economy was fought as hard as any gridiron encounter." More than two hundred and fifty people attended the meeting, including the five bishops who were to draft the letter.

The Common Good and U.S. Capitalism (1987)

Catholic Social Teaching and the Common Good was the theme of a 1986 symposium to explore the possible retrieval of the notion of "the common good" in philosophical-economic discourse. Ralph McInerny saw the concept of the common good as needed "to draw attention to flaws in our economic thinking and policies as well as to make positive suggestions that will be manifestly in line with our tradition." *New Catholic World* wrote: "a collection of eighteen essays . . . by social scientists, theologians, philosophers, business faculty, and television producers. The essays represent different points of view from both theoretical and practical perspectives. . . . It would be a valuable contribution to Catholic social teaching if all it did was to make people aware that a concept of the common good once was alive and well. It does much more than that."

Ethics and the Investment Industry (1989)

The 1987 symposium focused on ethics in the investment industry. Much has been written in the eighties about the misdeeds of actors in the investment community; suggestions for legislative reform abound. Very little has been said about the ethical vision and institutional bonding that form the context for a humane capitalism. It is these themes, as well as the appropriate market and legal aspects, that were explored at Notre Dame. *America* said of *Ethics and the Investment Industry* that it "will be an important reference for future participants in the international business community."

A Virtuous Life in Business: Stories of Courage and Integrity in the Corporate World (1992)

"I highly recommend *A Virtuous Life in Business: Stories of Courage and Integrity in the Corporate World*. . . . This book is not only valuable, it is readable and gets progressively better."

— *Commonweal*

Catholic Social Thought and the New World Order: Building on One Hundred Years (1993)

"With the recent demise of the Marxist alternative to capitalism, Catholic social teaching has assumed the role of the major international force challenging free enterprise to be more humane."

— *National Catholic Register*

Other Publications by the Center include:

Is the Good Corporation Dead? Social Responsibility in a Global Economy (1996)
Catholic Social Thought and the New World Order (1993)
A Virtuous Life in Business (1992)
The Making of an Economic Vision (1991)
Ethics and the Investment Industry (1989)
The Apartheid Crisis (1986)
Matter of Dignity: Inquiries into the Humanization of Work (1977)

as well as articles appearing in *California Management Review, Business Horizons, Theology Today, Business and Society Review, Horizons, Journal of Business Ethics,* and the *Harvard Business Review.*

A NEW ACTIVITY

The Center inaugurated an Executive-in-Residence Program in the fall of 1996. In this program, a senior executive comes to campus for a period of time and shares with our students his or her experience of the ethical dimension of business. David Collins, a contributor to this volume, was our first executive and taught two seminars. In the fall of 1997 there were four executives-in-residence: J. Neil Statler, former Vice President for Public Affairs, Campbell Soup Company; Joseph W. Keating, former President, Merck Pharmaceutical Manufacturing Division of Merck & Co., Inc.; Alfred C. DeCrane, Jr., former Chairman of the Board and C.E.O., Texaco, Inc.; and F. Byron Nahser, President and C.E.O., Frank C. Nahser Advertising Company.

Contributors

— ◉ —

EILEEN T. BENDER is a professor of English, special assistant to the chancellor, and university director of the Faculty Colloquium on Excellence in Teaching (FACET) at Indiana University–South Bend. She specializes in contemporary fiction and film, nineteenth- and twentieth-century American literature, Women's Studies, and Jewish–American literature. A Danforth Associate and Fellow of the Society for Values in Higher Education, Professor Bender is a graduate of Northwestern University and has a doctorate in English from the University of Notre Dame.

DAVID E. COLLINS was the Fall 1996 Executive-in-Residence in Business Ethics at the Center for Ethics and Religious Values in Business at the University of Notre Dame. He was senior executive of Johnson & Johnson during the Tylenol crisis and managed that problem for J&J; he was widely seen on television and in other media. Subsequently, Mr. Collins was executive vice president of the Schering-Plough Corporation. He has a B.A. degree from Notre Dame, an LL.B. from Harvard University, and is well known for his concern for ethics and social responsibility.

TIMOTHY L. FORT is an Assistant Professor from the University of Michigan Business School. Fort received his J.D. and Ph.D. (in theology with a business cognate) from Northwestern University, and his M.A. and B.A. from the University of Notre Dame. He has been at the University of Michigan since 1994. His work has appeared in the *Notre Dame Law Review, Journal of Corporation Law, Notre Dame Journal of Law, Ethics and Public Policy, Business Ethics Quarterly, American Business Law Journal,* and *Business and Professional Ethics Journal.*

MICHAEL L. GOLDBERG is a rabbi and ethicist at the B'nai Tikvah Congregation in Los Angeles and was the founding rabbi of the Congregation Lev Chadash in Indianapolis. Previously, he was a consultant on organizational design, values, and communications for McKinsey & Company, the Georgia Supreme Court and the State Bar in Atlanta. Rabbi Goldberg received his Ph.D. from the Graduate Theological Union in Berkeley, California, and his rabbinic ordination from the Jewish Theological Seminary of America in New York. He is the author of several books on Jewish studies, professionalism and the law, and new approaches to professional ethics.

JOHN W. HOUCK died in December 1996. He was a professor of management and co-director of the Notre Dame Center for Ethics and Religious Values in Business since its inception in 1975. A former Ford and Danforth Fellow, he earned both an A.B. and a J.D. degree from the University of Notre Dame, an M.B.A. from the University of North Carolina-Chapel Hill, and an LL.M. from Harvard University. He was also a Fellow of the Royal Society for the encouragement of Arts, Manufactures & Commerce. Professor Houck lectured and conducted workshops on the role of religious and humane values in business, wrote numerous articles and reviews, and published eleven books.

DENNIS P. McCANN is a professor of religious studies at DePaul University in Chicago and executive director of the Society of Christian Ethics. In 1992 he became the first annual holder of the Wicklander Chair in Professional Ethics at DePaul. He received his S.T.L. in theology from the Gregorian University in Rome and his Ph.D. in theology from the University of Chicago Divinity School. Professor McCann teaches Roman Catholic studies, religious social ethics, and business ethics. He has served on the board of directors of the Society of Christian Ethics and on the editorial board of the *Journal of Religious Ethics*. He is the author or co-author of four books.

MICHAEL MEDVED is the host of the *Michael Medved Show,* a daily radio talk show on KVI in Seattle, chief film critic for the *New York Post* and, for the past eleven years, co-host of *Sneak Previews*—the weekly half-hour film-review show that airs on more than 250 stations on PBS television. Mr. Medved is the author of seven nonfiction books, and his columns on media and society have been published in hundreds of periodicals, including the *New York Times* and the *Sunday Times* of London.

He was graduated from Yale University, attended Yale Law School, and is co-founder of the Pacific Jewish Center.

BERNARD G. MURCHLAND is the Guy Max Clarke Professor of Philosophy at Ohio Wesleyan University and the editor of the *Civic Arts Review*, a journal relating liberal learning to public life. His B.A. is from the University of Moncton in Canada and his Ph.D. from the State University of New York–Buffalo. In addition, he holds graduate degrees in religion and comparative literature. Professor Murchland has translated several books, edited and/or written several others, and has published over one hundred articles and reviews on philosophical and social themes. His academic interests are primarily in the areas of the history of ideas and the philosophy of social values.

ELLEN S. O'CONNOR is a research associate at FX Palo Alto Laboratory, Inc., in Palo Alto, California, having been previously on the faculty of the College of Business Administration at the University of Notre Dame and a Visiting Scholar at Stanford University. She holds a Ph.D. in humanities from the University of Chicago and an M.B.A. from the University of California-Berkeley. Her research explores the limits and possibilities of integrating the fields of literature and technology, in particular, how literary theory can contribute to theoretical and practical advancements in the field of high technology. Dr. O'Connor has lectured at universities in several European countries and her articles have appeared in a number of scholarly journals.

TERESA GODWIN PHELPS is a professor of law at the University of Notre Dame. She is the author of two books and has lectured and written extensively on gender issues and the law, law and literature, and legal writing. Professor Phelps received her B.A., M.A., and Ph.D. degrees from the University of Notre Dame and her M.S.L. from Yale Law School.

THOMAS L. SHAFFER is the Robert and Marion Short Professor of Law at the University of Notre Dame and the supervising attorney of the Notre Dame Legal Aid Clinic. He is a member of the bar for the Indiana Supreme Court, the U.S. District Courts for the Northern and Southern Districts of Indiana, the U.S. Court of Appeals for the Seventh Circuit, and the U.S. Tax Court. Professor Shaffer has published numerous books and articles. He was graduated from the University of Albuquerque and received his J.D. from the University of Notre Dame.

CHARLES VAN DOREN has been a senior associate and moderator of the Aspen Institute since 1973 and is the associate director of the Institute for Philosophical Research, with which he has been associated since 1960. He was consultant to the *Encyclopaedia Britannica* for over twenty years, rising to vice president/editorial. Dr. Van Doren is the author of numerous articles and books, including four novels for young readers and two children's books.

OLIVER F. WILLIAMS, C.S.C., is director of the Notre Dame Center for Ethics and Religious Values in Business and associate professor of management. He researches and teaches business, society and ethics, and has published and lectured extensively. He has studied the South African business and political landscape for many years and was a visiting professor at the University of Cape Town during the 1995–96 academic year. Currently, he serves as the chair of the board of directors of the United States–South Africa Leadership Development Program (US-SALEP) and is on the editorial board of *Business & the Contemporary World*. He has served as the chair of the Social Issues Division of the Academy of Management. Father Williams received a B.Sc. in chemical engineering from the University of Notre Dame and a Ph.D. in theology from Vanderbilt University Divinity School. He was ordained a Holy Cross priest in 1970.